MAY 2013

Pursuing the Good Life

Pursuing the Good Life

100 Reflections on Positive Psychology

Christopher Peterson

OXFORD

UNIVERSITY PRESS

Oxford University Press is a department of the University of Oxford.
It furthers the University's objective of excellence in research,
scholarship, and education by publishing worldwide.

Oxford   New York

Auckland   Cape Town   Dar es Salaam   Hong Kong   Karachi
Kuala   Lumpur   Madrid   Melbourne   Mexico City   Nairobi
New Delhi   Shanghai   Taipei   Toronto

With offices in

Argentina   Austria   Brazil   Chile   Czech Republic   France   Greece
Guatemala   Hungary   Italy   Japan   Poland   Portugal   Singapore
South   Korea   Switzerland   Thailand   Turkey   Ukraine   Vietnam

Oxford is a registered trade mark of Oxford University Press in the UK and certain other
countries.

Published in the United States of America by
Oxford University Press
198 Madison Avenue, New York, NY 10016

Library of Congress Cataloging-in-Publication Data
Peterson, Christopher, 1950 Feb. 18–
Pursuing the good life: 100 reflections on positive psychology / Christopher Peterson.
p. cm.
Includes bibliographical references and index.
ISBN 978–0–19–991635–1 (hbk.: alk. paper)
1. Positive psychology.   I. Title.
BF204.6.P483 2013
150.19'88—dc23
2012013999

1 3 5 7 9 8 6 4 2
Printed in the United States of America
on acid-free paper

The only freedom which deserves the name is that of pursuing our own good, in our own way, so long as we do not attempt to deprive others of theirs, or impede their efforts to obtain it.
—*John Stuart Mill*

Table of Contents

Preface

On April 22, 2008, I received an e-mail message from *Psychology Today* asking me if I would write for their website. The invitation sounded interesting, so I said yes. I had no idea where it would take me, but 800,000 hits later, I know the answer: anywhere on the Internet where people are interested in psychology—its theories, methods, findings, and applications.

Most of the entries I wrote for a blog titled "The Good Life" focused on *positive psychology*, an umbrella term for the scientific study of what makes life worth living. I learned that readers are hungry for what positive psychologists have discovered about the good life. I learned that readers like research findings. I learned that readers also like practical implications of positive psychology theory and research—the *so what*s. How might we pursue the psychological good life? I learned that terse is good, as is a bit of humor. I learned that readers like examples. And I learned that readers like occasional rants. All of this learning is represented in the present collection.

I have a day job as a psychology professor at the University of Michigan, and I wanted my efforts on behalf of *Psychology Today* to be noticed by the powers-that-be at my university. These powers do not understand Internet hits, but they do understand publications, so all along I had the goal of publishing my collected blog entries—*reflections*, as I term them here—in a book.

I waited until I had written more than a hundred entries, and then I chose those that were most relevant to positive psychology. I grouped them into sensible categories, and perhaps this book will be useful to students of positive psychology as well as to interested members of the general public.

Although many of these reflections were originally written for the *Psychology Today* website, the truth is that I have revised and updated virtually all of them. Where appropriate, I have provided some annotations, reflecting what I learned from the responses of Internet readers and my own further thoughts. I have also written some altogether new reflections for this collection.

I have organized these reflections under broad categories representing the concerns of positive psychology. The first section—"Positive Psychology and the Good Life"—contains examinations of positive psychology as a scientific perspective on the human condition. What is positive psychology? What has it accomplished? Where is it going? What are the potential pitfalls and problems with this perspective in progress?

Subsequent sections address different contributors to the good life: positive emotions and experiences; positive traits and talents; positive relationships; and enabling institutions such as families, workplaces, schools, sports, and geographical places.

I have also included some reflections on things I dislike under the heading of "Rants," which can be read as my take on what makes life *not* worth living.

Although all of these reflections have implications embedded within them, the final section contains reflections in which the relevance of positive psychology to pursuing the psychological good life is explicit.

I would like to acknowledge the encouragement of my *Psychology Today* editor, Lybi Ma, who always made me feel like my writing was appreciated. Thanks are also due to Abby Gross of Oxford University Press for shepherding and shaping this book.

I also express my gratitude to the many readers of my blog for *Psychology Today*, those who offered comments as well as those who simply read what I wrote. Their interest provided immediate and ongoing motivation as well as a way to gauge what I was doing well and what I needed to improve.

This collection is dedicated to my friend and colleague Nansook Park, who from the beginning encouraged me to write these reflections because it was patently obvious to her—if not to me—that doing so made me happy. Nansook also suggested a number of the topics and sources about which I wrote, and she also shared her wisdom about the content and style of specific reflections, as well as the overall organization of this collection.

Christopher Peterson
Ann Arbor, MI
February 18, 2012

Part I

Positive Psychology and the Good Life

Positive psychology is the *scientific* study of what goes right in life. I emphasize the science part of this definition to stress that positive psychology must be informed by what the evidence actually shows. If not, it is simply another armchair endeavor (see essay 10).

This first section focuses on positive psychology as a science, defining this new perspective and the topics to which this perspective has recently been brought to bear. I draw out some of the theoretical implications of a scientific study of the good life and discuss some of the challenges faced by positive psychology as the perspective develops in the years ahead.

1

What Is Positive Psychology, and What Is It Not?

Why always accuse, why always condemn? That's a sad ethics indeed, for sad people. As for the good, it exists...in the irreducible multiplicity of good deeds...and in the good inclinations to which tradition has given the name virtues, which is to say excellences.

—André Comte-Sponville

In little more than a decade, positive psychology has caught the attention not only of the academic community but also the general public. I just did a Google search for "positive psychology" and found 2,340,000+ hits. That is obviously impressive, although keeping all of us positive psychologists humble is that my searches for "Britney Spears" and "Lady Gaga" produced 57,000,000+ hits and 453,000,000+ hits, respectively.

It is still good that larger world is interested in positive psychology, and probably even better that this interest does not entail morbid curiosity or the wish to witness a train wreck.

Regardless, the downside of whatever popularity positive psychology enjoys is the temptation for those of us associated with this new field to run ahead of what we know in pursuit of further popularity. So let me slow down and explain what positive psychology actually is and what we actually know.

Positive psychology is the scientific study of what makes life most worth living (Peterson, 2006). It is a call for psychological science and practice to be as concerned with strength as with weakness; as interested in building the best things in life as in repairing the worst; and as concerned with making the lives of normal people fulfilling as with healing pathology.

Nowhere does this definition say or imply that psychology should ignore or dismiss the very real problems that people experience. Nowhere does it say or imply that the rest of psychology needs to be discarded or replaced. The value of positive psychology is to complement and extend the problem-focused psychology that has been dominant for many decades.

Several truisms underpin positive psychology (Seligman & Csikszentmihalyi, 2000). First, what is good in life is as genuine as what is bad—not derivative, secondary, epiphenomenal, illusory, or otherwise suspect. Second, what is good in life is not simply the absence of what is problematic. We all know the difference between not being depressed and bounding out of bed in the morning with enthusiasm for the day ahead. And third, the good life requires its own explanation, not simply a theory of disorder stood sideways or flipped on its head.

Positive psychology is psychology—psychology is science—and science requires checking theories against evidence. Accordingly, positive psychology is not to be confused with untested self-help, footless affirmation, or secular religion—no matter how good these may make us feel. Positive psychology is neither a recycled version of the power of positive thinking nor a sequel to *The Secret*.

Positive psychology will rise or fall on the science on which it is based. So far, the science is impressive. Consider what has been learned in recent years about the psychological good life, none of which was mentioned in any of the psychology courses I took a few decades ago:

- Most people are happy.
- Happiness is a cause of good things in life and not simply along for the happy ride. People who are satisfied with life eventually have even more reason to be satisfied, because happiness leads to desirable outcomes at school and work, to fulfilling social relationships, and even to good health and long life.

- Most people are resilient.
- Happiness, strengths of character, and good social relationships are buffers against the damaging effects of disappointments and setbacks.
- Crisis reveals character.
- Other people matter mightily if we want to understand what makes like most worth living.
- Religion matters.
- Work matters as well if it engages the worker and provides meaning and purpose.
- Money makes an ever-diminishing contribution to well-being, but money can buy happiness if it is spent on other people.
- As a route to a satisfying life, eudaimonia trumps hedonism.
- The "heart" matters more than the "head." Schools explicitly teach critical thinking; they should also teach unconditional caring.
- Good days have common features: feeling autonomous, competent, and connected to others.
- The good life can be taught.

This last point is especially important because it means that happiness is not simply the result of a fortunate spin of the genetic roulette wheel. There are things that people can do to lead better lives, although I hasten to say that all require that we live (behave) differently... permanently. The good life is hard work, and there are no shortcuts to sustained happiness (see reflections in Part XI).

My goals for the reflections that follow are several. First, I will discuss research findings about the psychological good life. Second, I will explore the most promising practical applications based on these findings. And third, I will use positive psychology as a vantage to make sense of the world in which we live. I hope you find what I say interesting.

REFERENCES

Peterson, C. (2006). *A primer in positive psychology*. New York: Oxford University Press.

Seligman, M. E. P., & Csikszentmihalyi, M. (2000). Positive psychology: An introduction. *American Psychologist, 55*, 5–14.

2

Parsing Positive Psychology

It is paradoxical that many educators distinguish between a time for learning
and a time for play without seeing the vital connection between them.
—Leo Buscaglia

In addressing the purpose of life, Sigmund Freud famously said, "Work and love, love and work—that's all there is." With all respect to Dr. Freud, I disagree. He left out play.

Play is not the silly sibling of work and love. Play is built as deeply within people as are work and love. Ethologists have addressed the function of play among the young of many mammalian species The specific behaviors that these youngsters rehearse and perfect in their rough-and-tumble play are precisely those they later use as adults to hunt, to escape predators, and to establish a dominance hierarchy. Said another way, play teaches lessons that make possible the serious tasks of work and love.

Although we have been taught not to attribute human motives to our animal cousins, it is difficult to watch kittens or puppies gambol about without concluding that they are having "fun" in the process. Suffice it to say that *we* derive pleasure from watching them.

And at least among people, play can take on a life of its own. We certainly enjoy play, not only as children but also throughout our lives. Leisure activities (play) are a common source of flow and a robust predictor of how satisfied we are with our lives. In play we find and pursue our passions (see reflection 15).

I propose that work, love, and play provide yet another useful way to organize the concerns of positive psychology.

Since the beginning of positive psychology, theorists have distinguished its various pillars, like positive experiences, positive traits, positive relationships, and enabling institutions (e.g., Peterson, 2006). But these are not literally pillars. They are psychosocial states, traits, mechanisms, and contexts, and most play a role in everything that we actually do.

In an important article, Paul Rozin (2006) took psychology to task for what he dubbed *domain denigration*, ignoring the important domains of behavior (like eating and sleeping, or for that matter work, love, and play) as a way to organize the field. Instead, psychologists have long parsed the field in terms of the presumed processes that give rise to behavior (e.g., cognition, emotion). The problem with this organizational strategy is that there is little evidence for cross-domain processes. The further problem is that what we actually do may be treated as arbitrary.

What makes like worth living is not a psychological process. It is work, love, and play.

ANNOTATION

After I originally wrote this reflection, my colleague Nansook Park has convinced me that there is yet another important contributor to makes life worth living: service to others. My initial reaction to her suggestion was that *service* could be subsumed under *love*, but further reflection convinced me that she was right. *Love* is one-to-one, referring to relationships with specific others—spouses, children, colleagues, and neighbors—whereas *service* is more general, referring to connections with larger groups or purposes. We may not even know those we serve, as in the case of future generations, but doing what we can to improve their lot makes our own life worth living.

Let us study all of these domains explicitly.

REFERENCES

Peterson, C. (2006). *A primer in positive psychology.* New York: Oxford University Press.

Rozin, P. (2006). Domain denigration and process preference in academic psychology. *Perspectives on Psychological Science, 1*, 365–376.

3

How Do Americans Spend Their Time?

The only reason for time is so that everything doesn't happen at once.
—Albert Einstein

Psychology is conventionally defined as the scientific study of behavior—what people do—which is ironic given that psychologists seldom study behavior that really matters. Oh sure, survey researchers may study what people report about their activities, and in laboratory studies, researchers may study people's eye movements or reaction times (Baumeister, Vohs, & Funder, 2007). In a technical sense, these are all behaviors— meaning observable actions by a person that are measurable in reliable ways.

But these behaviors do not matter in themselves. They are studied only as convenient means to an end, and for most psychologists, the end is to understand the psychological states, traits, and processes presumably leading to behavior that matters. However, few psychologists take the additional step to investigate directly behavior that matters. It is as if psychology has spent more than a century drawing up an invitation list for a party without ever sending out the invitations, much less throwing the party. "Further invitations are needed."

Indeed, the subfields of psychology have long been defined according to the underlying processes that are the real concern of most research psychologists: perception, memory, judgment, emotion, social influence, and the like. And the psychology curriculum at most colleges and universities features courses devoted to these processes as opposed to what they are intended to explain.

As noted in the previous reflection (2), Paul Rozin (2006) has criticized psychologists for not studying directly the real domains of behavior except in occasional studies relegated to one or another field of applied psychology. Roy Baumeister and his colleagues (2007, p. 399) made the same point in a more provocative way, after noting that the study of actual behavior was at one time somewhat more common by psychologists:[*]

> Whatever happened to helping, hurting, playing, working, talking, eating, risking, waiting, flirting, goofing off, showing off, giving up, screwing up, compromising, selling, persevering, pleading, tricking, outhustling, sandbagging, refusing, and the rest? Can't psychology find ways to observe and explain these acts, at least once in a while?

If psychologists should study what people actually do, then what are those things? One answer is provided by the interdisciplinary field of *time use* that documents—literally—how people spend their time. One might think that time use researchers follow people around and record what they do, but that is not usually feasible and in any event might influence what people do given that there are observers present (think "reality" television shows). Time use researchers instead rely on surveys, contacting respondents at the end of a day and getting a detailed account of what they did during that day and how much time each activity took.

For example, a 2009 survey of a nationally representative sample of U.S. adults found that the most frequent activities

---

[*] Baumeister et al. (2007) documented the occasional use of the phrase "actual behavior" by research psychologists, who apparently use it when they all so rarely study it! The point is that such investigations are unusual enough to earn this qualification.

of people were as follows: sleeping; working; doing household chores; eating and drinking; caring for others; engaging in leisure activities or sports; and providing service through formal organizations (e.g., volunteer, religious, and/or civic tasks; U.S. Bureau of Labor Statistics, 2010). There was also a category of miscellaneous "other" activities, into which were placed shopping, grooming, caring for pets, talking on the telephone, and dealing with e-mail (ugh; see reflection 80). You are not supposed to be surprised by these results—after all, they probably describe how you spend your own time. But when these unsurprising results are juxtaposed with what psychologists usually study, they become remarkable.

There are of course individual variations in what people do and how much time they spend at each activity, depending on their age, gender, and life circumstances. *Service* in particular is highly variable, with many Americans doing absolutely nothing for the greater good and others spending hours per day serving others besides their immediate family members. I also note, with considerable disappointment, that "frittering away one's life" was not an explicit activity category in this survey, although perhaps that is too subjective a description of the activities in which many of us engage.

That said, these results are important. If positive psychologists aspire to study what makes life worth living, we should have an inkling about what life actually entails. Time use surveys give us a glimpse of what is missing in most studies by psychologists. These results tell us where we should look if we want to understand, at least for most people, what makes life worth living.

Indeed, the major time use categories fit exactly the formulation of work, love, play, and service as the domains in which the well-lived life occurs, as described in my previous reflection (2). Sleeping and eating are additional categories, but at the risk of being flip, I note that these are more enjoyable when done with someone else, so perhaps they can be subsumed under the category of love. More seriously, they deserve their own emphases.

If someone participates in "work, love, play, and service," he or she has a *full life*, and if someone participates in none, what we see is an *empty life*. But these time use results have made me think that these ideas are too facile. Most people are already doing these sorts of things. On the one hand, maybe most people have a full life. But on the other hand, some qualifications may be in order in we want to zero in more exactly on the good life.

Positive psychologists should probably speak about *good* work, *good* love, *good* play (e.g., not watching television), and *good* service. Qualifications that move an activity from the typical to the notable include how well the activity is done; whether it is done with enthusiasm and joy; whether the activity is engaging; whether the activity has a larger meaning and purpose; and so on.

REFERENCES

Baumeister, R. F., Vohs, K. D., & Funder, D. C. (2007). Psychology as the science of self-reports and finger movements: Whatever happened to actual behavior? *Perspectives on Psychological Science, 2,* 396–403.

Rozin, P. (2006). Domain denigration and process preference in academic psychology. *Perspectives on Psychological Science, 1,* 365–376.

U.S. Bureau of Labor Statistics (2010). *American Time Use Survey user's guide: Understanding ATUS 2003 to 2009.* Washington, DC: Author.

4

Blaming the Science Versus
Blaming the Victim

A Third Alternative

If I'd known I was going to live this long, I'd have taken better care of myself.
—Eubie Blake

A downside of positive psychology research, especially when results are disseminated in the popular media, is that people can become dismayed when they compare conclusions about their own and acquaintances' lives to the conclusions they have just read. For example, we may read that happy or optimistic people are more successful at school and work, that they are more attractive and have better relationships, or that they are healthier and live longer. So what does it mean when we see happy or optimistic people who are doing poorly and unhappy or pessimistic people who are doing well? We may become dismayed, especially if those faring poorly happen to be us.

"But I did what I was supposed to do! I was cheerful. I looked on the bright side. I counted my blessings, I identified my strengths, and I did volunteer work. I took a sincere interest in other people. I identified the purpose for my existence. And my life is a mess."

Such dismay does not occur just with respect to the conclusions of positive psychology. It occurs even more frequently with respect to research about healthy habits and assets. We may exercise daily and eat sensibly, refrain from drinking, and never touch a cigarette. Our telomeres may be long, and our cholesterol may be low. And our health may still be terrible, whereas our great-uncle Fred—an unrepentant couch potato who smokes and drinks and avoids vegetables like the plague—is hale and hearty at age 93! He'll attend our funeral, not vice versa.

What are the possible reactions to this dismay? One reaction is to blame the science and conclude that it is all nonsense because we can so readily think of exceptions to the conclusions that supposedly follow from research. I encounter this reaction frequently among my skeptical first-year college students but also among some of the critics of positive psychology.

Another reaction is to blame one's self. Here the person accepts the science but concludes that the failure somehow lies within the self, for not being happy enough, or optimistic enough, or resilient enough. "If only I had…," goes the refrain, "I would be satisfied and successful and healthy." Here the guilt occasioned by self-blame only compounds the bad feelings experienced about whatever has gone wrong.

We know that we should not blame the victim (Ryan, 1978). The "positive" corollary of this insight is that we should not congratulate the victor (Peterson, 2006). But we often do both.

Here I suggest a third alternative that entails neither blaming the science nor blaming the victim. How about *understanding* the science? What does it mean, for example, to say that happiness leads to a longer life (Diener & Chan, 2011)? Simply that on average happiness at an earlier point in life foreshadows being alive at a later—sometimes much later!—point in life. However, the relationship is far from perfect. It is not a guarantee, and exceptions should be expected. The exception, alas, may be you or someone you love.

If you have a headache, you probably take an aspirin. The aspirin may help, but if it does not, you probably do not throw out your bottle of aspirin or sell your stock shares in the Bayer company. You conclude, reasonably, that the aspirin did not work this time. It happens. Oh well. And the next time you have a headache, you probably take another aspirin or two.

I urge the general public to be similarly smart about the conclusions from positive psychology studies. Sometimes they hold, and sometimes they do not. If a researcher concludes that X indeed leads to Y, all he or she means is that it does so more often than could be expected by chance. When an exception occurs, it does not mean that the researcher is a charlatan or that the exception deserves condemnation. It happens. Oh well. But the conclusion—a generalization—remains a perfectly good one, even if misunderstood.

The conclusions from positive psychology research reflect correlation coefficients (or their statistical equivalents) computed between predictors (e.g., happiness, optimism) and outcomes of interest (e.g., success, health). We all know that "correlation is not causation," but here I am focusing on correlations that really do reflect causation. Even in these cases, causation is inherently probabilistic, with exceptions to be expected. However, the exceptions are not the occasion for moral condemnation.

So, the general public may hear typical conclusions about X leading to Y as if they reflect the sort of relationship shown in Figure 4.1a, an essentially straight line. But in fact, virtually all of the conclusions in social science, including positive psychology, reflect the sort of relationship shown in Figure 4.1b.

We should not ignore these less-than-perfect relationships. All things being equal, we live longer if we do not smoke. All things being equal, we are more successful if we are happy. All things being equal, we accomplish more if we are optimistic. But there are no guarantees. Exceptions happen. Oh well.

I do not fault the general public for misunderstanding the results of research when they are presented without these qualifications and considerations. Rather, I fault positive psychologists who write exaggerated trade books and science writers who favor sound bites over sensible reporting.

People should heed good advice, like that based on research, when it is available. Perhaps we can blame them for not heeding the advice. But we should blame neither the good advice

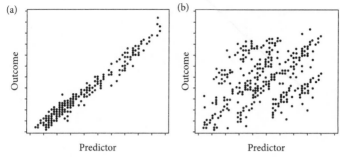

Figure 4.1 Predictors and Outcomes

nor the person who heeds the advice if it doesn't work out. That happens.

REFERENCES

Diener, E., & Chan, M. Y. (2011). Happy people live longer: Subjective well-being contributes to health and longevity. *Applied Psychology: Health and Well-Being, 3*, 1–43.

Peterson, C. (2006). *A primer in positive psychology*. New York: Oxford University Press.

Ryan, W. (1978). *Blaming the victim* (Rev. ed.). New York: Random House.

5

Perfect People

One of my favorite songs is "You Never Even Called Me by My Name" by Steve Goodman. His goal was to write the perfect country song, but when he showed his first draft to his friend David Allen Coe, he was advised that the perfect country song needed to mention getting drunk, and mothers, and rain, and trains, and trucks, and prison, and death. Hence he added lyrics that mentioned all of these topics, in rapid-fire succession, which indeed make the song perfect ... perfectly silly.

I thought of this song during a conversation with Martin Seligman about whether positive psychology (or psychology itself) has natural categories, notions that "carve nature at the joints" as constructs in the biological and physical sciences do. My off-the-top-of-my-head response was "No, because psychology studies jointless jellyfish, and there is nothing to carve. All we can do is describe, and we do so from a given sociocultural perspective."

Not a bad answer, but Seligman went on to describe a centuries-old critical experiment by Isaac Newton that revealed the basic structure of white light by using one prism to break natural light into a rainbow and a second prism to reconstitute the rainbow into natural light.

That led me to muse about positive psychology. Research has described the psychologically healthy person in terms of various components that make up the good life, including the following:

- Experiencing more positive feelings than negative feelings
- Being satisfied with life
- Identifying and using talents and strengths
- Being engaged in activities
- Having close relationships with neighbors, colleagues, friends, and family members
- Being a contributing member of a social community
- Having meaning and purpose

There are no doubt gaps here, but this list seems a reasonable start to a positive psychology rainbow. Now do a thought experiment: Reconstitute a person from these components, and imagine what she would be like. (By the way, for me to imagine that the reconstituted person would be a male, I would really need to be convinced.)

Is this creation credible, if not as a real person then at least as an ideal toward which we should strive? Would she be a composite of Mother Teresa and Angelina Jolie, or a caricatured Stepford wife—phony, boring, or downright creepy?

Positive psychology practitioners are trying—with success I believe—to cultivate the various components of the good life. Suppose we succeed beyond our wildest dreams and someday create the perfect person per positive psychology by building up in the same individual every identified component. Would the whole be greater than or equal to the sum of the parts or somehow less or just perfectly silly, like Steve Goodman's song? I suspect that the final possibility is the correct one.

Perhaps flaws and hassles are needed, if only to pose challenges and make us human as we fail to surmount them. Maybe "being human" should be added to positive psychology's list of the components of the good life, but doing so is a huge caveat that would render the other components neither necessary nor sufficient and leave us where we started: jellyfish in search of joints.

REFERENCE

Coe, D. A. (Performer). (n.d.). *You never even called me by my name* [Music video]. Retrieved from http://www.youtube.com/watch?v=9coh7mBH wr4&feature=related.

6

The Future of Unhappiness

In his book *Happiness: A History*, Darrin McMahon (2006) explained that once upon a time, happiness was seen as something that simply "happened" to a person.* Things have since changed. Happiness, or at least the pursuit of it, became a human right. And with the advent of positive psychology interventions that demonstrably bolster well-being, many can now do more than pursue happiness. They can actually achieve it.

Where does this leave unhappiness and those who regularly experience it?

My thinking on this subject was sparked by a conversation I had with a sinus surgeon, who described (in too much detail) sinus surgery, past and present. Several decades ago, surgeons would literally open up a patient's face. Now they can perform sinus surgery by going through the patient's nose. The procedure is much simpler, with the effect that the number of sinus surgeries has increased exponentially.

An additional effect of these new surgical procedures is that less-than-perfect sinuses—once simply endured with a box of

---

* The English word *happiness* comes from the Old Norse *happ*, meaning "chance" or "luck." Interestingly, the Chinese character for *happiness* also means "chance" or "luck."

tissues—are now seen as a medical problem, a disorder or illness, just *because* they can be treated.

So, if we can now "treat" unhappiness with positive psychology interventions, how will we as a society come to regard a less than ideal mood and below-average life satisfaction?

Will these become illnesses, literal or metaphorical?

Will we—as my friends in the humanities like to say—*problematize* unhappiness?

Will stigma ensue? (Some might say that unhappiness already carries a stigma, at least in the United States.)

Moral condemnation?

Legislation against unhappiness, at least when displayed inside a building (like smoking)?

Unhappiness activists protesting ever so listlessly against this legislation?

I am being silly in these extrapolations, but a serious point lurks. It is not that unhappiness can have occasional benefits, which it does (see reflection 19). It is not that happiness is an unalloyed good, which it is not (see reflection 20). Rather, it is that positive psychology, despite its stance as a descriptive science, may have unforeseen and inevitable prescriptive consequences.

Will these make us happy?

REFERENCE

McMahon, D. M. (2006). *Happiness: A history.* New York: Grove Press.

7

Positive Psychology and Bullshit

Develop a built-in bullshit detector.
—Ernest Hemingway

Is positive psychology bullshit?

Someone asked me this the other day—gently—so the question deserves a thoughtful answer, and not the one that immediately came to my mind.

As I noted in my very first reflection here (1), *positive psychology* is an umbrella term that organizes the work of those of us who have heeded the recommendation to study scientifically what makes life worth living. Specific examples of positive psychology theory, research, and practice can be good or bad or ugly, just like anything else. The umbrella cannot be bullshit—that's a category mistake.

But what about the person holding the umbrella—for example, me—and whatever it is that that the umbrella is covering—in other words, the body of basic and applied work done by positive psychologists?

Harry Frankfurt's (2005) well-known essay "On Bullshit" provides a perspective for understanding what BS is, as well as what it is not. Frankfurt defines bullshit not as a lie but as an indifference to truth.

By this definition, the science of positive psychology does not qualify, not when the research on which it is based is published in peer-reviewed journals, not when these papers contain appropriate qualifications and caveats, and not when other researchers weigh in with their own data that support different conclusions. The truth—at least the way that social scientists try to grasp it—is always of prime concern.

However, also by this definition, a self-identified positive psychologist could qualify. If someone presents himself as a positive psychologist and then proceeds to say things that are indifferent to what has been learned from research, then that is BS, even if it happens to be true, and especially if it is not.

Examples certainly exist. Anyone who promises the secret to happiness or six easy steps to bliss should trigger a BS detector, assuming one is legal in your state. Positive psychologists have identified many of the determinants of happiness, but they're hardly a secret—they're described in scientific books and journals readily found in any college library. And anyone who says that happiness is easy is not reading any of the journals where the research has been published.

By the way, I give a pass to positive psychology book authors and science writers when their book subtitles and headlines qualify—which they often do—because these are typically not written by them. Readers should be forewarned that they should not judge a book by the nonsense on its cover or a newspaper story by the nonsense in its headline.

Anyway, the positive psychologists I know and respect are not glib. To be sure, they elaborate, extrapolate, and conjecture—as do I—but they all acknowledge what they are doing, as I also do, I hope. That's not BS, even if the riffs are wrong. That's good clean intellectual fun, and it's what makes positive psychology so interesting to so many people.

When I give a talk about positive psychology, I am always struck by the curiosity of the general public about what the data actually show. By far the most common questions I am asked are about the specific studies I have mentioned, as well as those I have not. People do not want my uninformed opinions—an invitation to ignore the truth to which it would be easy to succumb. Rather, they want more details, from which they can and do draw their own conclusions. That keeps my head in the game of truth, and I do not think I am a special member of the positive psychology posse.

Then again, why should you believe me? The answer is that you should not, until you check out the truth for yourself and think about it. Positive psychology is fertile, but it is not fertilizer.

REFERENCE

Frankfurt, H. G. (2005). *On bullshit.* Princeton, NJ: Princeton University Press.

8

The Bad Company of Positive Psychology

It is better to be alone than in bad company.
—George Washington

When positive psychology was beginning, some of us clucked our tongues about the threat posed by *bad company*, meaning people with various intentions, bad or good, who might be attracted by the positive but indifferent to the science. Positive psychology has since grown, and I believe that its bad company has also proliferated.

What I do here is update my worries about bad company by expanding the idea and proposing a taxonomy. In his more recent writing, Howard Gardner (1999) suggested that the ability to taxonomize—to categorize the world—is one of the distinct multiple intelligences. Linnaeus and Gardner himself certainly qualify as geniuses at creating taxonomies. Whether I belong in that select group is doubtful, but here goes.

Within the general category of positive psychology's bad company are what I call

- The **stupid company**—those who pay attention to the science of positive psychology but dumb it down.
- The **mean company**—those in and out of psychology who mount a relentless attack on positive psychology and more generally on anything positive (e.g., happiness, optimism).

Even when their criticisms are correct, I am always confused about what they are urging on the rest of us (see reflections 25, 26, and 27). In any event, I wish they would actually read what positive psychologists—meaning the nonstupid ones—have written about the need for a balanced psychology that acknowledges and studies what goes right as well as what goes wrong.

- The **one-trick-pony company**—those who seize on a single positive psychology exercise or intervention (e.g., counting one's blessings, identifying and using one's character strengths) and suggest it as *the* cure for all that ails us.
- Ironically, the **happy company**—those who acknowledge that positive psychology is not simply happiology but then write books only about happiness and how to achieve it. I realize that "happiness" in a book title translates into sales (check out Amazon.com's sales ranks for evidence), but why are positive psychologists letting the marketplace dictate the public face of the field?
- And, most insidiously, the **complacent company**—those who treat positive psychology—its theories and findings—as a done deal. Where are the new topics worthy of study? Where are the new applications and interventions?

When I give a lecture on the future of positive psychology, I usually end with this quote: "I feel uneasy about the company I'm with...religionists, philosophers, yearners, utopians, Pollyannas, etc., rather than the tough-minded scientists I admire so much more." Then I ask who wrote it.

The answer is Abraham Maslow (1979, p. 113), uneasy founder of humanistic psychology. Maslow distinguished *safety science*, a complacent approach to inquiry, and *growth science*, a bold approach willing to ask new questions and to be wrong. Positive psychology needs to be a growth science, and the bad company does not help.

REFERENCES

Gardner, H. (1999). *Intelligence reframed: Multiple intelligences for the 21st century.* New York: Basic Books.

Maslow, A. (1979). *The journals of A. H. Maslow.* Monterey, CA: Brooks/ Cole.

9

Taking on the Criticisms of Positive Psychology

Better to light a candle than to curse the darkness.
—CP (Chinese Proverb)

Better to light a candle than to curse the candle that others light.
—CP (Christopher Peterson)

I recently received some feedback about my writing on positive psychology, like the reflections in this book. Simply put, the feedback is that I am too nice. I sidestep criticisms. I do not take on the critics of positive psychology except with humor and occasional innuendo, and I do not call them out by name.

I own the criticism because it is valid. I abhor controversy, and I do a great job avoiding it in my professional (and personal) life. But I am a self-identified positive psychologist, and I am deeply invested in this perspective. So maybe I should take a stand against the critics. Why should I be nicer than they are? More forthrightly, I should defend what I believe. Otherwise, what's it all about?

Those who write popular stories in the media try to be fair and balanced, and every time a story appears about positive psychology, a small number of usual suspects, in and out of academics, are interviewed to criticize what is going on. They invariably say the same things, even as positive psychology itself has changed over the years. Maybe their criticisms are timeless, but maybe they are immune to the facts.

Anyway, here I will not take on the critics of positive psychology. I don't want to be an *ad hominem* kind of guy.* Instead, it makes more sense to take on the criticisms. So here goes with my responses to some of the common criticisms. You readers can decide how successful I am.

First, positive psychology is nothing new. This is a criticism usually heard from academics who fault positive psychologists for failing to acknowledge the many intellectual predecessors of the perspective. There are instances in which positive psychologists present their work as thoroughly original when it is not, and doing so of course deserves criticism. But in general, this is not a valid criticism.

Plenty of positive psychologists acknowledge what came before and even build directly on it. Consider Jonathan Haidt's (2006) book *The Happiness Hypothesis: Finding Modern Truth in Ancient Wisdom*. And other positive psychologists may fail to mention a predecessor for all sorts of reasons that make good sense, like the space limitations imposed by most publication venues.

The real issue, I think, is determining when it is intellectually necessary for positive psychologists to focus explicitly on predecessors and when it is simply distracting to do so. When I give lectures in my college classes, I usually spend a lot of time on the predecessors, because that is what a college lecturer should do. But when I am giving a brief interview with a magazine writer interested in happiness and character, I usually do not quote at length from Aristotle.

In any event, none of the specific topics that positive psychology studies is new, and anyone who claims otherwise warrants criticism. But I would argue that the umbrella term *positive psychology*

---

* Some critics of positive psychology have launched *ad hominem* attacks against me. I try to be philosophical. I spent most of my career writing papers and books about which no one cared. Now people care, often in good ways but sometimes in bad ways. Would I want a do-over? No way.

itself is new and has considerable power for drawing together previously disparate topics and encouraging their simultaneous examination.** That's new and a large part of why positive psychology is popular (see reflection 1).

Second, who is to say what is positive? This criticism is frequently voiced, but it usually fails when we talk specifics. Yes, there are gray areas, but there are genuinely good things and genuinely bad things in the world. And anyone who lives in the world can make a judgment about what the good things might be, including—I would hope—positive psychologists. If these judgments are informed by evidence, like survey data about what most respondents value or observation of the choices that most people make, all the better. The good things are what positive psychologists study.

So, I believe happiness is better than depression, a long life better than a short life, and a healthy life better than an unhealthy one. I believe love is better than hate, meaning and purpose better than alienation and anomie, social connection better than loneliness, and success better than failure. I believe that optimism is better than pessimism.

And on Valentine's Day, I urge you to send your sweetheart chocolate and roses rather than Brussels sprouts and poison ivy. Who is to say what is positive? All of us, and there is a lot more consensus than the critics of positive psychology would have us believe.

Third, focusing on the positive gets us in trouble. It has been claimed that optimism is undermining America, leading to the mortgage crisis, to people eschewing health care, and to the country's high divorce rate. Yes and no, as I have discussed in other reflections (25, 26, and 27). There is foolish optimism

---

** Whether we want to credit Martin Seligman or Abraham Maslow for coining the term *positive psychology* is a legitimate debate (Peterson, 2006). Both used the phrase, Maslow much earlier than Seligman, but they used the term in different senses, and Maslow soon abandoned it.

that is thoroughly unrealistic, and that form of it indeed gets us in trouble. But there is also optimism that galvanizes activity in an uncertain world and leads to changes for the better that would not have occurred had we hunkered down and embraced the pessimistic view that things could never be better than they are. Hundreds if not thousands of studies show that optimism leads to better consequences than pessimism does. Exceptions notwithstanding, it is a focus on the negative that gets people in trouble more than a focus on the positive.

Fourth, positive psychology is indifferent to human suffering. Moreover, the very existence of positive psychology is a distraction from what we as individuals and a society should really be doing—solving the pressing problems that people experience (see reflection 1). These criticisms are heard less nowadays than they once were, because positive psychologists have recognized that one of the best ways to help someone solve a problem is to identify the person's assets and strengths and then use these in the service of solving the problem. You have to stand somewhere to paint a floor, so why not stand on a part of the floor that does not need painting?

Fifth, it is premature to do interventions based on positive psychology findings. This criticism urges "further research" in the lab before applying results in the field. There are plenty of examples, from psychology and other disciplines, of interventions supposedly based on science that either failed or did actual harm—think lobotomies, assuming you have not had one (cf. Valenstein, 1986).

That said, I have a different perspective on basic and applied work in psychology that echoes Kurt Lewin's (1946) idea of action research and more contemporary calls for translational research (Woolf, 2008). Applied work need not—and should not—follow basic work at a polite and cautious distance. Rather, at least when done well, basic research and applied research are synergistic; they reinforce one another and should be undertaken in tandem.

What is needed is an attitude toward interventions that is as skeptical and hardheaded as the attitude more often seen toward basic work. Interventionists need to consider the possibility that they are wrong (Campbell, 1969). And if they are wrong, they need to change or abandon the intervention that failed. That's how progress is made, not by waiting for an unspecified time before doing an intervention.

Potential participants in a yet-to-be verified positive psychology intervention should of course be told that it is experimental. No guarantees. Then they can make an informed choice about whether they want to give it a try. This is how my colleagues and I have recruited participants for our intervention studies (Seligman, Steen, Park, & Peterson, 2005), and I see nothing to criticize about such an approach.

Sixth, positive psychologists exaggerate the implications of results. The glib response to this criticism is that exaggeration is human nature and that researchers in and out of psychology are not immune to the tendency. But this response acknowledges the validity of the criticism, so a more thoughtful examination is in order.

Unlike many other domains of life, in which exaggeration takes on a life of its own, science is self-corrective, which means that exaggerations are eventually brought down to earth by follow-up studies. Of course, these studies need to be done, and here we have another strong justification for testing out interventions.

Critics sometimes lump together trade books (for the general public) by positive psychologists and peer-reviewed journal articles (for the scientific community) describing research by positive psychologists. It is difficult to defend some of the claims made in trade books, even when these claims are ostensibly based on scientific evidence. But the journal articles are another matter. Criticizing all of positive psychology for occasional excesses in some quarters is akin to criticizing all of music based solely on what one hears in an elevator.

We need to privilege findings (and applications based on them) that appear in reputable journals with a peer-review process. However, positive psychology ideas appear not only in scientific journals but also in popular books, Internet blogs, and iPhone apps. Some of these are reasonable, others not. It can be difficult for the general public to sort through what is actually known versus what is simply hoped. Exaggerations do occur, and they tarnish all of positive psychology.

I am completely in favor of "giving psychology away" through accessible media. But I urge responsibility on the part of those doing the giving. Include necessary qualifications and cautions. Distinguish what is known from what is not. Invite the general public along for a very interesting ride.

By all means, positive psychologists should keep writing books for the general public. The problem is not with the books per se but in how some of the books are framed and marketed. Positive psychology trade books should not be written as happiness cookbooks, replete with strong guarantees about the five easy steps toward lasting bliss.

According to Aristotle, "Criticism is something we can avoid easily by saying nothing, doing nothing, and being nothing." Positive psychologists have opted for a different approach to science, a positive one—pun intended. Criticisms should be heeded when correct and valued even when incorrect because they are a sign that people are paying attention.

REFERENCES

Campbell, D. T. (1969). Reforms as experiments. *American Psychologist, 24*, 409–429.

Haidt, J. (2006). *The happiness hypothesis: Finding modern truth in ancient wisdom.* New York: Basic Books.

Lewin, K. (1946). Action research and minority problems. *Journal of Social Issues, 2*(4), 34–46.

Peterson, C. (2006). *A primer in positive psychology*. New York: Oxford University Press.

Seligman, M. E. P., Steen, T. A., Park, N., & Peterson, C. (2005). Positive psychology progress: Empirical validation of interventions. *American Psychologist, 60*, 410–421.

Valenstein, E. S. (1986). *Great and desperate cures.* New York: Basic Books, 1986.

Woolf, S. H. (2008). The meaning of translational research and why it matters. *JAMA, 299*, 211–213.

10

The Future of Positive Psychology

Science and Practice

As for the future, your task is not to foresee it but to enable it.
—Antoine de Saint-Exupery

What comes next for the field of positive psychology? It is of course impossible for me to make predictions about the future with any certainty—if I could, I'd move to Las Vegas or Wall Street and set up shop—but here are some of my ideas. If your diet allows, take them with several grains of salt.

First, positive psychologists will expand the so-called natural homes of the field: settings where doing well is recognized, celebrated, and encouraged. Contrary to our original thinking about natural homes, they should include the psychological clinic in addition to those initially suggested, like schools and businesses. One way to help people with problems is to base solutions on what they do well.

And I for one never thought that the military would be a natural home for positive psychology, but at present, there is there considerable interest, especially in the United States Army. I predict that this interest will grow in the years ahead (Novotney, 2009).

My reflection on third places (75) suggests yet another natural home—or, more exactly, a community of natural homes for positive psychology: cafes, taverns, recreation centers, and maybe even Internet chat rooms as one reader suggested to me.

Second, positive psychology will continue to be criticized—which, up to a point, is a good sign that the field is taken seriously—and I hope that the criticisms will be heeded when apt and politely countered when not (see reflection 9).

Along these lines, I hope—but do not necessarily predict—that positive psychologists will challenge some of the emerging myths about the field, especially those concerning positive psychology interventions. As I see these interventions, they are neither light-handed nor foolproof. Change is always difficult, even if it is change for the better, and positive psychologists should not expect one-size-fits-all interventions to be the final and best-practice contribution, a point to which I return shortly when I mention culture.

Third, positive psychology will follow the directions of psychology per se, inward to neuroscience and outward to culture.

What is the neurobiological basis of the good life? More generally, what is the role of the body? To date, positive psychology has been very much a neck-up endeavor, but dance and music and sport and sex make life worth living, and we need to know more about these topics from the perspective of positive psychology.

Martin Seligman (2008) and others, including me, are starting to grapple with what can be called *positive health*, trying to do for the domain of physical well-being what positive psychology has productively done for the domain of psychological well-being. If "good" emotional health entails more than the absence of distress and unhappiness, does "good" physical health similarly entail more than the absence of symptoms and disease? I predict greater attention to what I dub *super health*: living not only long but well, with vigor and engagement, bouncing back quickly from illness.

Culture is not a veneer on human nature. It *is* human nature, and cultures differ in important ways. As positive psychology research and especially applications spread throughout the world, this growth cannot be simply an export business from the United States. Interventions that "work" in individualistic cultures may or may not be suitable in collectivist cultures (see reflection 73). Indeed, positive psychology interventions to date are usually one-on-one, following the model of psychotherapy or executive coaching. When "group" interventions are undertaken, the rationale is often one of mere efficiency. But we all live, love, work, and play in groups, so why not make the group an explicit focus in our attempts to build the good life? I predict that this will happen (Peterson, Park, & Sweeney, 2008).

And as important as the individualistic-versus-collectivist distinction may be, it is not the only cultural difference that deserves attention (Cohen, 2009). Cultures differ in how hierarchical they are, in terms of how norms for male or female behavior differ, in terms of their orientation to the future, in terms of their tolerance for uncertainty, and so on. I predict that these sorts of distinctions will be found valuable as positive psychology grows.

Positive psychologists should also remember the venerable distinction by Ruth Benedict (1934) between Apollonian and Dionysian cultures, which respectively emphasize moderation and restraint versus emotion and exuberance. Many self-identified positive psychology practitioners seem Dionysian, which of course is fine given that they work in a Dionysian setting. But at some point, they will encounter Apollonian groups and cultures, and they should adjust their interventions and styles accordingly. As I always mutter to myself when I go off to talk with members of the U.S. Army: "Don't hug the colonels."

REFERENCES

Benedict, R. (1934). *Patterns of culture*. New York: Houghton Mifflin.

Cohen, A. B. (2009). Many forms of culture. *American Psychologist, 64*, 194–204.

Novotney, A. (2009, December). Strong in mind and body. *Monitor on Psychology, 40*(11), 40–43.

Peterson, C., Park, N., & Sweeney, P. J. (2008). Group well-being: Morale from a positive psychology perspective. *Applied Psychology: An International Review, 57*, 19–36.

Seligman, M. E. P. (2008). Positive health. *Applied Psychology: An International Review, 57*, 3–18.

Part II

Positive Emotions and Experiences

Positive psychologists sometimes worry that the field will be seen as a celebration of shallow pleasures and thus be dismissed as another version of hedonism. So, positive psychologists emphasize that the field encompasses a variety of phenomena involved in a life well lived, and most of the reflections in this book address these sorts of topics.

That said, feeling good—experiencing pleasure, happiness, satisfaction, and engagement—is part of the good life, and the reflections in this section tackle positive emotions head on. What has been learned about positive experiences small and large, simple and complex? Are there ways to enhance or prolong our satisfaction?

11

What Do You Think About in the Shower?

While recently reading a newspaper, I came across a survey—thoroughly informal—the outcome of which was intriguing. The survey question was simple: "What do you think about while taking a shower?" The data lingered, like the smell of Irish Spring soap, because it was a rare example of me being more evolved than the typical respondent.

So what did the typical respondent say? He or she ran through a to-do list for the day ahead!

And what do I do in the shower? On occasion, I think about the importance of rinsing shampoo out of my hair. But I usually think, if that is even the right word, that I am really enjoying the shower.

Showers are not guilty pleasures. They are not among the seven deadly sins. They are neither immoral nor illegal. They are simply enjoyable. So why don't more of us just enjoy them?

There are few pleasures that we can savor without qualification or misgivings. Showers are among them. So savor your shower already! Research into savoring by positive psychologists Fred Bryant and Joseph Veroff (2006) is very clear that we can best savor a pleasurable experience—make it last—by throwing ourselves into it without distractions.

To-do lists, however important they may be outside of a shower, are a major distraction when you are naked and wet. Do you take a paper and pad into the shower? Can you actually check off anything on your list? Are you thoroughly alienated from pleasure?

(An occasional response to the survey, by the way, was that people in a shower thought about sex. I won't touch that.)

The good life is richly local. Some of it resides in the shower.

Enjoy your next shower. And do not think about anything, even this reflection.

ANNOTATION

One of the responses to this reflection when it was originally posted on the *Psychology Today* website was an advertisement for a waterproof product that allowed people to take notes in the shower. I try to take comments on my reflections with a grain of salt, but in this case, I lost it and fired back a reply about the importance of reading—however casually—what someone writes before trying to piggyback a commercial product onto it.

REFERENCE

Bryant, F. B., & Veroff, J. (2006). *The process of savoring: A new model of positive experience.* Mahwah, NJ: Lawrence Erlbaum.

12

Savoring and Dampening Positive Feelings

I have written several reflections here on *savoring*: the strategies people use to enhance and sustain their positive feelings (11 and 13). It is clear that savoring contributes to well-being, in the moment and thereafter. Different strategies are available, including sharing positive experiences with others, building memories (e.g., taking photographs or souvenirs), and immersing one's self in the experience. It is also clear that people vary in their spontaneous use of these strategies (Bryant, 2003). Some of us do a lot of savoring, and some of us do very little—with predictable effects on our life satisfaction and happiness. And some of us even show *dampening*: dealing with a positive feeling by trying to feel worse. Dampening entails snatching hedonic defeat, as it were, from the jaws of victory (Langston, 1994).

Why would anyone dampen a positive feeling? I can think of reasons—not wanting to show off to others, not wanting to get one's hopes up that the future will be as wonderful as the present, and so on (cf. Parrott, 1993). But a paper I just read suggests another reason, and this one is supported by a series of research studies and thus deserves to be taken more seriously than my mere speculation (Wood, Heimpel, & Michela, 2003).

It turns out that someone's self-esteem influences tendencies to savor versus dampen a positive feeling.

Using a variety of methods—surveys and experiments—researchers at the University of Waterloo showed that those with higher self-esteem savor positive feelings by using one or more of the strategies for enhancing and sustaining good moods. In contrast, those with lower self-esteem dampen positive feelings by deliberately muting them or distracting themselves from them. These patterns held even when the personality traits of extraversion and neuroticism were measured and statistically controlled. The psychologically rich become richer.

Using other data obtained in their studies, the researchers argued that these effects occurred because people are motivated to sustain a consistent view of themselves. Those with higher self-esteem—people who like and value themselves—see happiness as a state consistent with who they are, and thus they savor their good feelings. Those with lower self-esteem—people who neither like nor value themselves—analogously see unhappiness as a state consistent with who they are, and thus they dampen their good feelings.

If this interpretation is correct, then consistency is a more potent influence on feelings than is hedonism, a conclusion with interesting implications.

I have always thought that some people are unhappy because they do not know how to be otherwise. It is pointless to tell someone to cheer up if he or she does not know how to do so. But perhaps another reason that some people are unhappy is that they are motivated to be unhappy—or at least not happy—in order to preserve the view they hold of themselves.

Positive psychologists have devised a host of strategies to make people happier; most of these instruct people what to do in order to be happier (e.g., Seligman, Steen, Park, & Peterson, 2005). The results of the research program I have described suggest that skills are not always enough. People also need to have reasons to be happy, and the task of the applied positive psychologist becomes more daunting.

Have a good day. Or perhaps I should say, See a good day as consistent with who you are.

REFERENCES

Bryant, F. B. (2003). Savoring Beliefs Inventory (SBI): A scale for measuring beliefs about savouring. *Journal of Mental Health, 12*, 175–196.

Langston, C. A. (1994). Capitalizing on and coping with daily-life events: Expressive responses to positive events. *Journal of Personality and Social Psychology, 67*, 1112–1125.

Parrott, W. G. (1993). Beyond hedonism: Motives for inhibiting good moods and for maintaining bad moods. In D. M. Wegner & J. W. Pennebaker (Eds.), *Handbook of mental control* (pp. 278–305). Upper Saddle River, NJ: Prentice-Hall.

Seligman, M. E. P., Steen, T. A., Park, N., & Peterson, C. (2005). Positive psychology progress: Empirical validation of interventions. *American Psychologist, 60*, 410–421.

Wood, J. V., Heimpel, S. A., & Michela, J. L. (2003). Savoring versus dampening: Self-esteem differences in regulating positive affect. *Journal of Personality and Social Psychology, 85*, 566–580.

13

Who Most Enjoys the Small Things in Life?

I'd like to live as a poor man with lots of money.
—Pablo Picasso

The relationship between money and happiness has long been of interest to those of us in the modern world, and in the past few years, positive psychologists have conducted a number of intriguing studies showing—if nothing else—that the link between them is complicated (see reflection 18).

Yet another intriguing line of research has been explored by researchers Jordi Quoidbach, Elizabeth W. Dunn, K. V. Petrides, and Moïra Mikolajczak. In 2010, they investigated whether wealthy people were less likely than others to savor small pleasures (see reflection 14). As you might imagine, given that I am writing about this research, the answer to this question is an interesting *yes*. Wealthy people apparently take less pleasure in the small things in life. Is this because they already have the big things? I'll return to what this finding might mean, but first let me describe the research.

Two studies were done. The first study used a mixed-methods procedure: survey and laboratory. Adult research participants (from Belgium) filled out standard surveys assessing their income, their disposition to savor positive emotions, and their overall happiness. Half of the participants were primed by exposure to a photo of euros; the other half were not. In one set of analyses, wealth (income) negatively predicted scores on the savoring measure, and so did exposure to the money prime. In another set of analyses, the statistical link between income and happiness was weakened when the tendency to savor was taken into account.

The second study again primed adult participants (from Canada) with a picture of money or not, and then asked them to eat a chocolate bar. Ratings were made of how long it took participants to eat the chocolate (presumably, a longer time meant more savoring) as well as how much they appeared to enjoy the chocolate. Because women spent more time eating the chocolate, gender was controlled in the statistical analyses. Exposure to money reduced both eating time and the observed enjoyment.

The researchers concluded that a simple reminder of wealth undermined the ability of participants to savor the small things in life, like a chocolate bar.

Can we quibble with these studies? Absolutely. *Psychological Science*, the high-impact journal in which this paper was published, often privileges "oh my goodness" studies with their share of loose ends.

In the first study by Quoidbach and colleagues, I wondered about confounds like age and experience with savoring. And in the second study, along these lines, I wondered about the unidentified "chocolate bar" the research participants ate. As my own income has increased over the years, I have discovered designer chocolate bars—those with flavors of chili peppers, sea salt, or wasabi. Oh my! I still eat Hershey bars and on occasion scarf down half a pound of M&Ms in a single sitting, but that's all about the sugar rush. Can I savor the "good" chocolate? You'd better believe it.

But let's take the results of these studies at face value. What does it mean—for sake of argument—that those with money don't appreciate the smaller things, like a Hershey bar? Lots of things. It means they have habituated to the smaller pleasures of life, which I suspect are the more numerous ones. It means that their happiness is likely attenuated unless they always spend top dollar. It means that they don't understand other people and what satisfies them. And it means that their quest for the good life will be ongoing and ultimately frustrating.

The Bible tells us that it is more difficult for a camel to pass through the eye of a needle than it is for a rich man to enter the kingdom of God (Matthew 19:24). To this perhaps we should add that the rich may not even enjoy their time here on earth, at least when their wealth is salient to them.

REFERENCE

Quoidbach, J., Dunn, E. W., Petrides, K. V., & Mikolajczak, M. (2010). Money giveth, money taketh away: The dual effect of wealth on happiness. *Psychological Science, 21,* 759–763.

14

Fast Food and Impatience

Most of us know that fast food is not all that healthy, even if we can't resist it. A paper by Chen-Bo Zhong and Sanford E. DeVoe (2010) shows yet another downside of fast food—this one psychological. According to these researchers, even the subliminal reminder of fast food can make people impatient.

Three experiments with college students were conducted. In the first experiment, researchers flashed ever so briefly (below conscious thresholds) on a computer screen the logos of well-known fast food franchises (McDonald's, KFC, Subway, Taco Bell, Burger King, and Wendy's) while research participants worked on another task. A comparison group did the same task without the fast food logos appearing. Then all participants were asked to read a brief passage. Although there was no time pressure or time limit mentioned, the "fast food" participants read more quickly. That in and of itself may not be bad. The researchers did not measure recall or enjoyment of the passage.

But consider the other experiments described.

In the second experiment, participants were asked to remember either the last time they ate fast food or the last time they went grocery shopping. They all then completed an ostensibly unrelated marketing survey. Exposure to fast food reminders led participants to express a preference for time-saving products.

And in the third experiment, participants were asked to rate the aesthetic appeal of different corporate logos, some of fast food franchises and some not. Exposure to fast food reminders reduced the willingness of participants to delay gratification at a later task.

The researchers concluded their report by noting the apparent irony of their findings: Fast food, which supposedly helps us save time in one domain of life, leads us to be time urgent—impatient—in other domains of life. What's the point of saving time if we don't use it to savor what makes life worth living?

As W. H. Auden wrote, "Perhaps there is only one cardinal sin: impatience. Because of impatience we were driven out of Paradise, because of impatience we cannot return."

REFERENCE

Zhong, C.-B., & DeVoe, S. E. (2010). You are how you eat: Fast food and impatience. *Psychological Science, 21*, 619–622.

15

Passion and Positive Psychology

If there is no passion in your life, then have you really lived?
—T. Alan Armstrong

Positive psychology is concerned with what makes life worth living, and since its beginning, positive psychologists have done a good job of moving more and more relevant concepts under their umbrella. Passion is one of the recent notions claimed by positive psychology, and my purpose in this reflection is to talk about research into passion by psychologist Robert Vallerand at the University of Quebec (Montreal).

First a little background about *passion* that is relevant to contemporary research. The word apparently comes a Latin verb—*patoir*—meaning "to suffer and endure," an intriguing origin considering that nowadays we often use the term to describe pursuits that we enjoy and—indeed—to describe active pursuits as opposed to the passive endurance of painful events.

The term was used to describe the suffering of Jesus (cf. Mel Gibson's 2004 movie *The Passion of the Christ*) and Christian martyrdom. Following these uses, *passion* came to mean more generally very strong emotions, not only suffering but also what sustained the person who suffered. Even today, I suspect that one indicator of how passionate someone is about a pursuit or goal is the willingness to sacrifice in order to achieve it. In one of the memorable lines from *The Last Lecture*, Randy Pausch told his audience that the barriers in our lives are put there so that we can show how badly we want something (see reflection 24).

Throughout Western history, passion has often been juxtaposed with reason, implying that passion—at least from the viewpoint of an outside observer—is irrational, a point to which I will return.

Somewhat more recently in etymological history, passion was used more narrowly to describe strong sexual desire, a still common use, although nowadays we also see passion referring to any and all strong emotions: love or joy or hatred or anger.

Vallerand (2008) defines passion as "a strong inclination toward a self-defining activity that one likes (or even loves)." Note that he limits *passion* to activities that people like or love, which is why his work fits under the positive psychology umbrella. I suppose it would be interesting to explore the darker passions, those marked by hatred or anger, but that has not been Vallerand's purpose. I refer interested readers to AM talk radio.

Vallerand's qualification that our passions define us is important and distinguishes his work from superficially similar investigations of notions like persistence and perseverance. So, I persist doggedly every April to complete my income tax returns, but I would never use the word *passion* to describe what I do (except when I feel like an IRS martyr).

Vallerand uses the examples of playing the guitar and playing basketball. Many of us do these things, but they become passions when we start to think about ourselves as guitar players or basketball players.

Is passion as Vallerand defines it a topic for positive psychology to address? Obviously. The activities about which we are passionate make our lives worth living—usually—even if psychologists have typically neglected them. (There is an extended psychological literature on "interests" that strike me as the tepid relatives of passions.)

Where do we find our passions? Some folks are passionate about their work, and others passionate about their loved ones. In my opinion, these folks are fortunate but not typical.

Leisure activities are where many of us find our passions. Because he is my friend, I happen to know that Robert Vallerand is passionate about playing the guitar and about playing basketball (not at the same time, to my knowledge). And I am passionate about playing Scrabble and rooting for the University of Michigan football team. One need not be all that skilled at an activity to be passionate about it; I am at best a mediocre Scrabble player, although I am better at playing tiles these days than the Wolverines are at playing in the Big Ten.

Leisure activities may lend themselves readily to passion because they are voluntary and intrinsically motivated. It is much easier to define yourself in terms of an activity that you choose to do as opposed to one that you must do.

In any event, I suspect Robert Vallerand is also passionate about his research as a psychologist because he has carried out an impressive line of work into passion, one that he writes about and speaks about with great enthusiasm.

His early work entailed surveys. He found that 85% of his adult respondents could readily identify at least one activity about which they were passionate. As I have suggested, most of these activities are recreational. People on average spend 8.5 hours per week on their most passionate pursuit, and they had done so for many years, usually starting in adolescence. (It can't be a coincidence that the central Eriksonian task of adolescence is to create an identity for one's self.)

Then he developed a self-report scale to measure passion, and its important wrinkle is the distinction between two types of passion: a "healthy" type that Vallerand dubs *harmonious passion* and an "unhealthy" type that he labels *obsessive passion*. Although distinguishable, they can co-occur and—interestingly—both contribute to one's self-image. The difference is that a harmonious passion has no psychological strings attached other than its enjoyment. In contrast, an obsessive passion entails dependence on the passionate activity. Consider two passionate joggers who injure themselves. The one who has harmonious passion about running will take time off and heal. The other who has obsessive passion will keep running and make the injury worse.

Not surprisingly, harmonious passion is linked to the usual suspects that comprise the psychological good life: positive affect, life satisfaction, physical health, and good performance (at the passionate activity). Obsessive passion in general shows the opposite pattern of correlates and furthermore can interfere with social relationships. And those with an obsessive passion may experience shame during or after the activity.

Do the empirical findings about obsessive passion contradict the etymological history of passion that highlights one's willingness to suffer in pursuit of an activity? I don't think so. What makes a passion obsessive is that it actually gets in the way of itself. A hobbled jogger is not much of a jogger and will become ever less so as his or her jogging continues. Someone obsessively passionate about gambling will likely run through his or her money and not be able to place future bets.

In sum, passions make life worth living but need to be pursued in ways that sustain themselves. That passions can entail sacrifice actually define them as passions. They are healthy when the sacrifice is as freely undertaken as the activity itself and does not undercut the goal of the passionate activity. That passions may strike others as irrational is irrelevant in describing them as harmonious or obsessive, healthy or unhealthy. After all, passions are personal and what matters about our passions is whether they make sense to us.

As a Scrabble player, I love the words QAT, QAID, and QI—among the Q words that can be played without having a U (see reflection 100). Whether these words matter to you is not all that important to me, unless you happen to be my opponent, in which case I hope that you do not know them.

REFERENCE

Vallerand, R. J. (2008). On the psychology of passion: In search of what makes people's lives most worth living. *Canadian Psychology, 49,* 1–13.

16

The Positive Analogue of a Phobia

I don't just write essays—I also read them—and I have learned that the title can draw readers more than the content, which is why I try to title my own reflections in provocative ways, sometimes even stooping to using profanity or near-profanity in them (see reflections 7 and 52). I have drawn the line at writing about the shenanigans of sex-crazed celebrities.

Accordingly, when I came up with the idea for this particular reflection, I hesitated about writing it because I didn't know how to title it. The obvious title would be "Soteria," but who would read that? Most don't even know what it means.

But here you are, so let me explain. A *soteria* is the positive analogue of a phobia. A phobia is an irrational fear of some object, whereas a soteria is an irrational attraction to some other object. In popular U.S. culture, the most famous soteria is Linus's blanket, but I'd bet that most of us have our own examples, even if we don't have a label for them.

Indeed, last semester, when I offhandedly mentioned the notion of a soteria to my large lecture class, I saw more light bulbs turning on above students' heads than I had ever seen before. And students started to raise their hands and talk excitedly. They got it because they had it. Mind you, this kind of excitement is not the norm in large lecture classes at a university.

The stimulus for me writing about soterias was the aftermath of the attempt by an airplane passenger to detonate his underwear as the plane was landing in Detroit. He was unsuccessful, but one of the apparent decisions in the wake of this near-tragedy is that airplane passengers will no longer be allowed to have anything in their laps during the last hour of a flight.

I'm a nervous flier, so you might think I would welcome one more effort to make flying safer. But my reaction was to become even more anxious as I thought ahead to future flights...and landings. When my planes land, I am always clutching something close to me, usually my jacket or a pillow if available or sometimes just my well-worn briefcase.

Why do I do this? It makes me feel better. It is thoroughly irrational. The plane will do what the plane will do regardless of what I happen to be holding in my lap (and despite my vigilant scanning for the local equivalent of the Hudson River). But clutching something with a pleasing and familiar feel reduces my anxiety. That's one of the defining features of a soteria.

Some years ago, Martin Seligman and I were co-teaching a positive psychology class at the University of Pennsylvania. We came up with what we thought would be an interesting out-of-class exercise, or at least an interesting out-of-our-class exercise. Midterm exams were approaching in most of the classes our students were taking, and we suggested that they dress up for their exams—coats and ties, formal dresses, the whole nine yards. We told our students that—perhaps—if they looked good, they would do well.

And they told us that we were out of our minds. They were going to wear what they always wore for their exams: torn T-shirts, sweatpants or tattered jeans, and even in a few cases bedroom slippers. As to a further suggestion we made—that they get their hair styled right before the exam and put on makeup—they simply laughed. Some of them said that they went into an exam as uncombed and as unwashed as possible.

Many of the students described their exam gear as lucky, and we didn't persist.

I didn't put my finger on it at the time, but now I think that what the students were telling us was not about superstitions in the form of "lucky" clothes but rather about soterias. If it were simply about superstition, we would not have seen the incredible convergence that our students reported.

A soteria may be irrational, but it is not arbitrary. It invariably entails a pleasing texture and a familiar smell. Like a phobia, a soteria is biologically potent. Remember Linus's blanket: Next to losing his blanket, the worst imaginable thing for Linus is to have it washed. Laundry detergent advertisements notwithstanding, sometimes we don't want our things to smell fresh.

What's the positive point? In the psychoanalytic literature, there are discussions of soterias and their near relatives, so-called transitional objects, as well as their sexual cousins, fetishes. These discussions typically underscore the immaturity that soterias are thought to reflect as well as their link to psychopathology.

Here I won't touch transitional objects or fetishes (although doing so would feel good, I am sure). I will simply say from a positive psychology point of view that soterias are benign until proven otherwise. Indeed, they may be helpful in reducing anxiety and producing comfort, thereby contributing to the good life. Soterias may be quite common if we look beyond blankets, Teddy bears, and sweatpants to Lazy-Boy recliners, shag carpets, and turtleneck sweaters. *Not* to have a soteria may hamper one's ongoing life. Maybe students do well on exams not when they look good but when they feel good. Or maybe a soteria makes our oxytocin surge. Those are interesting empirical issues.

I'll let you know how my next flight goes. Suggestions are welcome.

ANNOTATION

At least on my recent flights, this ban on having things in one's lap during the last hour of a flight was not enforced.

17

Sunday Afternoon with
Daniel Kahneman

On December 19, 2010, the University of Michigan had its 2010 winter commencement, and the featured speaker was Princeton University professor of psychology and public affairs Daniel Kahneman, recipient of the 2002 Nobel Award in Economics and an important contributor to all sorts of fields, including behavioral economics and the perspective of positive psychology.

The winter commencement is much smaller than the spring commencement. It is held in the basketball arena and is attended by several thousand family members and friends of graduates as opposed to the tens of thousands who come to the football stadium in May.

But I like the smaller graduation ceremony more than the larger one precisely because it is smaller and more personal ... and certainly more convenient. Parking is not much of an issue, and neither are entrances nor exits. All Ph.D.s have their names called, and all degree recipients move across the stage and shake the hand of the dean of their college, the university provost, and/or the university president.

And I enjoyed the commencement speaker this December as much as I enjoyed the commencement speaker last May, which is saying something because the latter speaker was Barack Obama (see reflection 59).

I do not personally know Professor Kahneman, although I have long followed and appreciated his work. This past semester, during my positive psychology course, I spoke about his ideas constantly, so much so that many of my students—when they heard that he would be the winter commencement speaker—became very excited and told me they planned to attend, even though it was not their own graduation.

After receiving an honorary degree, he spoke for about 10 or 15 minutes, and he did so in his typically wonderful way, meaning that he was clear and provocative—and about the smartest person on the planet. To judge from his image on the JumboTron above the stage, he also had a twinkle in his eye.

There was snow on the ground outside, and he started by discussing a study of life in Michigan versus life in California. Everyone, in Michigan and in California, believes that people are happier on the West Coast than in the Midwest because—after all—the weather is so much better. The audience chuckled. And as if we needed further convincing, he added to the audience still garbed in winter coats, gloves, and mufflers, "It really is better, you know."

But he went on to the punch line, which is that people in California are not happier than people in the Midwest. Weather may influence happiness, but whatever effects it may have are lost among all the other factors that influence happiness (but see reflection 68). When asked, people believe Californians to be happier than Midwesterners because the question leads them to focus on differences between California and the Midwest, and weather is an obvious difference. This phenomenon, called the *focusing illusion*, has broad applicability. When making comparative judgments, we are overly influenced by those things on which we focus—in this case, weather.

To sum up the point, he said, "Nothing is as important as you think it is, at least when you are thinking about it." I was sitting next to a colleague, and upon hearing this one-sentence summary, we spontaneously turned toward one another, and each of us silently mouthed, "Wow."

The rest of his talk was about the experiencing self versus the remembering self. The happiness of each self matters, but the happiness of the two selves may have different determinants. The advice to the graduates (and to the rest of us) is to make appropriate choices about what we value and to behave accordingly. He summed up the differences tersely. To paraphrase, "The happiness of the remembering self is influenced by our achievements, and the happiness of the experiencing self is influenced by our positive emotions, which in turn result from other people" (see reflections 37, 38, and 43).

To mention one more of Professor Kahneman's important ideas, what we remember about our good experiences is how they end. In the case of the University of Michigan December 2010 graduates, their college careers ended with a great commencement address by one of the most important thinkers of our time.

As for me, it was also a wonderful afternoon, as I experienced it and as I have remembered it.

18

Money and Happiness

One of the popular conclusions supposedly stemming from research in positive psychology is that money cannot buy happiness. The problem with this conclusion is that it is wrong. Research shows that income has a positive relationship with happiness (life satisfaction), although it is not a straight line. As income increases, its added contribution to life satisfaction becomes smaller. The impact of additional income is greatest among those who have little money, but it does not stop mattering, even after someone is able to meet basic needs. The very least we can do as positive psychologists is to take our own data seriously.

Income may not be the most important contributor to how happy most people are, and there are good reasons—psychological and moral—to decry rampant materialism. But money matters, if only a bit. As Mae West once said, "I've been rich, and I've been poor; believe me, rich is better."

Here is another finding about money and happiness. When we compare the average life satisfaction of people who live in different nations, the wealth (GNP) of the nation is a strong predictor of the happiness of its citizens. With exceptions, the least happy nations are the poorest, and the most happy nations are the richest.

There are some data implying that as nations become richer, the happiness of their citizens does not rise. This finding is termed a paradox, but it may be based on an incomplete sampling of nations.

As my own salary has increased over the years, my life has certainly become more comfortable, and here may be some insight into the relationship between money and happiness. Positive psychologists distinguish between pleasures and comforts. Pleasures by definition are short-lived—we adapt to them. In contrast, comforts are not front-and-center in our consciousness, until they are absent. I call this the *Big Yellow Taxi Effect*, after Joni Mitchell's song about not knowing what we have until it's gone.

I can remember when my family was first able to purchase an air conditioner, and when the family was first able to purchase a color television. For a while, life was very pleasurable ... very cool and vivid (puns intended). Now we take these for granted, except when they break. Then life is miserable. Maybe for those of us who are fortunate enough to have extra income, the value of that income vis-à-vis happiness is to afford comforts. Is comfort good? I think so. Regardless, I would never tell someone who is uncomfortable that it does not matter.

Here are some additional findings about money and happiness.

A study by Hilke Plassmann, John O'Doherty, Baba Shiv, and Antonio Rangel, published in 2008 in the *Proceedings of the National Academy of Sciences*, measured brain activity while research participants were drinking wine. Regions of the brain responsible for the registering of pleasure were more active when the wine was identified as expensive as opposed to inexpensive. Here's the punch line: It was the same wine in both cases! Perhaps wealthy people are happier because they spend more money on things. In any event, I wish the researchers had included a third condition in which participants were told they were drinking really expensive wine purchased at a really deep discount. That might have short-circuited the fMRI apparatus.

Another article by Elizabeth W. Dunn, Lara B. Aknin, and Michael I. Norton, published in 2008 in *Science*, concluded that money can buy happiness, so long as the money is spent on someone else. They described three studies. The first, a survey of Americans, found that the amount of money people spent in gifts to others or gave to charity was positively associated with general happiness, even when overall income was controlled. (By the way, they also found that overall income predicted happiness.). In their second study, they surveyed employees at a company who had received profit-sharing bonuses. The amount of the bonus spent on others predicted happiness 6 to 8 weeks later, whereas the amount of the bonus spent on themselves did not. Their third study was a true experiment: Research participants were given either $5 or $20 and instructed to spend the money either on themselves or on others. Then their happiness was ascertained. Those who spent the money on others were happier, and the amount of money did not matter. One more finding was reported: Additional participants were asked to predict what would make people happier, and they mistakenly said that the most happiness would result from spending $20 on themselves.

Putting the findings from all of these studies together, might the most happiness be derived from expensive gifts to others? Admittedly, this is not what Dunn and colleagues found in their experiment (remember that $5 versus $20 made no difference), but as we are fond of saying in the science business, further research is needed. The most telling study would ask people to give away a substantial amount of their own money, not simply a relatively small amount of extra money provided by researchers.

Perhaps the Native American potlatch ceremony, marked by the ritualized giving away of one's most valued possessions, deserves attention from the perspective of positive psychology.

Maybe we should devise and carry out our own versions of the potlatch ceremony ... so long as they do not involve color televisions or air conditioners.

REFERENCES

Dunn, E. W., Aknin, L., & Norton, M. I. (2008). Spending money on others promotes happiness. *Science, 319*, 1687–1688.

Plassman, H., O'Doherty, J., Shiv, B., & Rangel, A. (2008). Marketing actions can modulate neural representations of experienced pleasantness. *Proceedings of the National Academy of Science of the United States of America, 105*, 1050–1054.

19

Does Happiness Have a Cost?

Do you understand that along with happiness, in the exact same way and in
perfectly equal proportion, man also needs unhappiness.
—Fyodor Dostoevsky

Positive psychology theory and research have helped dispel
the long-standing "happy and stupid" stereotype. From
Fredrickson's (2001) broaden-and-build theory of positive emotions to the literature review by Lyubomirsky, King, and Diener
(2005) linking life satisfaction to positive outcomes in many
important domains of life, we now have solid grounds for concluding that feeling good has desirable consequences.

A paper by Simone Schnall, Vikram Jaswal, and Christina
Rowe, published in 2008 in *Developmental Science*, therefore
deserves attention because it is at odds with this conclusion. Two
experiments with children were reported.

In the first, 10–11-year-olds listened to looped segments of
music, either a piece known to induce a happy mood or a piece
known to induce a sad mood. (A manipulation check verified the intended effects.) Then all the children were given an
embedded figures task, performance on which reflects attention to detail. Children in a happy mood performed worse than
children in a sad mood.

In the second, 6–7-year-olds were shown brief video clips
that induced happy, neutral, or sad moods. (Again, a manipulation check verified the intended effects.) As in the first study,
all were then tested on an embedded figures task. Children in

a happy mood performed worse than those in the other conditions, who did not differ from one another.

Before the media gets hold of these results and reports them under a misleading headline (e.g., "Why Grief Is Good"), let us put the research—which I hasten to say is well done, interesting, and important—in context.

First, these studies do not show that happy children are bad students. We already know that they are not. Furthermore, we also know that happiness is associated with more creative thinking, which Schnall and colleagues acknowledged. Attention to detail is an important skill, but it does not exhaust the skills that lead to good academic performance or success at life.

Second, these studies do not show that sad children are good students. No way.

Third, more generally, these studies do not necessarily speak to happiness or sadness as traits. The research is about what psychologists call *states*, temporarily induced moods.

The results show that a happy mood can have costs in certain circumstances, specifically those in which attention to detail is required.

Why am I going on and on? I want to head off rampant generalization of these findings, especially by those in the media who get an apparent kick out of sadness, depression, and pessimism, and studies showing that they can have benefits in certain circumstances (just as happiness, zest, and optimism can have benefits in other circumstances).

Positive psychology is sometimes criticized for urging relentless cheerfulness and happiness on people. I do not think any responsible positive psychologist does this, but regardless, let's not overreact in the other direction by using studies like this one to justify sadness or glorify depression.

My evenhanded recommendation is that people be encouraged to take charge of their moods and adjust them according to the demands they face. Don't proofread your dissertation or check your 1040 calculations when you are giddy. And don't plan profound changes in your life or brainstorm new projects when you are sad.

REFERENCES

Fredrickson, B. L. (2001). The role of positive emotions in positive psychology: The broaden-and-build theory of positive emotions. *American Psychologist, 56*, 218–226.

Lyubomirsky, S., King, L. A., & Diener, E. (2005). The benefits of frequent positive affect: Does happiness lead to success? *Psychological Bulletin, 131*, 803–855.

Schnall, S., Jaswal, V., & Rowe, C. (2008). A hidden cost of happiness in children. *Developmental Science, 11*, F25–F30.

20

Does Happiness Have a Cost?

Part Two

In my previous reflection (19), I discussed some studies showing that experimentally induced happiness can have a cost. I cautioned that state research is not the same as trait research. That is, experimentally induced emotions (like happiness) may not have the same consequences as habitual dispositions associated with these emotions (like life satisfaction).

But sometimes state research and trait research point to the same conclusion. An important paper by Shigehiro Oishi, Ed Diener, and Richard Lucas (2007) showed that dispositional happiness (rendered as life satisfaction) can have costs. These are not across-the-board costs; they depend on the specific outcome on focus.

These researchers looked at cross-sectional and longitudinal data from several large samples in which adult respondents had completed a life satisfaction measure and for whom other information about "success" in a variety of domains was available. The researchers were interested in how success varied as a function of life satisfaction.

Important finding number one: Happy (satisfied) people were more successful than unhappy (dissatisfied) people regardless of outcome.

Important finding number two: When the comparison was between the most satisfied and the merely satisfied, the outcome mattered. For success at close relationships, the extremely happy did better than the somewhat less happy. But for success at school, work, and political participation, the happiest people did not do as well as those who reported slightly less satisfaction. (But please remember important finding number one.)

The researchers concluded, "Once people are moderately happy, the most effective level of happiness appears to depend on the specific outcomes used to define success, as well as the resources that are available."

Okay. There are apparently circumstances in which one can be too happy. These findings admit to different interpretations. In some cases, the data were all obtained at the same time from respondents, leaving unanswered legitimate questions about what comes first: the reported satisfaction or the success. In other cases, though, these patterns held across time, strengthening the conclusion that satisfaction actually results in given outcomes. In these cases, perhaps the moderately happy among us are hungrier than the fully satisfied—more motivated—and thus put more effort into achievement domains.

Or perhaps considerable happiness more readily translates itself into good relationships than into good grades or a high income, if only because happiness is contagious and thus attractive to others.

Or it could simply be that there are but 24 hours in a day, resulting in necessary tradeoffs in what anyone can achieve. As Ed Diener reminded me when I spoke to him about this possibility, "Newton got so much physics done because he did not like social interaction."

We all make choices, or they are made for us. As a college student, I worked like a dog and had nothing that resembled a social life. My good grades opened doors for me not otherwise ajar. I walked through them, if not happily then at least purposefully. But 30 years later, as a tenured professor at a top university, I now have all the dog biscuits I could possibly want. And I also have wonderful friends. Maybe we can have it all—just not at the same time. Bow wow.

REFERENCE

Oishi, S., Diener, E., & Lucas, R. E. (2007). The optimal level of well-being: Can we be too happy? *Perspectives on Psychological Science, 2*, 346–360.

21

Heritability and Happiness

One of the frequently cited conclusions from positive psychology research is that happiness results from a combination of genetics, circumstances, and voluntary activities. This is reasonable enough. Indeed, it is a virtual tautology that applies to most any human characteristic.

Some positive psychologists go further and propose a happiness formula, typically a weighted sum of its components, with weights based on research with large samples of individuals. A representative set of weights is 50% genetics, 10% circumstances, and 40% voluntary activities. Again, this is reasonable enough, reflecting the research literature as I read it, although the exact weights are always a function of the samples from which they are derived.

So where am I going? To the conclusion that it is *thoroughly unreasonable* to think that we can parse the happiness of an individual, in the moment or in general, in the same way that we can parse the happiness of samples of individuals.

For people in the aggregate (a sample), we can perhaps say that 50% of the variation in their happiness is attributable to genetic differences. But we cannot say that Joe's short-term happiness following a raise at work or the victory of his favorite sports team or a wonderful weekend with his family is 50% due to his genes. That makes no sense. Which 50% are we talking about—the first 50%, the second 50%, or some other 50%? This is a category mistake of the first order.

I am reminded of the old question "Which contributes more to the area of a rectangle—its height or its width?" We can readily see that this is a silly query. Sure, given a "sample" of rectangles of different sizes, we can provide an answer that summarizes the sample as a whole. But we would not expect the "weights" to generalize to other samples of rectangles, and, in any event, we know that for given rectangles, the answers might vary widely.

The same point applies to thinking about happiness and its determinants, even if the point is harder to grasp.

Let's start with genetic influences. The technical meaning of the *heritability* of a characteristic is the proportion of its variation across people due to variation in genetic factors across people. Heritability estimates (like the 50% happiness heritability figure) therefore apply to groups and not to individuals.

Along these lines, please do not equate heritability with any simple notion of *inherited*. Perhaps we can say that Joe inherited his blue eyes from his mother,* but we cannot say that he inherited his happiness from her ... or half of it ... or any of it for that matter.

The same argument applies to the other components of happiness and their weights. So, *circumstances* include the nation where one happens to live. If the weights are based on a comparison between, for example, Norway and Sweden, the conclusion would follow that where one lives matters little. But if the weights are based on a comparison between, for another example, Scandinavian nations and sub-Saharan African nations, then the weight accorded to circumstances would be much larger.

---

* I believe that the "inheritance" of eye color, although a familiar example, is hardly this simple, so just appreciate the larger points about the heritability of happiness.

Moreover, we cannot say how much of the happiness of a given person results from the nation in which he or she happens to live. We can only offer generalizations about groups of people.

It is not clear to me whether positive psychology authors who present such formulas intend these formulas and their weights to apply to individual people or to the specific moments of happiness that individuals experience. I do know that their readers often make these leaps because I encounter this notion with incredible frequency among my students who have read popular trade books on happiness. I spend a lot of time trying to explain heritability to them.

Ed Diener (2008) made the same point in his important discussion of the myths of happiness, under the heading "Myth 2: The Causes of Well-Being Can Be Understood as a Pie Chart of Influences." He used a great example that I have found useful—mortality. It is possible to say, for a sample of individuals, what the typical causes of death are: cancer, stroke, accident, murder, malaria, and so on. Some causes are much more likely than others, and these can be deemed the more important causes of death—for the sample.

In most parts of the world, malaria does not lead to a large percentage of people's deaths. But that is little comfort to the person who happens to die from malaria, and it would be foolish for someone who lives in an area where malaria does occur, however infrequently, not to take appropriate precautions.

As Diener (2008, p. 499) concluded,

These figures [weights] are sometimes offered to the public as a guide to what might be most worthwhile to change in order to achieve greater happiness. However, the causes for change in an individual's happiness might diverge from what causes differences in happiness between individuals....[O]ne person might gain an enormous boost in happiness from becoming religious, even if the amount of individual differences in due to religion in a population is modest. The pie-chart way of thinking is seductive, because it is clear and simple, but...[it can be]...misguided.

Positive psychology is important because it is based on research. But the research needs to be understood correctly.

REFERENCE

Diener, E. (2008). Myths in the science of happiness, directions and for future research. In M. Eid & R. J. Larsen (Eds.), *The science of subjective well-being* (pp. 403–514). New York: Guilford.

22

Smiles and Longevity
Game Faces and Life Faces

One of the parable studies of positive psychology is the investigation of Duchenne smiles and marital satisfaction reported by LeeAnne Harker and Dacher Keltner (2001). These researchers analyzed 114 pictures from the 1958 and 1960 yearbooks of a women's college in the Bay Area. All but three of the young women were smiling, but the smiles varied. Some showed what is called a Duchenne smile: a genuine, full-faced expression of happiness indexed by the degree to which the muscles surrounding one's eyes are contracted—crinkled, as it were. Others did not, smiling with only their mouths, displaying what are dubbed flight attendant smiles. On a 10-point scale reflecting the "Duchenne-ness" of these yearbook smiles, the average rating was 3.8.

The researchers chose these particular pictures for analysis because the women in them were participants in a long-term study of important life events. Specifically, the researchers knew—decades after the yearbook photos—whether the women were married and if they were satisfied with their marriage. As it turns out, the Duchenne-ness of their yearbook smiles predicted both of these outcomes. Young women who expressed positive emotions (happiness) in yearbook photos, and presumably in other venues of their lives, as middle-aged women had better marriages.

The skeptic might wonder if these results reflect the operation of some confound such as physical attractiveness. Leaving aside the fact that physical beauty is not much of a route to happiness for people in general, prettiness did not account for the results in this particular sample. Harker and Keltner rated how attractive the pictures were, and this rating—largely independent of the Duchenne-ness rating—did not predict who had a satisfying marriage.

This is a provocative study, and I always mention it when giving a talk on happiness or positive psychology.

It was thus with interest that I read a more recent study that also looked at Duchenne smiles, in this case those shown in photographs of Major League Baseball players from the 1952 season (Abel & Kruger, 2010). The degree to which a player evidenced a Duchenne smile was coded, from no smile to partial (non-Duchenne) smile to full (Duchenne) smile. The percentages of players in each category were 42%, 43%, and 15%, respectively.

Analyses focused on the 150 players who had died as of June 2009, and the outcome measure of interest was longevity. Players who did not smile at all on average lived for 72 years. Those who smiled a bit on average lived for 75 years. And those with Duchenne smiles on average lived for 80 years. These are statistically significant differences, and possible confounds were controlled, including attractiveness. But these are also what I call *significant* significant differences. If we take these results at face value (no pun intended), a Duchenne smile is worth 5 to 8 extra years of life…happy years.

I have been a sports fan forever, and maybe it's just me, but it seems as if what it means to "put on a game face" has changed. Once upon a time, players in a variety of sports did their best to look confident and in control, whereas others tried to convey nothing (a poker face). But more recently, many athletes have been scowling and looking incredibly angry. During the last few NCAA basketball tournaments, I felt that I was watching a series of 40-minute unsynchronized *haka* dances.

One's game face is a tactic used to intimidate the opponent and to bolster one's own self as a player. If a game face is simply a tactic, then who cares? But if one's game face also reflects one's typical approach to life—if the game face is also the life face—then I worry about today's athletes. I wish they would smile more often, if not during games and matches then at least before and after.

Mind you, the smiles were not causes of longevity in the study just described, simply markers of how these men presumably lived their lives, happily or not. Pasting a phony smile on your face is not going to make you live longer (see reflection 90). But perhaps doing the sorts of things that positive psychologists have shown to produce lasting happiness might be beneficial.

And even if not, you'll have a better time more along the way, and so will everyone else who sees you.

REFERENCES

Abel, E. L., & Kruger, M. L. (2010). Smile intensity in photographs predicts longevity. *Psychological Science, 21*, 542–544.

Harker, L. A., & Keltner, D. (2001). Expressions of positive emotion in women's college yearbook pictures and their relationship to personality and life outcomes across adulthood. *Journal of Personality and Social Psychology, 80*, 112–124.

23

Happiness Outliers

Like many of you readers, I read Malcolm Gladwell's (2008) book *Outliers*, which presents his perspective on success and the people who achieve it. Like his previous books, *Outliers* is well written and provocative. We should all pause for a positive psychology moment and be grateful that such a talented writer is among us.

Gladwell's concern is with celebrated accomplishment like that attained by John D. Rockefeller, the Beatles, and Bill Gates. Prodigious achievement is an often overlooked member of the positive psychology family. Getting much more positive psychology attention are the warm and fuzzy family members, the ones we want to hug because they hug back: happiness, hope, kindness, and love. In contrast, accomplishment is elite and exclusive and for many of us not nearly so embraceable.

Nonetheless, accomplishment matters mightily and obviously contributes to the life worth living.

The arguments advanced in *Outliers* square with the research as I know it.

First, prodigious achievement does not simply happen because of an individual's genius. Talent matters but is not sufficient. Rather, achievement results from the alignment of all sorts of factors external to the individual: being born in the right time and place, having access to appropriate resources, and receiving instruction and encouragement. No one does it alone. There are no self-made men or women. Rugged individualism is ruggedly wrong.

Second, before success is achieved, someone needs to put in years of work perfecting a craft, whatever it may be. Gladwell suggests 10,000 hours as the minimum commitment, and this may be an underestimate. Psychologists who study achievement talk about the 10-year rule, meaning that people who make important contributions to a particular field have usually devoted a full decade to the mastery of necessary knowledge and skills. Psychologists also talk about the 12–7 rule, meaning that this decade needs to be filled with 12-hour work days, 7 days a week. Sound daunting? Of course, but *American Idol* notwithstanding, there are no shortcuts to excellence.

This conclusion may not be what many young people want to hear. The other day I sat on a train next to a young woman. We talked about her career aspirations, and I gently mentioned the 10-year rule. She kept changing the topic to "positive imaging" as a better principle to follow. I persisted because it is irresponsible for those of us who know better to let young people think that success comes easy or overnight, that it is just a matter of finding one's passions and interests, printing business cards, starting websites, or—heaven forbid—simply wishing and hoping for success.

Third, Gladwell stresses the role of legacy in achievement, by which he means the affordances of the cultural group into which one is born. In given times and places, legacy enables achievement in particular domains. For example, Gladwell discusses Jewish lawyers from a generation past who were not hired by elite (i.e., WASP-y) law firms and thus had to start their own firms. These elite law firms also did not handle certain sorts of cases—like the occasional corporate takeover—which necessarily fell into the laps of the "other" law firms. As business and legal landscapes changed to make corporate takeovers more common and exceedingly lucrative, it is not surprising who flourished.

In closing, I would like to suggest that the ideas in *Outliers* may apply to another sort of achievement: happiness. Here I mean more than somewhat above-the-scale midpoint life satisfaction. I mean prodigious happiness, not extraverted mania but a life that entails walking on sunshine, one that makes onlookers shake their head and say, Wow.

Each of us probably knows a few people who are happy in this prodigious way. Were they simply born that way? Would they be happy in any and all circumstances?

Extrapolating from Gladwell's book, I say *no*. A cheerful temperament and secure attachment may set the stage, but a happiness outlier, no less than an achievement outlier, further represents a perfect storm of enabling factors, many external to the person, as well as the absence of disabling factors.

This sounds fatalistic and is certainly not the starting point for a self-help book. But remember the role played by sustained practice in the lives of achievement outliers. There are things we can do to be happier, but these probably take many years to perfect. Research suggests that happiness and life satisfaction do *not* increase with age. If we take these data at face value, they mean either that people are not trying to be happier or—more likely—that they do not know how to do so (see reflections 90 and 91). Perhaps this can be a long-term contribution of positive psychology. However, positive psychologists need to do more than provide a reasonable formula. We also need to provide the warning label: This will take a really long time!

Can we speak about a happiness legacy? Gladwell's discussion of legacy is the most interesting part of his book but also the most tenuous. *Culture* is a sprawling term, and in focusing on one aspect of culture to explain achievement, he necessarily ignores all of the others that may also be crucial.

So, he attributes the mathematical accomplishments of East Asian schoolchildren to the fact that China, Japan, and Korea are rice-based economies. It takes a lot of hard work to grow rice, a cultural lesson presumably carried into the classroom even if a student is not the child or grandchild of rice farmers. True. But there are other features of East Asian cultures that might also matter. Gladwell mentions some of these—for example, "number" names in East Asian languages are short and consistent. He does not mention that the written languages of China, Japan, and (until 1446) Korea engage different parts of the brain from the Western alphabet. He does not mention Confucianism, which has infused East Asia for centuries and not only extols hard work but also places the teacher at the top of the respect pyramid.

But I digress. What does a happiness legacy look like? It would be a culture that stresses the sorts of things that lead to a good and satisfied life: family, friends, community, freedom, tolerance, engagement, meaning, and purpose (see reflection 70). It would likely not be a culture that stresses hedonism, materialism, or ruthless competition. It would certainly not be one that tolerates or rewards meanness (see reflections 50 and 52).

That said, I suspect that happiness legacies can be more local. Indeed, to paraphrase Tip O'Neill, perhaps all happiness legacies are local.

What is encouraging is that local cultures can be changed. Gladwell provides several intriguing examples of legacy change. He describes how South Korean airlines, once quite dangerous because of culturally mandated deference that led copilots never to challenge pilots, even as their planes flew dangerously off course, became much safer by mandating the use of English—and all the bluntness that entailed—in the cockpits. Gladwell describes how the acclaimed Knowledge Is Power Program (KIPP) schools have changed the cultural legacy of their students. As I see it, the KIPP schools in effect have created East Asian classrooms in the inner cities of the United States. Wow.

How can we create a cultural legacy of happiness? If you have read any of my other reflections here, you know my answer: Let other people matter. And that means moving beyond the slogan and working diligently over the years to make it so.

REFERENCE

Gladwell, M. (2008). *Outliers: The story of success.* New York: Little, Brown.

Part III

Positive Traits and Talents

Positive experiences and emotions are relatively fleeting. Positive psychologists are also interested in more enduring characteristics like traits and talents that make the good life possible. My own career as a research psychologist has for decades focused on styles of optimistic and pessimistic thinking. What are the consequences of thinking positively? Can this style be encouraged? I would have thought that decades of research showing conclusively that hope and optimism are beneficial would have closed the book on this issue, but there is an ongoing skepticism in some quarters about the value of positive thinking that led me to write several of the reflections in this section. Together, they argue—yet again—for the power of positive thinking, at least when hope and optimism are viewed with some sophistication and subtlety.

More recently, I have studied strengths of character, morally valued traits like curiosity, kindness, and teamwork. The most important takeaway from this research is that character needs to be approached not in either-or terms but rather as a family of positive dispositions, each of which exists in degrees. No one has it all, character-wise, but no one lacks it all either. Several reflections in this section describe recent research on strengths of character.

There are two traditions in positive psychology—a soft and cuddly one that focuses on feelings and happiness (see reflections in Part II) and a tough and challenging one that focuses on achievement and accomplishment (Bacon, 2005). Both matter when we are concerned with the good life, and they need not trip over one another. The concluding reflections in this section address talent and how to encourage it.

REFERENCE

Bacon, S. F. (2005). Positive psychology's two cultures. *Review of General Psychology*, *9*, 181–192.

24

The Last Lecture

A Positive Psychology Case Study

When we're connected to others, we become better people.
—Randy Pausch

Some years ago, my colleague Ben Dean and I conducted an Internet survey of 1,464 adults interested in positive psychology that asked what they would most like to know about this new field. A large number wanted compelling case examples of actual people who lived life well, who embodied the strengths of character that we have been studying with quantitative methods. The world's greatest teachers, from Socrates and Jesus to the present, have always used parables to instruct and inspire others, and in the disciplines of business and law, the detailed examination of particular cases is the preferred method of teaching. Psychologists have also relied on cases, but these have been psychiatric histories that centered on people's problems. With exceptions, such as Howard Gardner's (1997) psychobiographies of exceptionally talented historical figures and Anne Colby and William Damon's (1992) multiple case studies of contemporary people of striking moral commitment, positive psychologists have made insufficient use of cases to understand what makes life most worth living.

Here is another exception, a marvelous example of what it means to live well: Carnegie Mellon computer science professor Randy Pausch (2007), whose "last lecture" has been all over the Internet. Lots of universities, including my own, feature an annual "last lecture" in which award-winning teachers are asked to imagine that they are near death and to convey their final thoughts to students. I hope we all have the decency to retire the title, because now there is but one last lecture, the one by Professor Pausch.*

In case you have been living under a rock, at the time of the lecture, he really was dying, the victim of an aggressive pancreatic cancer. His last lecture was not maudlin, not saccharine, not filled with false bravado. It was simply wonderful. Five minutes into my watching, I forgot that he was dying. What captivated me was how he was living.

I watched his last lecture wearing many hats. As a teacher, I was inspired. As a lecturer, I was filled with admiration. As a human being, I was proud.

Watch it yourself. No summary I could offer would do it justice.

However, I do want to make a few observations. Positive psychologists, including me, intone that there are multiple routes to happiness and fulfillment: through pleasure, through engagement, and through meaning. If so, then Randy Pausch scored the hat trick of happiness. He is wickedly funny; he loves his work; and he contributes mightily to the larger world.

Other people matter to him, and he to them. When he received tenure at his university, he took his entire research team to Disney World to express his gratitude. One of his colleagues later asked him, "How could you do that?" He responded, "How could I not?"

---

* Irony of ironies, on March, 9, 2010, I received a teaching award at the University of Michigan and was asked to deliver a "last lecture." I was honored and excited, but I did not get with the agenda, remembering what I had had written in this reflection. Instead, I gave what I called a "first lecture." It went well enough, although it was not remotely Pausch-like. And that was okay.

All of us who are instructors should teach the "case" of Professor Pausch. The best-known cases in psychology should not be Little Hans and Little Albert.

It has been said, by the late Elizabeth Edwards and by others, that living is what you do until you die. Randy Pausch showed us that living well is the right way to do it. Yes, we encounter brick walls, sometimes frequently. But as Professor Pausch reminded us, brick walls are there to remind us how badly we want something.

ANNOTATION

Randy Pausch died July 25, 2008, at the age of 47.

REFERENCES

Colby, A., & Damon, W. (1992). *Some do care: Contemporary lives of moral commitment.* New York: Free Press.

Gardner, H. (1997). *Extraordinary minds.* New York: Basic Books.

Pausch, R. (2007). *Really achieving your childhood dreams.* Retrieved from http://www.cmu.edu/randyslecture/.

25

Is Optimism Undermining America?

The way to be nothing is to do nothing.
—Nathaniel Howe

Optimism has never had a good name, at least among the intellectually elite. We actually know when the word *optimism* entered common parlance—with the publication of Voltaire's (1759) *Candide* and the embodiment of foolish optimism in the annoying character Dr. Pangloss.

Empirical research over the past few decades showing that optimism has many benefits—for achievement, social relationships, and health—is therefore interesting and important (Peterson, 2000). Studies of optimism helped usher in the field of positive psychology by demonstrating the importance of "positive" constructs above and beyond the absence of "negative" constructs.

A recent backlash is apparent, reprising the centuries-old suspicion of optimism as indicative of stupidity or denial (Ehrenreich, 2009). Both scholarly and popular discussions have questioned optimism, positive thinking, and more generally positive psychology, suggesting that they are responsible for much of what ails the modern world, including ongoing economic crises in the United States.

When I lecture about these criticisms, which of course need to be considered, I sometimes am tempted to be glib and ask, "What's the point? Are the critics urging pessimism and hopelessness on people?" I could cherry-pick quotes from the critics that seem to imply this, but that would entail taking their ideas out of context. That's not responsible, even if the critics seem to do that to make *their* point.

Instead, the critics usually urge people to be realistic in their expectations about the future. That is a thoroughly reasonable suggestion in cases where there actually is a right answer, a reality against which to judge our expectations as accurate or inaccurate. So, I am optimistic that I will finish this reflection. I am optimistic that people will read it. And I am optimistic that many readers will enjoy it. Past experience tells me these are thoroughly realistic expectations.

And I am pessimistic that I will ever play in the NBA, win a Nobel Prize, or be adopted by Angelina Jolie. Those things are simply not going to happen, even if I hope that they do. If I led my life as if these things would or could happen, my stupid optimism would indeed undermine my life. If everyone leads their life as if thoroughly implausible things would happen, then our world collectively would be undermined.

So are the critics of positive thinking correct? Not exactly. The issue that is sometimes overlooked by critics of optimism is that our expectations about the future do not fall cleanly into two groups: those that are correct and those that are incorrect. There is a third and fuzzy group of expectations: those that are neither correct nor incorrect at the present moment. They become correct or incorrect only in the future, depending on how we act in the present. Optimism galvanizes activity, and optimism as I conceive it adds agency to affirmation. Positive thinking is powerful when it characterizes this third group of expectations.

On average, optimistic individuals are healthier because they take care of themselves; optimistic students earn better grades because they go to class; optimistic insurance agents sell more policies because they make cold calls; and so on. There are no guarantees, except that passivity will lead to failure in domains where activity is beneficial.

We should also be very careful about branding someone's expectations impossible simply because they strike us as unlikely. Unrealistic does not always mean impossible. Was Christopher Columbus unrealistic when he set sail on tiny boats across the Atlantic Ocean? Was Jackie Robinson unrealistic when he wanted to be a Major League Baseball player? Was Mother Teresa unrealistic when she left Albania to establish a mission of charity in India? Was Bill Gates unrealistic when he dropped out of Harvard to write software? Was Barack Obama unrealistic when he announced his presidential candidacy? Probably yes in all cases, but we also know the rest of the stories.

Of course, these examples of optimism that paid off can be matched by other examples of optimism that did not. As the saying goes, the plural of anecdote is not data, which is why I pay more attention to the hundreds of studies that show optimism on average to be beneficial.

As I read this literature, optimism is not undermining America. Indeed, as Alexis de Tocqueville (1835/2003) observed long ago, optimism *defines* America. Bless the critics, but I wish they would zero in on stupidity as a problem for all of us, or greed, or sloth, or envy, or gluttony, and not brand positive thinking a deadly sin. The world is challenging enough, and no good is served by dismissing one of its most wonderful resources.

REFERENCES

Ehrenreich, B. (2009). *Bright-sided: How the relentless promotion of positive thinking has undermined America*. New York: Metropolitan Books.

Peterson, C. (2000). The future of optimism. *American Psychologist*, *55*, 44–55.

Tocqueville, A. de. (2003). *Democracy in America*. London: Penguin Classics. (Originally published 1835)

Voltaire, (1759). *Candide, ou l'optimisme*. Geneva: Cramer.

26

Optimism Goes Underground

In the previous reflection (25), I discussed criticisms of positive thinking and especially positive psychology. Is the United States being undermined by the tendency to look on the bright side? I concluded *no*, but maybe that was rash. It has come to my attention that "optimism" has infiltrated the New York City subway system. Along with giant alligators and rats the size of terriers, yet another potential horror lurks beneath the unsuspecting streets of New York. Optimism!

And this is not an urban legend. You can read about it on the Internet, so it must be true. In what is obviously a government-sponsored conspiracy, the Metropolitan Transportation Authority has issued seven million MetroCards to riders on which is printed a single word: **optimism**.

What's next? The slippery slope from optimism may lead to further messages urging kindness, love, and tolerance. Indeed, we live in dangerous times.

Intended as art on an unusual canvas, the MetroCards have stimulated a variety of reactions, some positive and some negative. I suppose that is an indicator of good art. According to Reed Seifer, the artist who designed the card, "I like that people can digest it in any way they choose. I accept all praise and criticism. I love artwork in which people perceive things beyond the intention of the artist" (Grynbaum, 2009).

I have never taken a NYC subway—I'm not optimistic enough to think I could figure out how to do it. But these MetroCards were brought to my attention by Eric Kim, one of my students here at Michigan who went home to the city for the holidays and took the subway.

He sent me a brief e-mail message saying,

> Whenever I pulled out the card to get on a subway and saw the word, it set off however briefly a cascade of pleasant feelings and probably even helped me reframe whatever random thoughts I may have had at the moment. Optimistically thinking, this was probably happening all over the city among the millions of subway riders. I think this was a great public health intervention that increased warm feelings for short bursts at a time throughout the city, maybe even accumulating into meaningful outcomes here and there.

As he acknowledged, Eric may have been guilty of foolish optimism in thinking that the MetroCards "intervention" would have beneficial effects. And he certainly overlooked the possibility that these effects might have a downside.

Well-intended critics of optimism can remind us that smiling subway passengers might start talking to strangers and then miss their stops, create safety hazards by getting up to offer their seats to other passengers, or—heaven forbid—take their smiles to work on Wall Street and lose the edge that has made the U.S. economy the envy of the world. Hmmm.

Resistance is needed, like counterfeit MetroCards that read "Abandon hope, all ye who enter here." That would make the world a better place and counteract the undermining of America.

Or maybe not. Art is in the eye of the beholder. So too is the good life, as well as the not-so-good life. You choose.

REFERENCE

Grynbaum, M. W. (2009, November 19). The days may be grim, but here's a good word to put in your pocket. *The New York Times.* Retrieved from http://www.nytimes.com/2009/11/20/nyregion/20metrocard.html.

27

Good Hope and Bad Hope

In reality, hope is the worst of all evils, because it prolongs man's torments.
—Friedrich Nietzsche

I just reacquainted myself with the Greek myth of Pandora because it sheds light on the always contentious notions of hope and optimism, subjects of previous reflections here (25 and 26).

As the story goes, Pandora was the first woman. After Prometheus stole fire from heaven, Zeus took revenge on humankind by giving Pandora a jar (sometimes identified as a box) with the warning not to open it. Curiosity overcame her, though, and she opened it, only to unleash all manner of evil upon the world. She quickly closed it, trapping only hope inside, as Zeus intended.

The version of this myth that I learned as a child depicted hope as an unalloyed good that allowed people to this day to overcome evil.

From the viewpoint of an adult, the myth is more complex, and hope especially so. Why would an angry Zeus place hope in the same container as evil things?

How does the old joke go?

Q: What's a nice person like you doing in a place like this?
A: The same thing everyone does in a place like this.

That is, hope must also be evil, especially when kept and embraced. Given all the evil in the world, hoping that things will be different is stupid and thus evil in its effects. As Nietzsche argued, hope prolongs whatever torments us.

So how do these ideas bear on ongoing debates about the pros and cons of optimism (aka hope)?

First, let's look at the data, which show—contrary to the myth—that hope and optimism can actually mitigate torment ... literally. People who are dispositionally optimistic are happier and healthier (e.g., Park, Peterson, & Seligman 2004; Peterson, Seligman, & Vaillant, 1988). They also avoid so-called accidents (e.g., Peterson, Bishop, et al., 2001; Peterson, Seligman, et al., 1998).

And in an interesting experiment, Carla Berg, Rick Snyder, and Nancy Hamilton (2008) used guided imagery in what they called a hope induction. For about 15 minutes, research participants were asked to think of an important goal and to imagine how they might achieve it. A comparison condition asked participants to read a home organization book for 15 minutes. All participants were then asked to immerse their nondominant hand in a bucket of ice water for as long as they could (up to 5 minutes). This is a standard measure of pain tolerance, and it is painful but not harmful. Participants receiving the brief hope induction kept their hand immersed for about 150 seconds, whereas those in the comparison condition kept their hand immersed for about 90 seconds. Hope did not affect reports on how painful the experience was, but it did increase the ability to tolerate it.

Second, let's revisit the point from another reflection that the effects of hope and optimism depend on the specific contents of the hopeful belief (25). Hoping for things that cannot possibly happen is indeed stupid. We can dub it *evil* if we are so inclined. But hoping for things that can happen is smart (good), assuming we are motivated by our optimism to act in ways that make the hoped-for thing more likely.

Third, let's remember that the myth of Pandora and its more modern elaborations by Nietzsche and by contemporary critics of positive psychology posit a world densely populated by bad things, with scarce mention of good things. In such a world, hope may well be evil simply because, by definition, nothing bad can ever change.

I believe such a world is only hypothetical. Yes, there are evil things in the world, but just as genuine are the good things in the world: like friendship, love, and service. The real world is more complex than a Greek myth or a *New York Times* op-ed piece, and we should approach it in its full complexity, acknowledging good and evil, and recognizing good hope and bad hope.

At least I hope that we do.

REFERENCES

Berg, C. J., Snyder, C. R., & Hamilton, N. (2008). The effectiveness of a hope intervention in coping with cold pressor pain. *Journal of Health Psychology, 13*, 804–809.

Park, N., Peterson, C., & Seligman, M. E. P. (2004). Strengths of character and well-being. *Journal of Social and Clinical Psychology, 23*, 603–619.

Peterson, C., Bishop, M. P., Fletcher, C. W., Kaplan, M. R., Yesko, E. S., Moon, C. H., Smith, J. S., Michaels, C. E., & Michaels, A. J. (2001). Explanatory style as a risk factor for traumatic mishaps. *Cognitive Therapy and Research, 25*, 633–649.

Peterson, C., Seligman, M. E. P., & Vaillant, G. E. (1988). Pessimistic explanatory style is a risk factor for physical illness: A thirty-five year longitudinal study. *Journal of Personality and Social Psychology, 55*, 23–27.

Peterson, C., Seligman, M. E. P., Yurko, K. H., Martin, L. R., & Friedman, H. S. (1998). Catastrophizing and untimely death. *Psychological Science, 9*, 49–52.

28

Strengths or Weaknesses?

Character isn't something you were born with and can't change, like your fingerprints. It's something you weren't born with and must take responsibility for forming.

—Jim Rohn

When positive psychologists advocate a strengths-based approach, I hear it as an important correction to decades of interventions (in clinics, schools, and workplaces) that focused on problems and their remediation. I do not hear it as advice to ignore weaknesses and problems or as an assertion that change is possible only if a person is already skilled at something. Somehow this completely reasonable advice has been morphed into the completely unreasonable proposal that only strengths matter, and I have been asked repeatedly about the evidence in favor of addressing only one's strengths if one wishes to achieve a good life.

We don't need studies to refute the claim that only strengths matter, just common sense. Regardless of what they do especially well, workers need to have the "strength" of showing up on time, and they need to have the "strength" of being minimally civil to their coworkers. And so on.

Should we put people in positions where they can make use of their strengths? Of course. In my university department, good lecturers are asked to teach large-enrollment courses. We can do this because there are enough faculty members with the requisite skills.

That said, none of my colleagues was born a good lecturer. Those who can keep the attention of a large class and convey information in a clear and engaging way have talents, but these talents were developed by a lot of practice, a lot of mentoring, and a lot of feedback that was taken seriously.

The other side of the coin is the assertion that talent is over-rated, which is equally silly. I can only assume that the statement refers to innate talents, not to those developed over time. And how many of these innate talents exist?

As a basketball fan, I know that the two of the most "talented" players of our time, Larry Bird and Michael Jordan, practiced incessantly. It didn't hurt their games that Jordan had springs in his legs or that Bird had uncanny visual ability, but even these ostensibly inborn talents were no doubt honed by practice.

It seems to me that either-or debates like these (strengths versus weaknesses; talent versus practice; nature versus nurture) will never be resolved because it *all* matters when we look at the whole person (see reflection 21).

One more point. The term *strengths* is a sprawling one, and it seems to include talents like perfect pitch, moral virtues like kindness, and the situated workplace themes of interest to the Gallup Organization (like WOO: winning others over). We should be careful when speaking about strengths and strengths-based approaches and to be specific about the sorts of strengths we mean. Ditto for problem-focused approaches.

Strengths and weaknesses both matter, and both are us. I had my own insight into this a few years ago when one of my positive psychology colleagues urged me to join a gym and lose weight. I responded, "Why don't you just pay attention to what I do well?" Her response stopped me in my tracks: "Do you want a fan, or do you want a friend?"

That was 45 pounds ago.

29

Character Is Sexy

When I'm happy inside, that's when I feel most sexy.
—Anna Kournikova

I have been a college professor since 1976, and an important part of my job is working individually with graduate students who are writing doctoral dissertations. Over the years, I have supervised about 50 of these, learning to be one part cheerleader and two parts crossing guard: Bring it on, but look both ways. Dissertations are difficult, if only because the first one a student writes is usually the last one. Doctoral students cannot learn from experience they do not have, and it falls to me to warn them of pitfalls along the way.

Without doubt, procrastination is the biggest threat, and there are lots of ways for a student to procrastinate. One can alphabetize one's spice rack. Or clean one's apartment. Or sharpen one's pencils. Or update one's computer software. Or read everything ever written about anything remotely related to the topic of one's dissertation. And a dissertating student can always check out the personal ads in the newspaper and dream about a "real life" that will begin when the "unreal life" of graduate school is finally over.

One of my best students at the University of Michigan was Tracy Steen, who never procrastinated while completing her dissertation, even though she spent a huge amount of time reading personal ads. The secret was that she was *researching* the ads for her dissertation to see how people described themselves to potential mates and to learn what they in turn wanted.

Other psychologists have studied personal ads, often from an evolutionary perspective that expects differences between males and females (e.g., Wiederman, 1993). Males presumably seek females who can successfully bear children—accordingly, women should be young and attractive; females presumably seek males who can successfully protect and provide for children—accordingly, men should be ambitious and successful. The data usually support these predictions.

However, the research findings also show a pattern even more striking than the "looks and a whole lot of money" exchange highlighted by evolutionary theorists. Character is sexy, and if we can judge by what the personal ads say, good character actually trumps physical attractiveness and occupational achievement, both in what the advertisers proclaim about themselves and in what they are seeking in a romantic partner. These results hold for men and women.

What Tracy Steen (2002) did was simple. She read hundreds of personal ads in a local Ann Arbor newspaper and coded what each said, about the person placing the ad and about what that person wanted. She used a positive psychology perspective and was especially interested in the mention of character strengths.

The language of good character figured in almost every ad. Even within the severe word limits imposed by these ads, it was notable that the young adults who placed them explicitly mentioned character as often as they did. The following positive traits were frequently sought in others: capacity to love (36%), a sense of humor (30%), enthusiasm (25%), kindness (24%), and curiosity (19%). When describing themselves, those seeking romance used similar character language: humor (39%), capacity to love (36%), enthusiasm (29%), curiosity (25%), and kindness (23%).

These findings are interesting in their own right, but I mention them to make a point about character. It is not a concern of fuddy-duddies. Character is sexy, and there is a reason that it is sexy. Good character makes relationships of all sorts possible, including romance but also friendship and the relationships that matter at school or at work, around the neighborhood, and of course in the family. Bad boys and mean girls are celebrated by the media, but they should be avoided like the plagues they are.

REFERENCES

Steen, T. A. (2002). *Is character sexy? The desirability of character strengths in romantic partners* (Unpublished doctoral dissertation). University of Michigan, Ann Arbor.

Wiederman, M. W. (1993). Evolved gender differences in mate preferences: Evidence from personal advertisements. *Ethology and Sociobiology, 14,* 331–351.

30

There Are No Saints

There are two kinds of people in the world, those who believe there are two kinds of people in the world and those who don't.
—Robert Benchley

Psychologists who study individual differences—for example, personality traits—have repeatedly concluded that there are few if any types of people, if by a *type* we mean a category with well-defined boundaries into which folks can be unambiguously placed or not. It is obvious that people differ, but these differences are almost always along dimensions. Said another way, psychological differences are of degree and not of kind.

We may speak casually about introverts and extraverts, or optimists and pessimists, or smart people and stupid people, but it is all shorthand. These terms should be heard as relative ones. For example, we call someone extraverted when he or she is more outgoing than whatever reference group we have in mind. That is all we mean because there is no firm line between introversion and extraversion. Most of us with respect to most individual differences fall somewhere in the middle.

What about people's psychological problems? They too usually fall along less-versus-more dimensions. For example, depression ranges along a continuum from the merely moody to the desperately despondent. Those who are extremely depressed may enter the mental health system, may receive psychotherapy or medication, and may take their own lives. All of these consequences of depression are either-or, but strictly speaking, their depression is not. It is impossible to draw a firm line along the continuum, despite heroic attempts by those who traffic in psychiatric diagnoses, which assume that there are types of people: those with a disorder and those without.

And what about people's positive characteristics, like happiness, strengths of character, or good social relationships? Again, we may use a shorthand way of describing people as happy versus unhappy, kind versus mean, or socially engaged versus alienated. As long as the relativity of these terms is understood, this is a perfectly reasonable way to describe individuals who are extreme in such characteristics. It is a mistake, though, to take the further step and assume that extremity by some implies discrete types or kinds of people.

In my own work on character strengths, I have inadvertently contributed to this misunderstanding. With our online survey of widely valued positive traits, feedback is automatically provided upon completion of the survey about a respondent's "top" strengths, what are sometimes identified as signature strengths. The feedback is relative (to one's other strengths, to the strengths of other folks, and so on), but some respondents hear the feedback as identifying the "type" of person they are. Oops. There are no character types except in theory, just people who have more versus less of a given strength.

My colleagues and I published a paper that makes this point with data (McGrath, Rashid, Park, & Peterson, 2010).

Let me provide some background. If there really were types of people defined by where they fall along the character strength dimensions we measure, then the frequency distribution of strength scores would show breaks or bumps or bunches. If not, then the distribution should be smooth, with no discontinuities.

For the sake of illustration, consider the distribution of height. For the most part, I assume, this distribution is the familiar bell-shaped curve. But there may be spikes at either end, an excess of very short people and an excess of very tall people, resulting

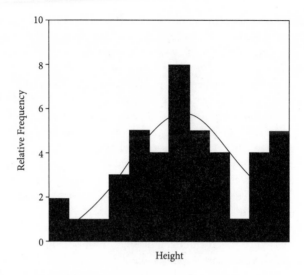

Figure 30.1 Frequency Distribution of Heights

from genetic and/or metabolic conditions. Here we have evidence for types of people; for example, some number of those at the left side of Figure 30.1 may have achondroplasia, and some number of those at the right side may have acromegaly.

There are statistical procedures for determining meaningful breaks or discontinuities in a frequency distribution and the latent constructs that underlie it. Without going into the details (where devils as well as saints reside), we used these procedures to analyze scores on our measure of character strengths from 83,576 adult respondents. The measure is notable because it is reliable and has been validated against informant reports. It includes a wide range of positive traits, based on our previous analyses of influential religious and philosophical traditions.

No matter how we looked at these data—no matter what character strength we considered—the results were unanimous in supporting a dimensional rather than a categorical view of character strengths.

We concluded our report by noting that in the real world, even the best of us are not wise, but wiser—not kind, but kinder—not brave, but braver.

These are not disappointing conclusions. There are no saints, but there are also no sinners. There are people who are more saintly (vis-à-vis a particular strength of character) and those who are more sinful, but the differences are of degree and not of kind. Our data may imply that all of us can move from the more sinful end of things to the more saintly end, no matter where we start, because there are no barriers of kind over which we must leap by transforming ourselves into an altogether different type of person. Finally, being a "good person" can and should remain a goal, but it is one we can only approach and never fully achieve.

REFERENCE

McGrath, R. E., Rashid, T., Park, N., & Peterson, C. (2010). Is optimal functioning a distinct state? *The Humanistic Psychologist*, *38*, 159–169.

31

Does It Matter Where We Live?

*We are like chameleons; we take our hue and the color of our moral character
from those who are around us.*

—John Locke

Nansook Park and I coauthored the lead article in the
September 2010 issue of the *American Psychologist*, which
described our ongoing research on psychological differences
among residents of cities across the United States. Although
many fields of social science focus on life in cities, psychologists
have rarely considered the possibility that people who live in
different cities have different psychological characteristics. And
when psychologists do occasionally study city differences, they
usually look at problems, such as crime, obesity, and mental
illness.

In contrast, we studied character strengths—positive dispositions like love of learning, kindness, and teamwork—among
47,000+ residents residing in the 50 largest U.S. cities who completed an online survey between 2002 and 2005 that measured
character strengths. Differences in character strengths were
found among cities and were strongly related to important
city-level features, including economic accomplishment and
2008 presidential voting.

To make sense of our findings, we distinguished between
strengths of the "head," which are intellectual and self-oriented
(e.g., curiosity, creativity), and strengths of the "heart," which
are emotional and interpersonal (e.g., gratitude, forgiveness).

U.S. cities like San Francisco and Seattle whose residents have greater intellectual and self-oriented dispositions—head strengths—are more innovative as gauged by such indices as patents per capita and the presence of high-tech industries. Residents of these cities tended to vote for Barack Obama—the liberal candidate—for president in 2008.

These cities have more colleges and universities. Cities with strengths of the head are also more crowded and have a higher cost of living. These features converge to suggest that the culture of head cities entails individual achievement, affluence, education, and change.

In contrast, U.S. cities like El Paso and Omaha whose residents have greater emotional and interpersonal strengths—heart strengths—are less innovative. Residents of these cities were more likely to vote for John McCain—the conservative candidate—for president in 2008.

Heart cities are smaller and less crowded. They have a lower cost of living, and their temperatures are warmer, perhaps allowing residents to go outside and interact with their neighbors. These cities are more likely to be populated by families with children. Their residents report more positive emotions and a greater sense of meaning. These features suggest that the culture of heart cities centers on other people and the emotional ties that bind people together. Heart cities are kinder and gentler because they afford greater opportunities for close relationships—and perhaps more pleasurable and more meaningful lives.

We concluded the following:

> Cities as a topic of explicit study deserve greater attention from psychology. Psychology researchers can contribute to future urban policy and the well-being of cities and their residents by addressing how cities create, enable, or allow the expression of different strengths of character among their residents. (p. 545)

Rather than trying to mimic cities such as San Francisco and Boston, mayors and chambers of commerce of other U.S. cities might instead emphasize the soft trade-off between strengths of the head and strengths of the heart implied by our results and stress that life may already be good in their own towns, simply in different ways. (p. 542)

Where we live does matter.

REFERENCE

Park, N., & Peterson, C. (2010). Does it matter where we live? The urban psychology of character strengths. *American Psychologist*, *65*, 535–547.

32

Resilience

Inside of a ring or out, ain't nothing wrong with going down. It's staying down that's wrong.
———Muhammad Ali

From writers and researchers, I receive a number of questions about resilience these days. It is a topic of ongoing interest to positive psychologists and—in light of economic and other challenges around the world—also a topic of current interest to people in general. What is resilience? How can we assess who has it? How can we cultivate it?

Before these questions can be answered, careful attention to the words is needed.

In an important review, Luthar, Cicchetti, and Becker (2000) observed that *resilience* is used inconsistently by theorists and researchers to refer to reactions to adversity ranging from not being devastated after a loss to doing okay in the wake of stress to being largely unaffected to actually flourishing. The range of definitions probably reflects the range of reactions people actually show in the face of adversity.

However, in many studies of resilience, researchers have neglected the details of the adversity of interest—for example, whether it is discrete versus chronic, specific versus diffuse, in principle controllable versus not.

Some studies do not even show that research participants experienced adversity in the first place, simply a life event that seems to be a bad one. We cannot speak of posttraumatic stress disorder or posttraumatic growth—or posttraumatic anything—if there were no experienced trauma!

Here are some definitions.

At least in its original—nonpsychological—sense, *resilience* refers to the return to original form by some entity following a disturbance. So, a squeezed tennis ball resumes its original shape when released.

Resiliency refers to those qualities of the entity that lead to resilience. I'm not smart enough to know why a tennis ball is resilient, but I assume that something about its material and design must be responsible. Is it the fuzz?

Invulnerability is a term once used in the psychological literature to refer to people unaffected by adversity or trauma. For example, children of mothers with active schizophrenia were termed *invulnerable* if they seemed normal. A close look reveals that such children invariably had some other adult in their life (relative, teacher) who took on the caregiving role of which their mothers were incapable, an important reminder not to seek resilience solely in the individual, as if it were no more than a coating of psychological Teflon.

Growth refers to someone doing "better" after adversity than before: "That which does not kill us only makes us stronger." It is akin to a squeezed tennis ball turning into a beach ball when released.

The possibility of posttraumatic growth has captured the attention of positive psychologists, including me, but the notion remains controversial. The relevant research usually primes the person by asking first about trauma and then about trauma's possible benefits. Not surprisingly, many people tell a survivor story, drawing on a common script for personal narratives that is framed in terms of redemption—triumph after and over misfortune. One should worry that the misfortune and its consequences may be exaggerated after the fact.

One of the better demonstrations of growth is my own work on character strengths following trauma, which found elevations of certain strengths—religiousness, gratitude, kindness, hope, and bravery—following potentially traumatic events (Peterson, Park, Pole, D'Andrea, & Seligman, 2008). Unlike most research, our study measured character strengths (the ostensible outcome) *before* trauma was ever mentioned. Priming was minimized, but the retrospective design was still not ideal.

I should emphasize that the effects, on average, were quite modest in magnitude. This is still good and interesting news, but we shouldn't get carried away and welcome bad events because of the benefits that may follow.

My own perspective on resilience is that the term is best used descriptively to refer to the bouncing back to "normal" following potential adversity. What is normal may or may not be all that good. It depends on where someone starts.

Remember the old joke:

Patient: Doctor, will I be able to play the piano after the surgery on my hands?
Doctor: Of course.
Patient: That's great, because I could never play before!

It needs to be recognized that resilience is multidimensional, meaning that one can bounce back in some domains but not others.

It also needs to be recognized that the length of time that needs to pass before resilience is evident may vary greatly, depending on the person and the domain.

My own perspective on resiliency is that it is not a singular thing, and certainly not a thing that people either have or do not have. Indeed, I rarely use the term in my own writing. Rather, *resiliency* is an umbrella term that covers a number of features— some internal to the person and some external—all of which exist along dimensions; for example, optimism, efficacy, meaning and purpose, life satisfaction and/or freedom from depression, social support, and group morale.

The assessment of resiliency needs to be appropriately analytic, measuring its specific components and describing people in terms of profiles of their characteristics.

Along these lines, the cultivation of resiliency needs to target its components, many of which we already know how to encourage.

The bottom line is this: Use the words carefully, and good answers to important questions will be possible.

REFERENCES

Luthar, S. S., Cicchetti, D., & Becker, B. (2000). The construct of resilience: A critical evaluation and guidelines for future work. *Child Development*, *71*, 543–562.

Peterson, C., Park, N., Pole, N., D'Andrea, W., & Seligman, M. E. P. (2008). Strengths of character and posttraumatic growth. *Journal of Traumatic Stress*, *21*, 214–217.

33

Growing Greatness

My first reaction when I heard about Daniel Coyle's (2009) book *The Talent Code* was sympathy. The author had apparently been scooped by Malcolm Gladwell in *Outliers*, which seemed to cover the same sorts of topics with the same thesis (practice, practice, practice), and has become a best seller (see reflection 23). But I bought and read Coyle's book anyway, and I am glad that I did. One should never judge a book by its cover or by other books—even really good ones—that seem similar.

Coyle's thesis is that greatness is grown, and his contribution is to explain how, at several levels.

First, he emphasizes extended practice but goes further to speculate that practice is important because it myelinates the nerves entailed in the practiced actions, making them much more efficient. I am not a neuroscientist and do not know if myelin bears the sole explanatory load. But maybe it does, and I like the idea of a neurological basis to expert performance. And I now have a rationale for my suspicion of the clichéd advice to "perform random acts of kindness and senseless acts of beauty" to be a better person. In my opinion, kindness is not—and should not be—random, and beauty is not—and should not be—sense-less. In any event, I doubt that too many people can perform

10,000+ hours of random and senseless acts and thereby alter the myelinization of their nervous systems.

Second, he discusses talent hotbeds, referring to places from which many talented people emerge at much the same time, like Athenian Greece circa 400 BCE, Florence in the 1400s, and in the more modern world, Brazil for male soccer players and South Korea for female golfers. Needless to say, these talented people did not simply emerge. They endlessly practiced their craft and learned from one another.

Third, Coyle talks about the importance of instigators, a talented person who first appears in a given time and place and gives other people in that time and place the idea that they too can do the same—citing, for example, the Russian tennis player Anna Kournikova who sparked so many other Russians to take up the game and excel at it.

Psychologists have been skeptical of the so-called great man/ woman theory of leadership, the notion that some people will be great leaders regardless of the setting or circumstance. But instigators are a different sort of leader, and I believe they exist. I was "instigated" to study psychology during college because of three graduate students at the University of Illinois who taught courses I took as breaks from my engineering major. Henry, John, and Stan seemed so much older then (now we're the same age), but not so old that I couldn't see myself, someday, doing what they did.

Fourth, in what I think is the most interesting idea of the book, Coyle emphasizes simulations as a way to log the necessary practice and thus lay down the myelin. And he means literal *simulations*, like flight simulators that turned American pilots into aces, the Brazilian game of *futsal* (described as soccer "played inside a phone booth and dosed with amphetamines") that transfers so readily to conventional soccer, and skateboarding in empty swimming pools in Southern California that created so many new moves for the new sport. All of these simulations, according to Coyle, allowed people to improve their neural circuitry at a ferocious speed, because the necessary actions could be done so quickly, over and over.

Positive psychology concerns itself with positive emotions, positive traits, and positive institutions. Institutions that enable excellence and well-being are the least understood member of this trinity, but I think that Coyle's ideas provide a blueprint for creating such an institution. The details will of course differ depending on what the institution is intended to enable, but in general terms, one can deliberately grow talent by having a group of like-minded people, an instigator or two, and an appropriate simulation. Expert teaching is important, and another interesting part of Coyle's book is what he has to say about great teachers, identified by him as talent whisperers.

And, of course, practice, practice, practice.

REFERENCE

Coyle, D. (2009). *The talent code.* New York: Bantam Dell.

34

David and Goliath and the Good Life

In the May 11, 2009, issue of the *New Yorker*, Malcolm Gladwell wrote an essay titled "How David Beats Goliath." The subtitle of the essay is provocative: "When Underdogs Break the Rules."

The essay was ostensibly about a California girls' basketball team from Redwood City coached by Vivek Ranadivé. He was originally from Mumbai and knew little about basketball before he became a coach for his daughter Anjali's team. He was familiar with cricket and soccer, and from his vantage point, basketball as played in the United States made no sense. Teams simply took turns bringing the ball down the court and trying to score. This strategy obviously favored the more talented team, the one with bigger players who could dribble, pass, shoot, and rebound. His team was not talented. In a phrase that is too Imus-like for me to embrace, he described his players as "little blonde girls" whose parents were computer programmers from Silicon Valley.

Ranadivé decided that his team would play a full-court press the entire game, an unusual strategy fully within the rules of the game. They did extremely well, winning most of their games and advancing to the championship game. If you can repeatedly force turnovers under your opponent's basket, you don't need to dribble, pass, rebound, or stick the J. All you need to do is shoot layups, and his team could do that.

As Gladwell is wont to do, he introduced into his essay other ideas and facts. He cited a study of military battles over the past 2 centuries that found that David beat Goliath 29% of the time. That's pretty good. But when the underdogs used unconventional tactics, they won 64% of the time. That's really good.

All's fair in love and certainly war. But apparently not in basketball. The story of the Redwood City team had an unhappy ending. When they advanced to the championship game, they encountered a referee—supplied by their opponent—who did not think that a full-court press for an entire game by 12-year-old girls was kosher. (I suppose he had never heard of the University of Arkansas men's team, coached by Nolan Richardson and famed for its "40 minutes of hell.") Foul after foul was called on the Redwood City team as they contested the inbound passes of their opponents. They eventually gave up their way of playing. They simply moseyed down the court after a made basket, waiting for their opponents to take their shot. And they lost. After all, they weren't as "good" as the other team.

So how should one play the game of basketball? The easy answer is to play to win and to play by the rules. Appreciate that there is no rule against a full-court press. But there are expectations about how one "should" play, and woe be it to a team that goes against these expectations. Whistles will blow.

Even though I care about basketball, many or most of you probably do not. And that is okay, because this reflection is about the game of life. Even though basketball has explicit rules, there are also powerful implicit expectations and norms that may trip up a team.

Life is even more complicated. We want to play to win—be happy—but there are few explicit rules (yet implicit rules galore).

Consider KIPP teachers, who earn the ire of their counterparts elsewhere because they make unannounced home visits to talk to the parents of their students. Teachers are not supposed to do that!

Consider workers who go the extra mile without putting in for overtime. They are called rate busters and scorned (or worse). Workers are not supposed to do that!

One of the few chilling moments of my life occurred when I was a teenaged letter carrier for the U.S. Postal Service. My first day on the job, I delivered my route in 2 hours less than the scheduled time. I lolled about the post office at the end of the day, feeling good about myself, until the union representative came up to me. "You will never do that again," he intoned. "Ever. Not if you enjoy being able to walk."

One of my colleagues at the University of Michigan teaches a course that enrolls hundreds of students every term. Every week during the semester, he invites a number of students over to his home for dinner, so that by the end of the semester he and his family have broken bread with almost every student in the class. The reaction by some of our colleagues is not acclaim but condemnation. "What's wrong with him? And what is his wife's problem? Is she a doormat or what?"

Consider those we know who are passionate, who live life fully. They laugh readily, and they cry just as easily. They hug us when we need it. They yell at us when we need it. They never—and I mean never—fail to say please and thank you. So, how do we regard them behind their backs? We may roll our eyes. People are not supposed to do that!

Shame on us.

Basketball player Wilt Chamberlain famously said, "No one roots for Goliath." Maybe. But we don't always root for David either, because he's not supposed to win, especially if he finds an unconventional way to do it.

What's the positive psychology point? Be tolerant of those who do things differently and well, as long as what they do is neither immoral nor illegal. Indeed, celebrate them. You might actually learn something about the good life.

Most of you, like me, are a David and not a Goliath. I hope we all have the requisite stones (as it were) to pursue a life worth living. It doesn't matter if we have a mundane job, an unremarkable spouse, or really ordinary children. Put a full-court press on life!

REFERENCE

Gladwell, M. (2009, May 11). How David beats Goliath. *The New Yorker*. Retrieved from http://www.newyorker.com/reporting/2009/05/11/090511fa_fact_gladwell.

35

Steve Jobs

Lessons for the Good Life

I just watched the 2005 Stanford University Commencement Address by Steve Jobs. Perhaps you have already seen it—the website reports hundreds of thousands of hits!—but it was new to me, and it contained some excellent points about the good life that I would like to mention here.

I know little about Steve Jobs, so I will focus on the message and not the messenger. That said, this particular message was also about the messenger. Specifically, his 15-minute talk consisted of three personal stories, and it is one of the best speeches I have ever heard, especially of the commencement address genre. Despite being well intended, such talks are usually platitudinous, tedious, and endless. Elderly relatives of college graduates often keel over during them. Heat stroke? Maybe. But boredom might play a role as well, and older audience members could simply be taking an easy way out. After all, life is short.

To judge from the audience shots that interspersed the speech, no one listening to Jobs keeled over. No one looked bored. Indeed, the entire audience was fully engaged. My day job is that of a lecturer, and I would be thrilled if half of the people listening to me in Ann Arbor were half as interested half the time as all of those listening to Jobs during his entire address in Palo Alto were.

Speaking of speaking, stories are always a good vehicle in a talk, especially when packaged in threes. Folks who study such things talk about the "law of three" as a powerful rhetorical strategy. Use three adjectives. Employ three examples. Make three points. And when you tell a joke about guys walking into a bar, be sure there are three of them—not two and certainly not four.

The first story he told was about dropping out of Reed College. More exactly, he stopped paying tuition for classes he didn't like but stayed on campus, dropping in on classes he did like. One of these was a calligraphy class. The relevance of this chance event is in front of me as I draft this reflection: different fonts for computer text and proportional spacing, innovations introduced by Jobs years later that made the first Macintosh computer the apple of so many people's eye. The point? Jobs told his audience to connect the dots in life, appreciating that you cannot do so looking forward. You can do so only when looking back. And you need faith—optimism?—that someday the dots will connect.

The second story he told was about getting fired from Apple Computers, the company that he had cofounded. Talk about coupling insult with injury! But hurt and dismayed though he was, Jobs realized that he still loved what he was doing, so he kept doing it. He founded Pixar. He founded NeXT, which was then acquired by Apple, and you know the rest of the story. The point? Find something that you love to do, because "The only way to do great work is to love what you do."

The third story was about his experience with pancreatic cancer, which made his own mortality more than an abstraction. According to Jobs, "Death is very likely the single best invention of life" because it allows you to sidestep the trap of thinking you have something to lose. The point? Jobs reported that he often asks himself, "If today were the last day of my life, would I want to do what I am about to do today?" When the answer is *no* for too many days in a row, he knows he needs to change something.

Steve Jobs ended his speech with the admonition "Stay hungry—stay foolish." Borrowed from the final *Whole Earth Catalogue*, this advice sounds good, and Jobs repeated it several times. But I don't buy it, or at least not all of it, maybe because it violates the law of three. Stay hungry? Sure. Stay foolish? No way. None of the lessons he conveyed about living a good life is remotely foolish.

REFERENCE

Jobs, S. (2005). *Stanford commencement address*. Retrieved from http://www.youtube.com/watch?v=UF8uR6Z6KLc&feature=related.

36

What Have You Done for Yourself Lately?

A *USA Today* story published in 2009 caught my eye: "Former comedian Al Franken is now a member of the United States Senate" (Schouten, 2009).

I was struck—not by the information that Franken was the winner of the prolonged election in Minnesota, an outcome that seemed inevitable given the trajectory of the repeated recounts and court challenges—but rather by the description of the new senator as a former comedian. I suppose if you become a senator, you stop being funny. Some would beg to differ, but that is not my point here.

Would we see a story that led with the sentence stating that a *former* doctor joined the Senate, or a *former* lawyer, or a *former* whatever?

It depends on the whatever. Certain occupational roles literally become the person, so much so that the person who once occupied the role always does so. A former athletic coach like Bobby Knight remains Coach Knight, even when he is a television commentator. A former president like Bill Clinton is still President Clinton regardless of what he is doing, even if it is not all that presidential. A former general like Colin Powell is always General Powell, except of course when he is Secretary of State Powell, former and forever.

These examples illustrate what sociologists call *person-role merger*, and the phenomenon has been discussed in the scholarly literature with respect to the features of the person or the role that lead to it, as well as the consequences for the person so defined.

Positive psychology suggests to people that they not define themselves as victims because such an identity ties them to a negative past. Can the same point be made about a past identity that is positive? Consider middle-aged men who still present themselves to the world as high school football stars, baby boomers who remind us all that they attended Woodstock, or people who manage to work their attendance at Harvard decades ago into every conversation they have (it's called "dropping the H-bomb," if you are interested). Such folks are lamentable clichés, and they illustrate the downside of person-role merger, even when the role is positive.

Positive psychology also suggests to people that they savor their good experiences, so my advice here is subtle. Yes, one should savor a past role that has provided positive experiences and may still provide status. However, one should not be that role and wallow in the experiences it provided or the status it still radiates to the exclusion of what one currently does and will do.

Another story I just read about Al Franken quoted him as saying that he wants to be regarded only as the junior senator from Minnesota. That is a bit disingenuous, of course, because we can assume that his status as a celebrity contributed mightily to his election. Still, I applaud the sentiment and the bravery it entails.

REFERENCE

Schouten, F. (2009, June 30). Franken wins court battle over Minn. Senate seat. *USA Today.* Retrieved from http://content.usatoday.com/communities/onpolitics/post/2009/06/68493202/1.

Part IV

Positive Relationships

Regardless of the topic that a positive psychologist studies, his or her findings usually come back to the importance of other people. We are, after all, inherently social, so it is not surprising that that other people figure so prominently in the characterization of the psychological good life.

The reflections in this section include some case examples as well as discussions of recent research findings about the importance of other people to us and of us to other people.

37

Other People Matter

Two Examples

"Other people matter." I say that in every positive psychology lecture I give and every positive psychology workshop I conduct. It sounds like a bumper sticker slogan, but it is actually a good summary of what positive psychology research has shown about the good life broadly construed. It is in the company of others that we often experience pleasure and certainly how we best savor its aftermath. It is through character strengths that connect us to others—like gratitude—that many of us find satisfaction and meaning in life. It is with other people that we work, love, and play. Good relationships with other people may be a necessary condition for our own happiness, even in markedly individualist cultures like the contemporary United States.

Let me go beyond these generalizations and provide two examples that illustrate that other people matter. Both were called to my attention by my friend and colleague Nansook Park. (Other people matter.)

I am reluctant to call these positive psychology case studies, as I did without hesitation in my reflection about Randy Pausch (24), because I do not know the rest of the stories. I know only what I was able to glean from some brief accounts that I read. So regard them as examples. But they're good examples and will probably stay with you as they have stayed with me.

Nancy Makin (2010) weighed 703 pounds, the result of a despair-driven spiral. The more she ate, the worse felt, and the worse she felt, the more she ate. For years, she was essentially housebound and allowed only her immediate family to see her. Then her sister gave her a computer as a gift. With Internet access and an interest in politics, Nancy Makin surfed through chat rooms and began to make friends, who of course did not judge her by her appearance.

She began to value herself and to look forward to each new day. According to her, "I was being loved and nurtured by face-less strangers....Friends accepted who I was based on my mind and soul." And she began to lose weight. No diet. No pills. No surgery. No special exercise program. She simply stopped eating to excess, and over the next 3 years she lost some 530 pounds. "I've heard so many times, I said it myself, if I could only lose 40 or 50 pounds, I'd be so much happier. I've found on this journey that the opposite is true." For her, feeling happier about herself started the weight loss, and feeling happier about herself was the result of her new friends.

Luke Pittard worked for McDonald's in Cardiff, Wales. When he won £1.3 million in the National Lottery, he followed a typical lottery winner script: He quit his job, bought a new house, threw a lavish wedding, and went on a dream vacation. After 18 months of his new lifestyle, he went back to work. Why? He missed his fellow workers, who welcomed him back. Said one, "Luke was always a great member of our team and when he won the lottery we were all so pleased for him....I'm glad he has had the time to enjoy his winnings but love having him [back] here....It's as if he never went away."

Luke Pittard acknowledges that some may think him mad for returning to a job where he makes less than the interest on what remains from his lottery winnings. But he explained that "a bit of hard work never did anyone any harm" and further that his job gave him something to look forward to every day.

These are hardly typical stories, which is precisely why I have written about them. Surfing the Internet is not a guaranteed way to lose weight, and returning to a job that pays £5.85 an hour is not a guaranteed way of avoiding the problems that can plague lottery winners. But for Nancy Makin and Luke Pittard, the good life they discovered or rediscovered was entwined with other people, who provided them with hope and meaning.

As the rest of us search for the good life, we would be well served by keeping in mind these examples and the lesson they teach. Other people matter. And we would also be well served by keeping in mind the cyber friends of Nancy Makin and the workmates of Luke Pittard. We are all the other people who can matter so much.

REFERENCE

Makin, N. (2010). *703: How I lost more than a quarter ton and regained a life.* New York: Dutton.

38

Gratitude

Letting Other People Know They Matter Benefits Us

Gratitude is when memory is stored in the heart and not in the mind.
—Lionel Hampton

I talked to a colleague the other day who told me that his 15-year-old son had taken our online measure of character strengths. The son's top strength was gratitude. My colleague shook his head and said wryly, "We're sure not seeing that."

I might have said that the survey was not working for his son, but instead I said, "Maybe you're not paying enough attention." I wanted to believe that the test was valid in this case, for the sake of my colleague's son as well as my colleague, because our previous research had shown that gratitude is one of the strengths of character most robustly associated with life satisfaction and all the good things that follow from that (Park & Peterson, 2006; Park, Peterson, & Seligman, 2004).

Gratitude is what we call a strength of the heart because it forges an emotional bond between people (see reflection 31). To be sure, not everyone expresses gratitude loudly and clearly (like 15-year-old boys), but we should listen hard for it, given how precious gratitude is.

A study by Jeffrey Froh, Giacomo Bono, and Robert Emmons (2010) clarified what might be going on for adolescents who are grateful, and why this disposition is a beneficial one. Their sample was 700 middle school students, who completed a self-report measure of gratitude at one point in time and measures of life satisfaction and social integration at subsequent points in time.

Results were clear: Consistent with previous research, gratitude led to subsequent life satisfaction, and one of the pathways was increased social integration. So, gratitude indeed bonds us to others.

I'm not sure why, but several years ago, I started to thumbtack the thank-you cards and notes I received on a bulletin board in my office. I call this the Wall of Gratitude. Before, I simply read such cards and notes, smiled, and tossed them in the garbage. How incredibly stupid of me. Displaying them on a bulletin board provides a constant reminder, not that I do good things for people (most of the thank-you notes were for mundane things that are part of my professional role, like writing a letter of recommendation or giving a guest lecture) but rather that people are appreciative. When I am down and troubled, I look at my bulletin board and feel grateful myself that other people are as well. What a wonderful world, and I mean specifically the social world in which we live.

Other people matter. But few of them are mind readers. Let them know that they matter. They might benefit. And you certainly will.

REFERENCES

Froh, J. J., Bono, G., & Emmons, R. (2010). Being grateful is beyond good manners: Gratitude and motivation to contribute to society among early adolescents. *Motivation and Emotion, 34*, 144–157.

Park, N., & Peterson, C. (2006). Character strengths and happiness among young children: Content analysis of parental descriptions. *Journal of Happiness Studies, 7*, 323–341.

Park, N., Peterson, C., & Seligman, M. E. P. (2004). Strengths of character and well-being. Journal *of Social and Clinical Psychology, 23*, 603–619.

39

Gender and Friendship

A Book Review

The friendship that can cease has never been real.
—Saint Jerome

The "Girl from Ipanema" walked alone, and her samba to the sea lasted a scant 2 minutes. In contrast, *The Girls From Ames* have walked together for 40+ years, and their journey is far from over.

Some years ago, journalist Jeffrey Zaslow wrote a column on women's friendships. He received many letters and e-mail messages in response, including one from a middle-aged woman who recounted the lifelong friendship of 11 women ("girls") from Ames, Iowa. He eventually wrote a book about them that I am happy to recommend, especially to male readers like me who might be curious about how the other half lives (Zaslow, 2009).

The book contains largely descriptive accounts of the women's lives separately and in particular together. It contains enough interpretation and reference to survey data to satisfy this social scientist, but it never bogs down in the "research shows" motif.

The theme of the book is that women are different from men with respect to their friendships. Exceptions of course exist, but women interact face-to-face, whereas men interact side-by-side. Women's friendships revolve around one another, whereas men's friendships revolve around shared activities.

I used to play a lot of pickup basketball with the guys. They were my friends, but when the games ended, so did the friendships. I used to play a lot of cards with other guys. They too were my friends, but when the dealing was done, so were the friendships. And I am embarrassed to say that I used to spend a lot of time in a bar drinking with still other guys. They were my friends as well, but not after the final last call some years ago.

My closest friends now are women, and I do not expect these friendships to end. I doubt that I am as good a friend to them as they are to me, and I am glad they also have close friendships with women. Those are the friendships that research shows to be healthy, lasting, and satisfying. Those are the friendships described in *The Girls From Ames*.

The women in the book are ordinary people with an extraordinary friendship. They are now scattered across the country. They are pursuing a variety of careers. Some are married, and some are divorced. They have all had triumphs and tragedies in their lives. But they remain friends. "Research shows" that a friendship established before age 40 is apt to last forever, at least for women. Too bad marriages are not that stable.

A few weeks before reading this book, I talked to a 20-something female student of mine about to leave for the summer for an internship far from home. She was excited but fretted than she knew no one in the town to which she was moving.

"And I'm so shy," she added.

I responded, "But no one there knows you are shy. Why not be outgoing?"

She liked that advice and said it was a good idea. But now I realize that it was just one perspective. After reading *The Girls From Ames*, another and perhaps better suggestion would have been for her to invite her friends—specifically her female friends—to visit her while she was away.

Friendships are not just in the here and now, and they cannot be created anew each time we relocate. According to one of the women from Ames, "You can tell people where you're from and who you were, which is who you are. But no one really knows you unless they were there."

REFERENCE

Zaslow, J. (2009). *The girls from Ames: A story of women and a forty-year friendship*. New York: Gotham Books.

40

Tears and Testosterone

Tears are the noble language of the eye.
—Robert Herrick

A paper published in *Science* in 2011 captured the attention of scientists and civilians alike on the Internet, for good reason: The research reported is really interesting. A group of Israeli researchers headed by Shani Gelstein investigated the biochemical effects on others of exposure to tears. Bottom line: Female tears reduced sexual arousal of males, assessed in various ways.

To paraphrase their summary of the research:

Merely sniffing negative-emotion-related odorless tears obtained from women donors reduced the sexual appeal attributed by men to pictures of women's faces. After sniffing such tears, men experienced reduced self-rated sexual arousal, reduced physiological measures of arousal, and reduced levels of testosterone. Finally, functional magnetic resonance imaging showed that sniffing women's tears selectively reduced activity in brain substrates of sexual arousal in men.

The researchers gathered "unhappy" tears from women watching sad movies and placed on absorbent pads, which men were asked to smell. Control participants sniffed a saline solution on the pads. As we all know, when we stop and reflect, tears have no discernible odor, but there were still effects of exposure to them—a reduction in sexual arousal. Many of the Internet reports of this research headline it by saying that "tears turn men off," which is strictly true if our focus is on sexual arousal.

But is this the whole story? Tears may turn men off sexually, but do tears turn men off in other ways? I suspect not, at least based on my own experience. Tears make me take someone's unhappiness seriously. Tears make me want to help. Tears make me want to be comforting, to offer a shoulder or a hand. And if sexual arousal is not getting in the way of that, all the better. Indeed, testosterone is linked not only to sexual arousal but also to aggression, which means that exposure to tears may make men kinder and gentler.

That such effects may have a biochemical basis is intriguing beyond belief.

The researchers concluded that tears must contain a chemical signal (I agree), although it remains unidentified. Further research is needed. And it will be conducted because the mark of interesting research is that it stimulates more research.

REFERENCE

Gelstein, S., Yeshurun, Y., Rozenkrantz, L., Shushan, S., Frumin, I., Roth, Y., & Sobel, N. (2011). Human tears contain a chemosignal. *Science, 331*, 226–230.

41

Dealing With the Pain of Romantic Breakups

Some Research-Informed Suggestions

I don't know why they call it heartbreak. It feels like every other part of my
body is broken too.

—Missy Altijd

Psychology researchers today increasingly use fMRI (functional magnetic resonance imaging) as a laboratory strategy. Research participants are placed in a large scanner that takes pictures of their brain and indicates which parts of it are more versus less active as gauged by blood flow while the participants are performing one or another activity, including doing nothing at all. This strategy makes sense given the growing interest of psychologists in locating what people do in terms of the structure and function of their brains, but the strategy has its own challenges.

Brain imaging is terribly expensive, and fMRI studies often enroll a very small number of research participants, limiting the power of the research design. The results of fMRI studies are often starkly empirical—merely determining what correlates with what—and critics have charged that researchers may simply be reporting associations that reflect chance, a possibility increased by the use of small sample sizes (Vul, Harris, Winkielman, & Pashler, 2009).

In my opinion, fMRI results—like those from any research strategy—are most useful when there is a theory to make sense of them, especially when the theory guides the research design and analyses. There are countless parameters of a brain image.

Theory can tell an investigator which parameters deserve attention and emphasis in a given study. In the absence of guiding theory, what we see are after-the-fact explanations of research results that may be simply that: after the fact. In the case of many fMRI studies, we may have examples of what biologist Stephen Jay Gould decades ago dubbed a "just-so story."

But there are exceptions, and these deserve our attention. An example of a theory-guided fMRI study was recently reported by University of Michigan psychologist Ethan Kross and his colleagues (2011). Their research has received widespread publicity, deservedly so.

Kross and his colleagues recruited 40 research participants who had recently experienced a romantic breakup and took pictures of their brains in different conditions. By the way, the participants were the breakees rather than the breakers, and they reported feeling quite rejected. Participants who were asked to look at photos of their ex-partner showed brain activity in exactly the same regions of their brains that were active when they were experiencing physical pain produced by thermal stimulation—heat, in plainer English. "Love hurts" was the unavoidable headline under which popular accounts of this research appeared.

Popular accounts went on to conclude that the pain following a romantic breakup is "real," which is a conclusion that deserves scrutiny. As virtually all of us know, the pain of a romantic breakup is real—in psychological terms—and fMRI research is not needed to show this. Furthermore, the pain of a romantic breakup of course has a basis in the activity of the brain and nervous system, just as all of our thoughts, feelings, and actions have a basis in the activity of the brain and nervous system. To believe otherwise is to endorse a strict mind-body dualism long ago rejected by psychologists. Again, fMRI research is not needed to show this.

But what is important about this research is that pain due to a breakup and pain due to physical stimuli *look the same* in terms of brain images and by implication brain activity.

That's really interesting, and an explicit hypothesis led to this finding, one with theoretical and perhaps practical implications.

Theoretically, if I may tell my own just-so story, perhaps in the course of human evolution, romantic breakups piggybacked onto existing brain structures and functions to register social rejection as painful...and to lead to the sorts of behaviors that pain from physical stimuli produces, like putting a distance between the self and the source of pain and then taking time to recover from the damage inflicted.

Practically, this research suggests ways to deal with the pain of social rejection. For starters, perhaps one should not "confront" the source of the pain—the breaker—at least not if one wants to feel less pain. We do not advise people who have burned their hand on a stove to "confront" the stove. We do not tell people who have burned their hand to "process" or "talk through" what happened. We tell them to turn off the stove and to be more careful in the future.

Relationship problems foreshadow substance use, and here people may be trying to deaden the accompanying pain (cf. Simon & Barrett, 2010). I surfed around this morning and found an Internet website devoted to the "best" drugs, legal and illegal, to use after a romantic breakup! Most of the suggested drugs had analgesic properties. All of this makes perfect sense, but there is a slippery slope between drug use and drug abuse that make this a dangerous long-term remedy, no matter how successful it may be in the short term. Alas, my caution pertains to chocolate ice cream as well as to alcohol and the opiates.

So, how about physical exercise? Research is clear that vigorous aerobic exercise can reduce physical pain. I bet that it reduces the pain of social rejection as well, although relevant research is needed. Perhaps it has already been done and escaped my searches. Regardless, we have a clear hypothesis, and that is good if science is to contribute to a life lived well, or at least not painfully.

REFERENCES

Kross, E., Berman, M., Mischel, W., Smith, E. E., & Wager, T. (2011). Social rejection shares somatosensory representations with physical pain. *Proceedings of the National Academy of Science of the United States of America, 108*, 6270-6275.

Simon, R. W., & Barrett, A. E. (2010). Nonmarital romantic relationships and mental health in early adulthood: Does the relationship differ for women and men? *Journal of Health and Social Behavior, 51*, 168–182.

Vul, E., Harris, C, Winkielman, P & Pashler, H (2009). Puzzlingly high correlations in fMRI studies of emotion, personality, and social cognition. *Perspectives on Psychological Science, 4*, 274–290.

42

Happiness, Small Talk, and Big Talk

Great people talk about ideas, average people talk about things, and small people talk about wine.

—Fran Lebowitz

We all talk—that's human nature. But do we talk about big topics or small topics? Do we engage in big talk, as it were, or simply small talk? And what does our style say about us?

I am a very good small talker. I can chatter away with almost anybody about almost anything: the weather, the local sports teams, or last night's television shows. Cocktail conversations are my forte, and I have always assumed that was an unalloyed good thing, an indicator of my glibness if not more profoundly my social skills.

So, I must be a happy camper, right?

Perhaps not, according to a study by Matthias Mehl and colleagues (2010). These researchers asked 79 college students to wear an audio recorder for 4 days as they went about their daily lives. At random intervals during waking hours, a 30-second recording was made of whatever was being said, resulting in almost 24,000 snippets, about 300 per participant. These snippets were then coded by the researchers into small talk—defined as the banal and uninvolved exchange of trivial information (about 18% of all recorded conversations)—or substantive talk—defined as the involved exchange of meaningful information (about 36%). (The remaining conversations could not be unambiguously coded into either category.)

Also known about the research participants was their happiness, assessed in several ways.

The results were straightforward. First, happier participants spent more time talking to others, unsurprising finding given the social basis of happiness. Second, the extent of small talk was *negatively* associated with happiness. And third, the extent of substantive talk was *positively* associated with happiness. So, happy people are socially engaged with others, and this engagement entails matters of substance.

The authors acknowledged that the causal direction of these results is not clear. Causality could run from big talk to happiness, or it could run from happiness to big talk. It could run from small talk to unhappiness, or from unhappiness to small talk. But regardless, the results are interesting, at least to me, because they are not what I would have expected. I would have predicted that chattering away—small talking—would be an indicator of greater happiness, and that big talking would mark someone's darker—or at least ponderous—side. *Au contraire*, which is why research is important to do.

Mind you, for a conversation to earn a score of "substance" from these researchers, it did not have to focus on the meaning of life or the disclosure of deep secrets. Rather, "substantive" conversations were involved—that is, the person with whom the researcher participant talked actually mattered vis-à-vis the conversation.

Assuming that causality runs from the topics of our conversations to our psychological well-being, the "so what?" of the research seems pretty clear. Talk about what matters, especially to those who care about what you say.

REFERENCE

Mehl, M. R., Vazire, S., Holleran, S. E., & Clark, C. S. (2010). Eavesdropping on happiness: Well-being is related to having less small talk and more substantive conversations. *Psychological Science, 21*, 539–541.

43

Having a Friend and Being a Friend

The only way to have a friend is to be one.
—Ralph Waldo Emerson

A literature review by Julianne Holt-Lunstad, Timothy Smith, and Bradley Layton (2010) summarized 148 prospective studies with a total of 308,849 research participants. The focus was on social relationships and longevity, and the results were clear and intriguing. Those with stronger social relationships—assessed by both quantitative and qualitative indices—had a 50% increased likelihood of survival. This finding held across age, sex, initial health status, cause of death, and length of follow-up period

So, it bears repeating that other people matter, and in this case, mattering shows up in terms of an increased life span.

Here is a simple multiple-choice test. What was your first reaction when you read about this finding, which is not only reliable but quite robust?

A. I thought about how many friends I had, and whether I had "enough" friends to make me live longer in a meaningful way.
B. I thought about how many people for whom I was a friend, and whether I had "enough" friends to help other people live longer in a meaningful way.

My immediate answer was A—I admit it—but as I thought further, I realized that B was a pretty good answer as well, and maybe a morally better one to boot. Note to students: Sometimes your first reaction to a test question is not the correct reaction!

Positive psychology can be criticized as much too focused on the individual. Many of the findings of this field are presented to the general public in terms of how they can benefit the individual: in other words, *your* increased happiness, success, health, and longevity. But sometimes doing the right thing does not always benefit the individual. It nonetheless remains the right thing.

In the case of friendship, there is no trade-off. Many (not all) friendships are symmetric, so my point here is mainly about how you frame the value of a friendship. Is it all about you, or is it also about the other person? In this case, according to the review, the answer is both.

So, what is the so what? Maybe we should think about the benefits of friendship, not for us, but for others. Who in our circle might most benefit from having a friend? Probably not those who are already popular. When was the last time you (or I) set out to befriend a person who was a bit isolated, a bit awkward, or a bit difficult? Maybe you are like me, and the answer would be *seldom* or *never*.

I intend to change that.

And given that I (and you too?) may be a bit isolated, a bit awkward, and a bit difficult, I hope others heed this moral message, based on the data, and do the right thing!

We're all in this together, dear readers.

REFERENCE

Holt-Lunstad J., Smith, T. B., & Layton, J. B. (2010). Social relationships and mortality risk: A meta-analytic review. *PLoS Med* 7(7): e1000316. doi:10.1371.

44

Infants Get It Right

Nice guys finish last.
—Leo Durocher

A colleague directed my attention to a fascinating line of research at the Yale University Infant Cognition Lab.

Researchers there have developed a paradigm that allowed them to show that infants prefer "nice" guys (Hamlin, Wynn, & Bloom, 2007). Very young children—so young they needed to be held on the lap of a parent during the experiment—viewed puppet shows in which one character in the show assists another character (by helping it climb a steep passage, open a box, retrieve a bouncing ball, and so on) versus another character who impedes these actions. The infants were then allowed to choose the character—the one who helped or the one who hindered—and some 80% of the time, they were oriented to the good guy, touching it first or grasping it first.

A video has been posted on the Internet describing these studies (Bloom, 2010), and I was struck that the babies touching or grasping the helpful character seemed always to be smiling when they did so.

This indicates that infants like nice guys, and that this preference may be wired into them, or at least it is present before language. Children are obviously not blank slates, and maybe they get it from the very get-go. It is obviously advantageous to prefer those who help as opposed to those who hinder.

This research has been discussed in the scientific and popular media under the rubric of "the moral life of babies," meaning that the results are taken to reflect an inherent preference among infants for moral goodness, to which I say, *yes* and *no*. What is morally right is not always what benefits us, and niceness—helpfulness—should not be confused with moral goodness. All things being equal, niceness characterizes many acts of moral behavior, but not necessarily.

Among my sins are some that result precisely from my attempts to be nice, by not setting the bar high enough for my students, by not telling someone a difficult truth, by doing something for others that they should be doing for themselves, and so on.

But the results of this research program are remarkable enough even if rendered more modestly, as showing that infants are oriented toward those who help rather than those who hinder—a behavioral style that I have chosen to call *niceness*.

As we mature (so to speak), some of us seem to forget our early preference for niceness. Leo Durocher's famous quote about nice guys as losers is paraphrased and applied in many domains of life. I even did this myself a few weeks ago, when I repeated a cynical quote I had heard to the effect that no one with an open door policy was ever elected to the National Academy of Sciences, an assertion that may or may not be true. We rationalize our own departures from niceness and excuse those on the part of others if they seem to contribute to a competitive edge (what an ugly phrase upon reflection). And many of us are romantically attracted to bad boys and mean girls, or their adult equivalents, despite the heartaches that will necessarily follow.

Most of us accept small acts of kindness from others—niceness—but maybe we think these are our just due. Do we thank nice people? Do we take obvious delight in them? Do we prefer the nice guys in the world? Infants get it right. What about the rest of us?

A great deal of contemporary character education tries to teach children what they do not know about morality . . . or niceness. I suggest that another goal of character education should be to leave intact what the young already know.

> It's not true that nice guys finish last. Nice guys are winners before the game even starts.
>
> —Addison Walker

REFERENCES

Bloom, P. (2010, May 3). The moral life of babies. *The New York Times Magazine.* Retrieved from http://www.nytimes.com/2010/05/09/magazine/09babies-t.html.

Hamlin, J. K., Wynn, K., & Bloom, P. (2007). Social evaluation in preverbal infants. *Nature, 450,* 557–559.

45

Viral Happiness

Thousands of candles can be lit from a single candle, and the life of the candle will not be shortened. Happiness never decreases by being shared.
    —Buddha

One of the well-established findings in positive psychology is that many of the important determinants of happiness and life satisfaction are social. A study by James Fowler and Nicholas Christakis (2008) reinforces this finding by showing that happiness spreads through social networks. We are likely to be happy to the degree that our friends or spouses are happy, and we are likely to become happier as they become happier.

These particular results are important because they expand the scope of positive psychology, which often has quite an individualistic—some would say selfish—emphasis. That is, we are told to be happy because of what will follow in its wake for us as individuals: good feelings, success, and health. The study by Fowler and Christakis provides an additional rationale for individual happiness: It can lead to the happiness of others and presumably produce desirable consequences for them. Accordingly, the pursuit of happiness may be more than a selfish journey.

Although this study has received widespread publicity, its details are worth reviewing, because some of the accounts in the media have apparently glossed over important nuances. For example, one of the deans of my university sent out an e-mail to faculty and staff urging us to be happy. He did not cite the study by Fowler and Christakis, but given the timing and content of his message, I believe that his well-intended exhortation was inspired by a media account of the study. He observed that happiness could spread throughout an office, so we should all "get happy" in order to benefit our colleagues and further the goals of the university. The problem is that the study did not show happiness contagion among those who work together. It occurred only among friends and spouses.

The study analyzed data gathered from thousands of individuals from 1983 through 2003 as part of the Framingham Heart Study. Information was available not only about target individuals but also their family members, close friends, neighbors, and coworkers. Target individuals included both men and women from the United States. They were mostly middle-aged and on average had completed several years of college.

Happiness was measured with four reverse-scored items from a depression inventory. That is, although intended to measure symptoms of depression, these items were phrased in terms of its opposite: "I felt hopeful about the future," "I was happy," "I enjoyed life," and "I felt that I was just as good as other people." These items cohere and are a plausible measure of happiness. In the research Fowler and Christakis reported, happiness was operationally defined as rating each of these four items at the top ("most or all of the time").

The first question of interest was whether the happiness of our associates is linked to our own happiness (or vice versa). The answer is *yes*. A happy individual with whom one is socially connected increases the likelihood of one's own happiness by about 9%, whereas an unhappy individual with whom one is connected decreases the likelihood of one's own happiness by about 7%. So, happiness is a bit more potent than unhappiness. And if I understand the data correctly, the relationship between happy associates and one's own happiness is strictly linear: the more, the better. But the relationship between unhappy associates and one's own unhappiness is not linear. One unhappy associate takes a toll, but additional unhappy associates do not.

The second question of interest was whether changes in someone's happiness in the social network led to subsequent changes in one's own happiness. A close look at the data in terms of the nature of the relationship and changes in happiness over time was needed. Again, the answer is *yes*, although with qualifications. Having a friend who lived nearby (within 1 mile) and became happy increased one's own subsequent happiness. The same result was found for a spouse with whom one shared a residence. Increasing happiness among friends at a greater distance did not lead to changes in one's own happiness, and neither did having colleagues at work who became happy.

The researchers acknowledged that their data do not speak to why these results occurred, although their findings are reliable and rather robust. Psychologists know that many emotional states are literally contagious. All that matters is mere proximity. In the present case of happiness, physical proximity may set the stage for the spread of happiness but is not sufficient. Otherwise the changing happiness or unhappiness of the people with whom we work would affect our own happiness. Perhaps we also need to like the person, and the unfortunate implication of this conjecture is that we may not really like the people with whom we work. Maybe we see them as competitors or akin to office furniture. If happiness is a virus, it is not spread by casual contact, no matter how frequent.

In my reflection "Happiness Outliers" (23), I speculated about what I called *happiness legacies*: groups of people united by an emphasis on living a psychologically good life. The first place to look for these legacies is probably not at the workplace, which is sad and interesting in equal measure. Someone needs to tell my dean, perhaps adding the advice that the university should go out of its way to hire our friends and spouses, at least those who are happy.

REFERENCE

Fowler, J. H., & Christakis, N. A. (2008). Dynamic spread of happiness in a large social network: Longitudinal analysis over 20 years in the Framingham Heart Study. *British Medical Journal, 338*, 1–13.

Part V

Enabling Institutions

Families

When positive psychology first began, the field was divided into positive experiences, positive traits, positive relationships, and institutions that enable positive experiences, traits, and relationships—an organization I have used in the present collection. Positive institutions were the acknowledged weak link, which makes sense because psychology per se looks at individuals much more frequently than at groups of individuals.

Things are changing, at least in positive psychology, and we are starting to learn more about positive institutions. The next few section in this book look at some of the institutions that have attracted the recent attention of positive psychology, starting with the family.

46

Books Matter

Books are not made for furniture, but there is nothing else that so beautifully furnishes a house.

　　　　　—Henry Ward Beecher

I don't know if I'm a materialist or not. I acquire lots of stuff, but I also get rid of lots of stuff. I routinely go through my closet and find clothes to put in Goodwill boxes around town, and I regularly purge my pantry of canned goods for local food drives. I take dishes and glasses to the Salvation Army. I have trashed a number of television sets, countless computers, and on two occasions, automobiles. I do not keep leftovers in my refrigerator or reprints in my file cabinets. I acquire knickknacks, and I soon disacquire them. I even get rid of my money, and I don't mean in bad investments. My friends, family members, and various nonprofit organizations would say that I am generous, but the truth is that as much as I like acquiring money, keeping it is not all that important to me.

But I never get rid of books, including books that I don't like, books that I'll never read again, and books that I'll never read at all. Books are different than other things, at least for me. I never get rid of them. I loan books to others, but I get them back!

I rack them. I stack them. I pack them. I have placed books not only next to my bed but also in it. There are books in the backseat of my car, and there are books in the trunk. On occasion, I've stored books in my refrigerator (don't ask). I haven't put them in my oven yet, but now that I think of it, that might happen, too. If there were ever a special episode of the A&E television show *Hoarders* devoted to books, I would be the star.

It was therefore with interest that I read a study showing rather conclusively that books matter (Evans, Kelley, Sikora, & Treiman, 2010). Mightily.

Researchers assembled survey data from nationally representative samples in 27 countries and looked at the eventual educational attainment of children who grew up in a home with "many" books (500 or more) versus few books. Across the 70,000 research participants, children growing up in homes with many books stayed in school 3 years longer than children from largely bookless homes. This finding was independent of parental education, occupation, and social class. The finding occurred in rich nations and poor nations. This finding occurred under communism and capitalism, in North America, Europe, Africa, and Asia.

Further research may not be needed, at least not if we want to know the empirical link between the presence of books and subsequent educational attainment of children.

Are books markers of a scholarly culture within a family (as the researchers suggested) or direct causes of educational attainment? Probably both. Books provide context. Unlike a cause in the Baconian sense, context is not a discrete event but rather an ongoing influence on what we value and what we do. Context lingers. It not only causes but maintains and sustains.

One of the oft-repeated stories about the Peterson family is that we grew up without much extra money for fancy clothes, vacations, a second car, or an air conditioner. But there was always money for books. And while we never visited the East Coast, the West Coast, or Europe, we visited the local library every week.

I grew up in the 1950s, and I have a twin brother. Our mother was exhausted by the demands of child-rearing times two, in an era without Pampers or day care. So she coped by plunking my brother and me down next to her in a chair, and she read to us, hour after hour, from the endless supply of books in our otherwise modest home.

Thanks Mom. I'm still at school!

REFERENCE

Evans, M. D. R., Kelley, J., Sikora, J., & Treiman, D. H. (2010). Family scholarly culture and educational success: Books and schooling in 27 nations. *Research in Social Stratification and Mobility, 28*, 171–197.

47

You May Now Kiss the Bride...and Would You Like Fries With That?

Anews story caught my attention one morning, and I have been thinking about it ever since. Along with its fast food, McDonald's is now offering weddings—McWeddings, I assume—in Hong Kong.

Apparently, restaurants are a common venue for Hong Kong weddings, but they can be pricey. McDonald's offers the whole package of invitations, decorations, and food for $1,282. The bride's dress costs extra, but it too is available. A wedding at McDonald's is a bargain, relatively speaking.

When I first heard about the story, I shook my head, rolled my eyes, and resolved to write about it. But what you are reading is not what I originally had in mind, which was going to be flip and critical. One of the accounts on the Internet that I read certainly followed this line, dubbing these weddings tacky and nauseating.

But I stopped and thought about the motives of couples who would get married at a McDonald's, realizing that I have no idea what they might be in any given case. I could think of some possibilities, though, and none of these is tacky.

So, perhaps those tying the knot under the golden arches have a sense of humor. That's a great way to begin life together, and good for them. Retelling the story of their wedding years later will certainly be fun.

Along these lines, perhaps these couples have a sense of irony and are deliberately contrasting the solemn occasion of a wedding with the frivolous setting of a fast food restaurant. Again, good for them, although they would probably need to spell out the irony for many folks.

Not far from where I live in Ann Arbor is a small town named Hell, Michigan, which has a wedding chapel that does a thriving business. One of my colleagues claims to have been married there—she may or may not be teasing—but I have always loved her wry comment: "My marriage began in Hell."

Or perhaps those who marry at a McDonald's actually like the place. The story I read quoted a McDonald's manager in Hong Kong who spoke about the couples interested in McWeddings: "They date here, they grew their love here, so when they have this important day, they want to come over here." Again, good for them. Getting married in a familiar and beloved place seems more sincere than—for example—getting married in a church one has rarely if ever attended.

Or maybe people get married at a McDonald's because this is what they can afford, or what they choose to afford. How dare we call anyone tacky who does not want to start a marriage by running up tens of thousands of dollars in debt, for themselves or for their families? I think an inexpensive wedding makes sense for those of modest or even not modest means, and again, I say good for them.

48

Living Happily Ever After

There is only one happiness in life—to love and to be loved.
—George Sand

The results of an ambitious longitudinal study spanning 25 years have been described by Bruce Headey, Ruud Muffels, and Gert Wagner (2010). The data came from the German Socio-Economic Panel (SOEP) Survey, an ongoing investigation of a large nationally representative sample of Germans, aged 16 and over, who have reported their life satisfaction every year from 1984 to 2008.

There are many interesting results, but Headey and colleagues emphasized how these data show that the *set-point theory* of happiness is wrong. According to set-point theory, people have a certain genetically determined level of happiness, which can be temporarily raised or lowered by life events, but only temporarily. In other words, people will revert to their characteristic levels of happiness, whatever they may be. By this logic, happiness cannot be boosted in a lasting way, and good-intentioned efforts by positive psychologists to do so are doomed.

The problem with set-point theory is that the data from the SOEP Survey—and other longitudinal studies—do not support the premise that people's levels of happiness are fixed. There of course is some stability in reported happiness, but for many people, happiness can and does change. Set-point theory predicts that across increasing periods of time, more stability in happiness should be found. The data show just the opposite pattern.

Indeed, Headey and colleagues concluded that psychosocial factors are more important than biology in determining happiness.

What should one do to live happily ever after, regardless of one's starting point? Among the factors implicated in the SOEP Survey are

- Having an emotionally stable (nonneurotic) marital partner;
- Prioritizing altruistic and/or family goals;
- Attending church; and
- Making a satisfactory trade-off between work and leisure—both are important, but need to be balanced.

In their article, Headey and colleagues dubbed these factors *choices*, which they may or may not be—it depends on how much of a determinist one is. However, I will observe that most of us have more control over such matters than we do over our genes.

REFERENCE

Headey, B., Muffels, R., & Wagner, G. G. (2010). Long-running German panel survey shows that personal and economic choices, not just genes, matter for happiness. *Proceedings of the National Academy of Science of the United States of America, 107*, 17922–17926.

49

What Good Are Fathers?

One father is more than a hundred schoolmasters.
—George Herbert

Those of you with access to a college or university library might be familiar with PsycINFO, a wonderful online resource of the American Psychological Association that allows a computerized search by keywords of English-language studies published by psychologists, from 1872 to the present.

One year, with Father's Day approaching, I did separate searches for the terms "mother OR mothers OR maternal" and for the terms "father OR fathers OR paternal." I found what I expected: 97,957 studies on mothers and 35,236 studies on fathers, an almost 3 to 1 discrepancy. Similar discrepancies arise if we compare the number of Mother's Day cards and gifts sent each year to the number of Father's Day cards and gifts sent each year.* And the number of phone calls to

---

* Mother's Day is a wildly successful commercial occasion in the United States. It is reportedly the most popular day of the year to dine out in a restaurant. Every Mother's Day sees Americans spend $2.6 billion on flowers, $1.5 billion on gifts (including 8% of all jewelry purchases), and $68 million on greeting cards. Comparable statistics for Father's Day are harder to obtain, which may reflect the point I am trying to make, but they seem to be lower in each and every case.

Mom on her day versus Dad on his day is similarly out of balance.**

So, are moms more important than dads? Of course not. Besides what I can glean from my Internet searches, I cannot speak intelligently to the epidemiology of cards, gifts, or phone calls, but I can say something about psychology research studies. Although psychologists have long been more interested in mothers than in fathers, things have changed in recent years, with studies of fathers dramatically increasing. The focus of studies has also changed. In the past, the most typically studied topic was father absence, but many of the newer studies look at the benefits fathers afford their children. What we see is a trend consistent with the premise of positive psychology to look at what goes right in life, including in this case the benefits of fathers who are present in the lives of their children. If you look, you will find.

There are procedural challenges in studying the effects fathers have on their children. A researcher may want to tease out the separate effects of mothering and fathering, which are of course related. Some mothers may encourage some fathers to behave in certain ways, thereby creating an apparent association between fathering and child outcomes, but the real action may be in what the mothers do. (And the same caution applies when looking at the effects of mothering without taking into account what fathers do.)

Along these lines, the family's financial resources must be taken into account, because poverty—or wealth—can influence both how someone parents and child outcomes of interest, with no direct link between them.

Per the research, what good are fathers? Carefully done studies show that fathers have positive influences on their children

----

** Indeed, the highest volume of phone calls made every year in the United States is on Mother's Day. Interestingly—really!—the largest volume of *collect* calls made every year in the United States is on Father's Day.

throughout life, although the details differ depending on the age of the child and whether the child is a boy or a girl. And the degree of positive influence depends on whether someone is a "good" father, an obvious but important qualification. Fathers who are abusive of course do not benefit their children, and all would be better off if those sorts of fathers were not around. But most fathers are good ones, and research suggests that good fathers are those who are actively involved in the lives of their children. *Active involvement* is a deliberately general term, reflecting the point that there is no one way to be a good father.

Active involvement is often defined in terms of (a) *engagement* (directly interacting); (b) *accessibility* (being available); and (c) *responsibility* (providing resources). Actively involved fathers have close and affectionate relationships with their children; they spend time with their children; they talk to them about things that matter; and they are the kind of person their children want to be as adults (e.g., Harris, Firstenburg, & Marmer, 1998).

In general, actively involved fathers provide their daughters and sons with a lifelong example of what it means to be a good man, a good husband, a good parent, and a good person, and their children make wiser choices in their own lives as a result of the lessons learned while growing up.

The important bottom line from research is that actively involved fathers have children who fare better physically, psychologically, and socially.

A difficult issue is the one captured by the phrase *quality time*. The point of quality time is a good one—what one does with one's child is more important than one's mere physical presence, even if prolonged. But there are boundary conditions, and time is a quantity as well as a quality. One minute a week of active involvement with a child likely has no beneficial effects. That said, the exact parameters of quality time are not known.

Many fathers are actively involved with their children as the breadwinners for the family, meaning that the amount of direct time they spend with their children is limited. In the 1950s and 1960s, my own father fit this model of a good father. He was not often around to change diapers, to wipe away tears, or to attend PTA meetings. Instead, he was at work 10–12 hours a day, commuting 60+ minutes each way from our north suburban home to the south side of Chicago and back. But he put bread on the table, and he paid tuition to the colleges my brothers and I attended.

When he was around, he also provided some of the wonderful and still memorable occasions of my childhood: Easter egg hunts featuring clues he wrote about where the eggs were hidden in our house, frequent visits to bookstores before there was a Barnes & Noble store on every corner, and countless shows and concerts ranging from classical ballet to raucous rock-and-roll.

Maybe as youngsters my brother and I did not fully understand what it meant to have a father who was primarily a breadwinner, but we do now. Because of our father, we are well educated and have reaped the benefits. Because of our father, we work hard, and we treat others well. Because of him, our lives have been much more worth living.

Looking back, I see that my father was always present, psychologically if not literally, and he was always involved. Always. Thanks Dad. I love you.

REFERENCE

Harris, K. M., Firstenburg, F. F., Jr., & Marmer, J. K. (1998). Paternal involvement with adolescents in intact families: The influence of fathers over the life course. *Demography*, *35*, 201–216.

Part VI

Enabling Institutions

Workplaces

Throughout our adult years, we spend many of our waking hours at work. Do we want to take our job and shove it, or are we among those who love it? The reflections in this section discuss recent ideas about the workplace seen through the lens of positive psychology.

50

Leadership Style and Employee Well-Being

I suppose *leadership* at one time meant muscles, but today it means getting along with people.

—Gandhi

An important literature review was published by Jaana Kuoppala, Anne Lamminpää, Juha Liira, and Harri Vaino (2008). They summarized studies linking workplace leadership to the well-being of those led. They located hundreds of potentially relevant studies, of which 27 were presented in sufficient detail to include in their meta-analysis.

A meta-analysis, by the way, is a relatively new arrival on the social science scene, and provides a quantitative way of summarizing the gist of different studies of the same topic. Meta-analysis is an attempt to solve the problem often encountered in reviewing a research literature that finds some studies supporting one conclusion, other studies supporting the opposite conclusion, and still others being inconclusive. Meta-analyses treat given studies as individual data points and then calculate an overall summary in terms of the robustness of effects, giving more emphasis to studies with larger samples, more rigorous designs, and so on. Meta-analysis requires assumptions that some would deem heroic, not the least of which is whether and how to regard the measures used in different studies as equivalent. Regardless, meta-analyses have become an important analytic tool in getting a handle on what research actually shows.

In their literature review, Kuoppala and colleagues included studies from different nations, with both males and females, that measured leadership style on the one hand and employee well-being on the other. The dimensions of leadership style on which they focused were consideration and support. A considerate leader is one who treats employees kindly and fairly. A supportive leader is one who treats employees with concern and provides encouragement. It may seem surprising, or at least disappointing, to learn that not all workplace leaders are considerate and supportive, but there was sufficient variation across these dimensions in the studies reviewed to allow their impact to be calculated.

Across the studies reviewed, employee well-being was assessed in various ways, depending on the study: job satisfaction, job well-being (defined as burn-out, exhaustion, anxiety, depression, or stress related to work), amount of sick leave, and early retirement due to disability.

In all cases, positive relationships were found. The robustness of effects—using meta-analysis jargon—ranged from small to moderate. But even small effects, multiplied over thousands or millions of millions of workers, imply that the impact of "good" leadership on employee well-being is potentially staggering.

Among the studies reviewed, there was no relationship between leadership style and work performance. I hasten to add that plenty of other studies do find such a link, but let us just for a minute consider that leadership style might be more related to employee well-being than to employee performance. There is considerable irony in this possibility given that the thriving pop leadership literature is invariably framed in terms of improving productivity. The literature review by Kuoppala and colleagues suggests that leadership style does affect the bottom line but does so indirectly, through its effect on the well-being of employees.

One can of course quibble with this meta-analysis. A meta-analysis is only as useful as the literature it summarizes, and many of the studies included were not ideal. For example, most studies were cross-sectional—all of the data were gathered at the same time, leaving unaddressed chicken-and-egg-issues. But can we afford not to take these findings and their implications seriously?

A theme running through my reflections is that "other people matter," and the take-home message of this article is that when leaders treat their employees as if they matter, everyone wins.

REFERENCE

Kuoppala, J., Lamminpää, A., Liira, J., & Vaino, H. (2008). Leadership, job well-being, and health effects-A systematic review and a meta-analysis. *Journal of Occupational and Environmental Medicine, 50*, 904–915.

51

Doing the Right Thing

Do the right thing. It will gratify some people and astonish the rest.
—Mark Twain

Positive psychology should study doing the right thing. All too often, this is not the focus of research. Rather, studies look at what makes people happy, healthy, or wealthy. Sometimes the right thing produces none of these wonderful outcomes. But the right thing remains the right thing.

It was therefore with interest that I read a literature review by Jennifer Kish-Gephart and colleagues (2010) about the determinants of doing the wrong thing—lying, cheating, stealing—in the workplace. The article had a great title—"Bad Apples, Bad Cases, and Bad Barrels"—and I am a sucker for great titles. The review was a meta-analysis (see reflection 50) of 170 different studies of unethical decisions at work and was organized under the rubric captured by the title: bad apples (characteristics of the individual), bad barrels (characteristics of the workplace), and bad cases (characteristics of the issue).

Guess what? They all matter, and none carries the burden of explaining the bad things that people do at work. Said another way, doing the wrong thing is complex.

Apple-wise, those who are Machiavellian are more likely to transgress, as are those who fail to see a relationship between their actions and outcomes (i.e., those who have an external locus of control) and those who embrace a relativistic moral philosophy. Interestingly—perhaps—demographic characteristics had nothing to do with lying, cheating, or stealing. However, those who were less satisfied with work were more likely to cross the line.

Barrel-wise, some characteristics of work organizations predicted unethical choices on the part of their employees: *not* being concerned with the well-being of the multiple stakeholders (e.g., other workers, customers, and community members) and a work culture that did *not* make clear what was acceptable or unacceptable. The mere existence of an explicit code of conduct was not as important in reducing unethical actions as was a code that was enforced.

Case-wise—and probably the most interesting findings of this meta-analysis—some issues at work predicted doing the wrong thing: those with little apparent consequence, those removed in time from their consequences, and those in which the negative consequences of doing the wrong thing were spread over a large number of people.

What's the point about doing the right thing? Positive psychology posits that the absence of a negative is not the same thing as the presence of a positive, although in the present case, perhaps we can make this assumption. I apologize for the black-and-whiteness of my argument, but I am after all addressing wrong and right. So, *not* doing the wrong thing probably means that one is doing the right thing.

Accordingly, by extrapolation, those who do the right thing are people who do not see others as means to ends, those who believe they are responsible for what happens to themselves, and those who are happy. The latter conclusion is certainly a positive psychology point. Those who do the right thing are in groups with strong social commitment to the welfare of all and clear—and enforced—guidelines about what are acceptable actions. Finally, those who do the right thing are aware of the large and immediate and specific consequences of what they do.

The implications are clear, for employers, teachers, parents, and everyone else. If we want people (including ourselves) to do the right thing, we need to encourage agency *and* communion. We need to do whatever we can to make people happy and satisfied. We need to put a human face on "those" people who may be affected by our actions. We need guidelines about what is acceptable, and we need to enforce these.

No one said that doing the right thing is easy. But the right thing remains the right thing.

REFERENCE

Kish-Gephart, J. J., Harrison, D. A., & Treviño, L.K. (2010). Bad apples, bad cases, and bad barrels: Meta-analytic evidence about sources of unethical decisions at work. *Journal of Applied Psychology, 95*, 1–31.

52

Positive Psychology and Assholes

A few years ago, I gave a talk on my campus about positive psychology in the workplace. I was pleased with how it went, although the questions were difficult. I am better at being conceptual than being practical, and some of those in attendance—staff members from different university units—wanted to know what to do about those in their midst who were relentlessly negative, pessimistic, and mean. A tough but good question, and all I could do in response was to mutter something about killing them softly with kindness.

Afterward, I saw a friend and mentioned my talk. I told her that I behaved well—no foul language—but that I had wished I could have answered the question about negative coworkers by talking about my recent conversations with the leaders of a company on the East Coast. They all said exactly the same thing about the reason for the company's success and high morale: "We don't hire assholes." This is apparently a very explicit company policy, even if it is not written down in a procedure manual. I joked with them that it should become the official company motto and appear on the letterhead of their stationery, rendered of course in Latin: *Non Rectum Intestinum*.

I had deliberately censored myself during my campus talk because I did not think *asshole* would be an appropriate word for a self-identified positive psychologist to use in public. My friend laughed at me and said, "Too bad...if you were more willing to use that word, you might have become a best-selling author." She then told me about a book by Robert Sutton (2007) titled *The No Asshole Rule: Building a Civilized Workplace and Surviving One That Isn't.* I confess I had not heard of it, but I immediately ordered it and read it with great interest that weekend.

I assume many readers here are familiar with the book, given its popularity. If not, its gist is simple to convey. Today's workplaces are filled with "bullies, creeps, jerks, tyrants, despots, and egomaniacs"—in short, assholes (p. 1). These folks usually direct their abuse at those over whom they have power. The cost—for the targets, for the workplaces, and even for the assholes themselves—is staggering. Sutton recounts one story of a company that decided to deduct from an employee's salary the financial costs incurred by his bad behavior: like anger management classes for him, legal fees to adjudicate complaints, time spent by senior management and HR professionals fretting over his misdeeds, and the cost of hiring and training a series of people who worked under him. The total in one year? $160,000! It would have been cheaper to fire him, but the point is made.

The book is a very good read, with memorable stories about actual people who perfectly fit the description used in the title, like the Hollywood producer who ran through 250 personal assistants in 5 years. (In fairness to the producer, he reportedly thought that the number was only 119!) But the book is more than entertaining. Suttons knows the research literature on workplace bullying and incivility, the sanitized labels for the topic that concerns him. He also knows a lot about psychology, and he bases a lot of his advice on what the research shows or implies.

Solutions are possible. First, don't hire these people, no matter how impressive their resumes. Second, don't keep them around, again no matter how impressive their objective performance indicators. Third, if you must keep them around, don't reward them. Sutton recommends that jerks be treated as incompetent employees, with all that entails. Fourth, to the degree possible, minimize status, power, and pay differences among all employees because larger discrepancies afford misbehavior among those so inclined.

In some cases, not all, confrontation may work because the difficult person may be clueless about his or her bad habits. In other cases, more drastic steps are needed, such as social isolation and censure. In all cases, it is important that a work organization avoid what Sutton calls "asshole poisoning." Bad behavior is contagious, and if there enough of it going on, it will become part of the organizational culture and perpetuate itself.

If a workplace adopts a "no asshole rule," Sutton urges that it be enforced vigorously. In my favorite line of the book, he says, "If you can't or won't follow the rule, it is better to say nothing at all.... You don't want to be known as a hypocrite *and* the leader of an organization that is filled with assholes" (p. 89).

Nowhere in the book is positive psychology mentioned, and you may be wondering why I am writing about it. After all, one of the truisms of positive psychology is that to understand what it means to live life well, we need to study people who exemplify the good life. So what's my point?

Every truism has exceptions, and I think that attention to really terrible people—assholes—is instructive, if only because they can make the rest of us so unhappy. The absence of such people may not be enough to make us happy, but it would certainly make us less unhappy, and that's a starting point for the pursuit of a fulfilled life.

But there are also some more specific positive psychology points contained in Sutton's book.

First is a caution not to be naïve, as positive psychologists are sometimes accused of being:

> Passion is an overrated virtue in organizational life, and indifference is an underrated virtue. This conclusion clashes with most business books, which ballyhoo the magical power of deep and authentic passion.... All this talk about passion, commitment,

and identification with an organization is absolutely correct *if* you are in a good job and treated with dignity and respect. But it is hypocritical nonsense to the millions of people who are trapped in jobs and companies where they feel oppressed and humiliated. (pp. 136–137)

For these people, Sutton recommends less passion and more detachment from their work.

Second is the importance of positive reframing in dealing with difficult people. In particular, an oppressed worker should look for small victories at work and relish those that occur. This strategy allows someone to maintain a sense of control until escape is possible.

Third is an interesting discussion, which Sutton says he included with reluctance, concerning the virtues of assholes. Even the worst among us have strengths, another positive psychology truism that becomes very compelling in this concrete discussion. These strengths may include gaining power and status, vanquishing competitors, bringing other people to their senses, and being left alone. But Sutton nonetheless believes that when assholes succeed, it is usually in spite of their style and not because of it. With tongue in cheek, he even suggests that his "no asshole rule" be supplanted by a "one asshole rule," meaning that workplaces should consider keeping one token creep around as a reminder to everyone else how *not* to behave.

Fourth is a suggestion by Sutton that one way to deal with assholes is to respond with consistent calmness, respect, and even kindness. I am reminded of Patrick Swayze's character Dalton in the movie *Roadhouse*. Dalton is the über-bouncer at a bar frequented by assholes, and he advises the other bouncers to "Be nice...be nice...be nice." The point is that someone who refuses to be contaminated by the style of a jerk may actually change the jerk. Perhaps my idea about killing negative people softly with kindness was okay advice after all, although Sutton cautions that the eventual death may be slow in coming.

Sutton ends the book by telling his readers that "assholes are us," meaning that we are all part of the problem but also part of the solution. There is a slippery slope between what he calls temporary assholes and certified assholes and between certified assholes and those of the flaming variety. Wherever we fall along the continuum, we can start to have a better workplace by being the change we want to see. And we can also help by not tolerating the bad behavior of others. Ever. That's what a rule means.

ANNOTATION

I originally posted this reflection on the *Psychology Today* website with the title that appears here: "Positive Psychology and Assholes," which not only captures the content but also is provocative. Perhaps readers thought I was going to slam some of my positive psychology colleagues or some of the critics of positive psychology (see reflection 9). In any event, some time after the posting, the title was changed by someone at *Psychology Today* to "The Jerk in the Corner Office." I guess that is censorship, although I understood the squeamishness and did not complain. After all, I usually censor myself while writing or speaking as a positive psychologist and refrain from using George Carlin's seven dirty words. Provocative is good, to be sure, but distraction is not (see reflection 85).

In the present case, though, I have chosen to use the original title, because the word *asshole* is not a distraction so much as a good description of people who are mean to others. In the relevant research literature, the phrase *workplace incivility* is often used to describe the behavior of assholes, but this phrase is so tepid that it blunts the outrage that we all should feel.

REFERENCE

Sutton, R. I. (2007). *The no asshole rule: Building a civilized workplace and surviving one that isn't*. New York: Business Plus.

53

Positive Psychology and Unemployment

My share of the work may be limited, but the fact that it is work makes it precious.

—Helen Keller

In recent years, with the ongoing economic woes in the United States, I have received inquiries from those in the popular media about what positive psychology has to say to people who have lost their jobs. I have by and large demurred, because I wasn't sure what to say other than to offer aphorisms about being optimistic and to conclude with "it's the economy, stupid." And none of that seemed very positive or very helpful.

My thinking has now changed, at least a bit, after reading a book written by European social psychologist Marie Jahoda (1907–2001).

As a positive psychologist, I was familiar with Jahoda through her 1958 book—*Current Concepts of Positive Mental Health*—which made the case for understanding psychological well-being in its own right, not simply as the absence of disorder or distress. Her argument is of course the premise of contemporary positive psychology, and one can wonder why it took 4 decades for other psychologists to answer her challenge.

In her 1958 book, Jahoda surveyed what previous thinkers—mainly clinicians—had to say about mental health and synthesized their views by proposing half a dozen underlying processes presumably producing or reflecting psychological health: acceptance of oneself; ongoing growth and development;

personality integration; autonomy; accurate perception of reality; and environmental mastery.

Her analysis of positive mental health is persuasive, although upon first reading it, I was puzzled that it did not include good relationships with other people or the strengths that make these possible. I decided to read more of what Jahoda written and came across her 1982 book *Employment and Unemployment: A Social-Psychological Analysis*. In it, she stressed social contact and shared purpose as vital for well-being. So, Jahoda foreshadowed my own summary of positive psychology that "other people matter."

But that's not why I'm writing this reflection. The book offers some genuinely good ideas about employment and unemployment from the perspective of psychology, and her ideas seem as relevant now as when the book was written some 30 years ago.

The thesis of the book is simple, something we probably all know but need to have pointed out: Employment is not the same thing as work. Employment is what people do in order to earn money. Work, in contrast, is what people do in order to live a fulfilling life. People without paid jobs can and do have fulfilling lives, so long as they have work. Conversely, people with well-paying jobs can be miserable, if they do not have work.

The problem in modern economies is that employment provides the sole source of work for many people. And unemployment, when it occurs, leaves them not only without income but also without work and the fulfilling life that work makes possible.

How does work enable the psychological good life? To answer this question, Jahoda surveyed the European and United States research literature from the 1930s and the 1970s on the psychological consequences of unemployment versus employment. She identified five important features of the employed life and thus of work:

1. It imposes a time structure on the day and thereby on our experience. Much as we celebrate leisure, leisure time is valued only when it is scarce, a complement to work as opposed to a substitute.

2. It enlarges the scope of relationships beyond those of the immediate family or neighborhood where one lives.
3. It provides meaning through the shared purposes and activities of a social group.
4. It assigns social status and clarifies personal identity. Work (or employment) need not be "high status" to meet this need.
5. It requires regular activity.

Note that none of these features requires a salary.

One implication of these findings is that positive psychologists might be able to help those who have lost their jobs, not by finding or creating jobs for them (worthy as those endeavors would be) but by suggesting ways to engage in work and thereby satisfy the basic psychological needs that may have vanished along with their jobs.

You readers are smart enough to deduce how this can be done for given people in given circumstances.

Jahoda was not naïve. (How could anyone imprisoned by fascists in the 1930s and later forced to flee her native Austria to avoid the Nazi death camps be naïve?) She concluded her book by observing that "work not in order to earn a living is for some, for some length of time, an appropriate alternative to employment if they can manage to live within their financial support from public funds or belong to the lucky few who have private means" (p. 94).

In the long run, most people need jobs. In the short run, maybe positive psychology has something helpful to say to those who are unemployed.

REFERENCES

Jahoda, M. (1958). *Current concepts of positive mental health.* New York: Basic Books.

Jahoda, M. (1982). *Employment and unemployment: A social-psychological analysis.* Cambridge: Cambridge University Press.

Part VII

Enabling Institutions

Schools

I am a teacher, and I am especially interested in positive psychology perspectives on good schools. My own school—the University of Michigan—is the focus of most of the reflections in this section.

54

Did You Bring a Stuffed Animal to College?

There's just something about a Teddy bear that's impossible to explain. When you hold one in your arms, you get a feeling of love, comfort, and security.
—James Ownby

I learned something interesting in my positive psychology class one semester. I was talking about *oxytocin*—aka the cuddle hormone—and its social benefits. Oxytocin is stimulated by human touch, and I believe research has shown a similar effect from contact with pets. I suppose that's why we call them *pets*, because we can and do pet them. I went off on a tangent about why turtles and goldfish are not pets in the literal sense. My students chuckled a bit, and then one of them asked a great question. "What about Teddy bears?"

I said I had no idea, but it would be interesting to conduct a study and find out.

Then I asked how many students brought stuffed animals with them to college. Some large number of the 250 students present raised their hands. Thinking I saw a pattern, I asked for shows of hands separately by females and males. Indeed, there was a striking pattern. About 80% of the females had brought a stuffed animal to college, whereas fewer than 10% of the males had done so—or at last admitted to it. But those few guys who raised their hands earned applause from their female classmates. I think they deserved hugs as well, but we don't do that in classrooms at my university.

This all surprised me, maybe because I am a male. In 1968, I brought a slide rule and a basketball to college, neither of which I ever cuddled. (And decades later, I am neither an engineer nor a professional athlete. Go figure.)

What does it all mean? Maybe carrying around a stuffed animal is not a sign of immaturity but something else related to contentment and comfort. With my tongue in my cheek, I wonder if women do better in college than do men because they are more likely to bring stuffed animals with them. Maybe I should write a million dollar grant request to fund a Teddy bear intervention with male college students.

55

Paying Students for Good Grades

When an actor comes to me and wants to discuss his character, I say, "It's in the script." If he says, "But what's my motivation?" I say, "Your salary."
—Alfred Hitchcock

A friend drew my attention to an article on the *Time* maga-zine website about ambitious programs in schools across the country that pay students for doing what we want students to do: achieve good grades, get high test scores, attend classes, stay out of fights, and the like (Ripley, 2010).

Sometimes the programs work as intended, sometimes not. There are plenty of subtleties and nuances in the results, depending on the city, the gender of the child, the reward scheme, and—most interestingly to me—just what activities earned paychecks. Apparently, the children have to be capable of the activity in question for rewards to influence it. Well, duh!

Paying students to get good grades doesn't have any effect if they have no idea about how to get good grades. Paying them to attend class or to read books—behaviors in the repertoire of most students—was more likely to have a positive effect.

As you can imagine, these programs are controversial. Indeed, the title of this article was "Should Kids Be Bribed to Do Well in School?" which sums up one perspective on the endeavor. I admit that my immediate reaction to these pro-grams was negative. They just don't seem like the "right" thing to do.

But I read the article while taking breaks from my annual routine of preparing income tax returns, which if nothing else remind me that I am paid (bribed?) for what I do as a teacher, researcher, writer, and speaker. Being paid for doing what I do strikes me as very much the "right" thing, so why should schoolchildren be different?

That's a rhetorical question, of course, and there are obvious differences between schoolchildren and working adults.

The article has kept me thinking, because these programs, at least at face value, embody a positive psychology heresy. A well-established line of research shows that extrinsic rewards can undermine intrinsic motivation. In a representative study, children are given rewards for what they spontaneously do; after some period of time, the rewards are withdrawn. And the children stop doing what they had previously done without a reward!

Do the "pay for grades" programs therefore undermine the intrinsic motivation of students to do well at school? Perhaps yes, perhaps no. The students in these programs may or may not have intrinsic motivation in the first place. Indeed, we can assume that many of them do not (for whatever reasons); they tend to be students in schools where the overall performance is poor. Paying them cannot undermine motives that do not exist.

Maybe that's why the programs sometimes work. Intrinsic motivation is desirable, but if it's not there, maybe external rewards can jump-start "good" performance among students. As I see it, the issue is not incentives per se. The issue instead is whether incentives stay in place.

The hope embedded in these programs, I think, is that once students are encouraged to do what we want them to do, these activities will take on a life of their own and continue without incentives. The research jury is out on that one.

Of course, the very large issue is how to raise our children in ways that programs like these—whether or not they work—are not needed.

REFERENCE

Ripley, A. (2010, April, 8). Should kids be bribed to do well in school? *Time*. Retrieved from http://www.time.com/time/magazine/article/0,9171,1978758,00.html.

56

Teaching Positive Psychology to an Entire University

Education is what remains after one has forgotten what one has learned in school.

—Albert Einstein

Although a new perspective, positive psychology has caught the attention of higher education, and undergraduate positive psychology courses are proliferating around the world. Students are eager to learn about the scientific study of what goes right in life, and instructors enjoy preparing and teaching these courses.

Is it possible to teach the theories, findings, and applications of positive psychology on an even larger scale? I think so. Here I describe an ambitious effort undertaken at the University of Michigan. Since 1980, the College of Literature, Science, and Arts (LSA) at the University of Michigan has sponsored theme semesters: groups of courses, lectures, and special events that center on a given topic. Over the years, the LSA theme semesters have focused on places (e.g., Detroit, St. Petersburg, China), historical periods and events (e.g., Victorian Europe; *Brown v. Board of Education*), and enduring matters of human concern (e.g., comedy, death, evil, diversity, education).

The fall 2010 LSA theme semester, which I proposed and helped to coordinate and direct, was "What Makes Life Worth Living?" This is a topic to which positive psychology directly speaks. For the theme semester, my colleagues (notably my codirector John Chamberlin in political science and my collaborator Nansook Park in psychology) and I identified relevant courses and mounted new ones, in psychology and other fields (*N* = 107 and counting), and invited expert speakers who addressed the topic in public lectures, including Martin Seligman from the University of Pennsylvania and Mihaly Csikszentmihalyi from Claremont Graduate University (*N* = 95).

What makes life worth living is not simply a topic for classes and lectures, and we also worked with university and community groups to highlight and in some cases create events centering on the well-lived life: art, dance, music, film, play, toys, food, religion, and service to others. We also invited speakers who walk the walk of the good life, like Ari Weinzweig (cofounder of Ann Arbor's own Zingerman's Delicatessen), Dr. Denis Mukwege from the Congo, and Sister Helen Prejean from New Orleans.

Campus groups that sponsor painting, photography, film, and writing competitions included award categories reflecting the semester's theme. Groups that offer film series chose appropriate movies, including those with Michigan themes, like *Bilal's Stand* and *The Big Chill*.

We also collaborated with the university's museums, learning communities, musical societies, student government, religious groups, college advisors, and athletic department to create events of concern to them that spoke to the semester's theme.

By a wonderful coincidence, our theme semester coincided with the 50th anniversary of then presidential candidate John Kennedy's proposal of the idea of the Peace Corps, which he conveyed on the steps of the Michigan Union October 14, 1960...at 2:00 AM! A weeklong celebration of this event occurred, including a 2:00 AM anniversary gathering (see reflection 57).

Even the essay that incoming Michigan students wrote to determine their placement in composition courses reflected the theme semester—so, in the essay they wrote (on robotics!), each student was asked to address the topic "What Makes Life Worth Living."

The theme semester had an inauspicious start, at least as judged by attendance. A public showing of *The Wizard of Oz* by the university's residential college had five of us there to do the introductions and behind-the-scenes work but only one person in attendance! We asked him if he really wanted to see the movie. His response was, "The show must go on."

And indeed it did, and things only got better. The following week was a public lecture by positive psychologist Mihaly Csikszentmihalyi and artist Chris Csikszentmihalyi from MIT. This father-and-son presentation was attended by more than 1,000 people!

We live in a T-shirt culture, and one of our good ideas about publicizing the theme semester was to design and distribute T-shirts describing the semester that allowed people to write in their own answer. These T-shirts became a hot commodity on campus.

The goal of the theme semester was to plant the theme in the mind of all students, faculty and staff members at the University of Michigan, and all Ann Arbor community residents. There of course is no single answer to the question of what makes life worth living, but our hope was to underscore the importance of the question and the variety of possible answers, which will take a lifetime to consider.

57

The 50th Anniversary of the Peace Corps

All this will not be finished in the first one hundred days. Nor will it be finished in the first one thousand days; nor in the life of this Administration; nor even perhaps in our lifetime on this planet. But let us begin.
—John F. Kennedy Inaugural Address

In the previous reflection (56), I wrote about the fall 2010 theme semester at the University of Michigan—"What Makes Life Worth Living?"—which happily coincided with the weeklong celebration by the university of the 50th anniversary of the birth of the Peace Corps, which occurred at 2:00 AM, October 14, 1960, on the steps of the Michigan Union.

What makes life worth living? My colleagues and students have discussed this question a great deal, and one answer that has emerged with which most readily agree is "work, love, play, and service" (see reflection 2). The Peace Corps of course represents service writ large, very large.

Those of us at Michigan are well familiar with the beginning of the Peace Corps on our campus, but for other readers, here is the story. Scant weeks before the 1960 presidential election, candidate John Kennedy made a brief appearance on campus and spoke to students gathered in front of the Michigan Union. For whatever reasons, Kennedy did not begin his speech until 2:00 in the morning. Maybe the fact that the third televised debate with Richard Nixon had just taken place explained the timing. Even someone as accomplished as John Kennedy could not be in two places at the same time.

In what he called the longest brief speech of his career, Kennedy asked the five thousand students in attendance the following:

> How many of you who are going to be doctors are willing to spend your days in Ghana? Technicians or engineers, how many of you are willing to work in the Foreign Service and spend your lives traveling around the world? On your willingness to do that, not merely to serve one year or two years in the service, but on your willingness to contribute part of your life to this country, I think will depend the answer whether a free society can compete. I think it can! And I think Americans are willing to contribute. But the effort must be far greater than we have ever made in the past.

He did not use the phrase *Peace Corps* during this speech, but what he said resonated with those in the crowd, so much so that many of them began a letter-writing and petition-signing campaign to Kennedy and his staff in support of his challenge. On November 1, in another speech, Kennedy dubbed the proposed organization the Peace Corps. Critics, including his opponent Richard Nixon, charged that the program would be nothing more than a haven for draft dodgers. Others said that young Americans lacked the skill, maturity, and will to do the right thing for the world. But Kennedy heeded the Michigan students and not the critics, and the Peace Corps was born.

From the vantage point of history and the perspective of positive psychology, I observe that it is useful to see what is right about an idea as opposed to what might be wrong about it. Since 1961, more than 200,000 Americans have joined the Peace Corps, serving in 139 countries. At the present time, there are 3,200+ Americans active in the Peace Corps, including 70 University of Michigan graduates.

Among numerous events on our campus focused on the Peace Corps was a celebration outside the Michigan Union at 2:00 AM, October 14, 2010—exactly 50 years after Kennedy's appearance. I urged my students to attend and resolved to go myself.

About 1:45 AM, I parked my car one block from the Union and walked to it. I started to worry because I heard nothing, which suggested that no one was in attendance or—horrors—that I had the date or time wrong.

No worries. When the Union came into my sight, so too did a crowd later estimated at 1,500. It was an excited and expectant crowd, but also a quiet and polite one, as appropriate given the occasion. Most of the people there were young college students, bright-eyed and bushy-tailed. I saw lots of my own students, including a large number of my international students. I'm not always sure what international students think about the United States, but I know for sure what they were thinking at 2:00 AM, October 14, 2010: "What a country!"

There also were a number of senior citizens in attendance, not quite so spry as the 20-year olds, but also with bright eyes perhaps magnified by tears of pride and joy. I assume that some of the senior citizens had been there 50 years ago, and that some of them had served in the Peace Corps themselves. To all of them I can only say, "Job well done."

What followed for the next 45 minutes or so were talks and films shown on a JumboTron, including excerpts from Kennedy's speech 50 years ago. The theme of the evening (morning?) was "passing the torch." My favorite talk was by a 73-year-old man who had been there 50 years ago that put it all in context, reminding us that what had happened in 1960 was not simply a maize-and-blue event but rather one that flowed naturally from rising student activism in the country and the growing civil rights movement. And I learned something new, that in 1960, the editor of the University of Michigan student newspaper was none other than activist Tom Hayden.

It was rainy; the sound system was funky; and the sight lines were poor at best. It was a wonderful event, and I'm looking forward to the 100th anniversary.

58

Doing the Right Thing...With a Business Plan

In 2010, I attended a symposium at the University of Michigan. It consisted of the presentations of final course projects done by students in a winter 2010 class titled Social Venture Creation. Taught by Moses Lee and Nick Tobier, the class was thoroughly hands-on. Teams of students—mainly from the colleges of business and engineering—used market principles to design a specific project to make the world a better place.

What impressed me about the presentations was that they were both idealistic and realistic. The students, throughout the term, had studied the realities of business, and every presentation addressed issues of start-up costs, competition, risks, and sustainability.

I sat and listened as an academic psychologist, one who often asks students in my classes to write papers "applying" the ideas covered in our course. The papers are always good but very much pie-in-the-sky, reflecting the "let George do it" (or at least pay for it) attitude of many well-intended psychologists. In the real world, any project needs to have a business plan, and the business plans I heard at the symposium were good ones.

Four projects were presented. A panel of judges was assembled, all with special expertise in entrepreneurship. They listened to what each group said, asked tough questions, and eventually awarded $1,000 to the best project.

The goal of the first project was to encourage the sharing of automobiles in Ann Arbor. Most cars sit idle most days, and if owners were willing to rent out their cars to others who needed them for a few hours at a time to run errands, then everyone would benefit—except perhaps the local Detroit auto industry, a risk that was acknowledged.

The second project had as its goal the dissemination of medical information to health-care workers around the world by providing them with laptop computers preloaded with relevant databases. Part of this project was to allow these health-care workers to pose questions to physicians about particular patients.

The third project focused on Kenya and how to allow teachers there to stay current with developments in their fields through Internet information and lesson plans. Appreciate that in Kenya, a typical classroom may have but one textbook, one that is often out-of-date. This project had to grapple with Internet access in Kenya. Most of us in the developed world take Internet access for granted, but elsewhere, the hardware—satellites or cell phones—must be put into place. The business plan by this group addressed these issues.

And the fourth project, my favorite and that of the judges as well, was to provide fresh produce for Detroit. Prepare dear reader, if you do not live in the Motor City, to be surprised by this fact: Detroit, with 800,000+ residents, has only 10 full-service grocery stores, which means stores that sell meat, fish, fruits, and vegetables. I live a mere 45 miles away, in affluent Ann Arbor, a city with about 115,000 residents and several dozen full-service grocery stores, plus all sorts of "specialty" grocery stores (those selling Latin American food, Korean food, Middle Eastern food, Indian food, and so on). The food we eat is critical for our health, but what Detroit residents have are neighborhood convenience stores that specialize in junk and candy.

This fourth project had a detailed plan about how to put fresh vegetables into these already existing neighborhood stores. You can read about their project at http://www.engin.umich.edu/newscenter/pubs/engineer/engineerfeatures/getfreshdet/. The students are going to make this happen, and the group leaders are moving to Detroit in May to work with the stores and community groups like churches. Wow.

These projects impressed and inspired me because they juxtaposed features that often seem at odds. They were all predicated on the idea that one could do good and make money, or at least break even. They blended lofty goals with hard-headed pragmatism. And the presentations by these young people were incredibly polished, among the best I have ever heard in any setting by any folks. By *polished*, I don't mean slick. I mean articulate, informed, and most importantly passionate.

I love the next generation. I think I will stick around a while and see what they will do. My parents are members of the greatest generation. I think my own generation—baby boomers—is a middling one at best. But perhaps my students will be another great one.

59

Saturday Morning with President Obama

I spent last Saturday morning with Barack Obama. And now that I have your attention, let me add that there were a few other people present—about 85,000 of them—because he delivered the 2010 Spring Commencement Address at the University of Michigan, the third sitting president of the United States to do so.

Attendance at the graduation ceremony, held in the Big House, doubled what is typical, despite rain, metal detectors, and protestors outside. Indeed, tickets were difficult to find, and rumor had it that some of our enterprising graduates were even selling their extras on eBay. Goodness.

Regardless, most everyone in attendance was visibly excited by President Obama's presence. I myself rolled out of bed at 5:30 AM to get to the football stadium for the 11:00 AM start of the ceremonies. I hadn't stood in line that long since the early 1970s, when I did so to buy tickets to a concert by the Moody Blues.

We would have been excited and honored to hear any president in person, but in particular this president. After all, we are a blue university (and I don't mean in the maize-and-blue sense), in a blue city, in a blue state.

After receiving an honorary degree, President Obama spoke for about 30 minutes. He broke no new ground on policy, but what

he said was still of interest. He called for increased civility in political conversation because we can't work together with those we
vilify. He called for an end to criticism of government per se. Are
those who despise "government" ready to forgo our public schools,
our national parks, and our interstate highways? He urged listeners to learn about points of view with which they might disagree,
whether voiced by Rush Limbaugh or by the *New York Times*.

President Obama is a gifted speaker. His inaugural address
and his speech on race during his campaign were among the
best speeches I have ever heard. His commencement address at
Michigan was good, but it did not measure up to these other
talks. Despite being intelligent, eloquent, and at times humorous, President Obama seemed tired. And he of course had reason to be tired.

But I don't end my blog entry on this note because there is a
larger point. Other speakers at the commencement included our
university president, our provost, and the dean of my college. I
have heard each of them speak on numerous occasions, and they
of course are good speakers. But in each case, their brief talks
at the 2010 commencement were the best from them that I had
ever heard. They were animated and passionate. Their talks
were from their hearts as well as their heads.

How come? I think the answer is obvious: They were sharing
the stage with the president of the United States. If I were ever
to do so, I too would give the best talk of my life. Guaranteed.

Perhaps this observation tells us what leadership entails.
Leadership is inspiring others to do their best, and last Saturday
morning, the speakers at the commencement ceremonies were
so inspired.

As President Obama implied in his commencement address,
we need to listen to our leaders to be inspired by them. There is
a lot of public discourse nowadays about the need for leaders to
listen to those they lead. I suggest that we who are led need to
listen as well to our leaders.

Part VIII

Enabling Institutions

Sports

From the perspective of positive psychology, leisure activities deserve serious attention as a contributor to the good life (see reflections 2 and 3). The reflections in this section are concerned with sports—playing them and watching them. I am a sports fan, but I hope I am an evenhanded one.

60

When Losing Isn't Losing

I just read a wonderful essay by Joe Posnanski (2011) posted on the Internet, to which I refer readers. Here I am just piggybacking, but I cannot help myself. Please read the original essay.

I classify my own reflection as being about sports, but that hardly captures the point. The real point is about life per se and what makes life worth living. My focus here is on the Washington Generals, a barnstorming basketball team whose name some of you will recognize. Long led by Louis "Red" Klotz—owner, player, and coach—the Washington Generals (who also went by other names) are the ones who played the Harlem Globetrotters hundreds of times per year, from 1953 until 1995.

And they always lost, right? Yes and no.

When the Globetrotters and Generals played, there were certain conventions about when the competition was real and when was it not. So, the Generals always played serious offense. And they played serious defense, too, except when the Globetrotters went into one of their famous routines; then the Generals were expected to stand by and let the routine unfold for the amusement of the crowd.

The Generals actually beat the Globetrotters six times but lost more than 13,000 games. The essay I read detailed the last victory of the Generals, which occurred on January 5,

1971, in what is remembered* as an overtime game in Martin, Tennessee. The Globetrotters could have elected to go into a comic routine and prematurely end the game, but they chose not to do so. Instead, they played the end of the regular game and the overtime period straight up, losing 100–99 when Red Klotz scored the last basket of the game. This victory ended the Globetrotters' 2,499-game winning streak, which makes the streaks of the UCLA men's college team and the UConn women's college team look paltry (see reflection 62).

Some spectators booed. Others cheered. Regardless, what the Washington Generals had done has to number among the largest upsets in sports history.

This upset is a feel-good story of the first magnitude—despite the boos of some of those present—and should hearten all of us who would most certainly play for the Washington Generals of life and not for the Harlem Globetrotters.

But this is not why I am writing about the story. Red Klotz was quoted extensively in the essay I read. Now 89 years old and retired, he has a philosophy born from his decades with the Washington Generals that we should all consider seriously.

First, Red Klotz always played to win. Obviously, this did not necessarily mean coming out ahead on the final scoreboard but rather by bringing out the best in the opponents. For Klotz and the Generals, winning meant making the Harlem Globetrotters play hard, with passion and with joy. My goodness, can we imagine what Congress would be like if the opposing "teams" there construed winning in this way?

Second, for the Washington Generals, and Red Klotz in particular, playing well meant playing the roles assigned to them. One of the famous Harlem Globetrotter routines is to yank down the pants of an opposing player. On every tour with the Globetrotters, Red Klotz took initial pants duty, as it apparently

---

*The details of the game are apparently a bit fuzzy, but not its eventual outcome.

was called, and he had his pants yanked down thousands of times. Again, imagine what the rest of the world would be like if leaders voluntarily took on pants duty before asking those they lead to do the same.

Third, although some reports said that Red Klotz got in trouble for beating the Globetrotters on that day in 1971, he disagrees. "It has never been our job to lose," he says. "It is the Harlem Globetrotters' job to win."

Finally, Red Klotz did what he did because he loved playing basketball. He had been a high school star in his native Philadelphia, but he was too short to succeed at the conventional next levels. Nonetheless, he played the game longer and in more places than anyone. He scored more points than Wilt, or Kareem, or Michael. Joe Posnanski thinks that Red Klotz should be in the Basketball Hall of Fame in Springfield, and I heartily agree. Will he make it? Probably not, but if you ask me, he is already in the Hall of Fame of the Good Life.

The day after the Washington Generals last beat the Harlem Globetrotters, they played again. And the Generals lost. Badly. The Globetrotters were sharper than ever. At the end of that game, Red Klotz looked around, and he saw that the crowd was happy.

In the words of Joe Posnanski, "It was the damnedest thing. His team had won again."

REFERENCE

Posnanski, J. (2011). *A basketball carol.* Retrieved from http://joeposnanski. blogspot.com/2011/01/basketball-carol.html.

61

I Love the NFL, But...

Being in politics is like being a football coach. You have to be smart enough to
understand the game, but stupid enough to think it's important.
—Eugene McCarthy

Here's a sports story that caught my eye. San Francisco 49er
offensive linesman Chilo Rachal missed 2 days of practice
and as a result did not start his team's November 14, 2010, game
against the St. Louis Rams. He eventually got into the game, following an injury to the player given his starting spot, and the 49ers
won an exciting game in overtime.

So what? NFL players should not miss practice any more
than the rest of us should miss work, and there should be some
consequences for absenteeism.

Except that Rachal alerted the team that he would likely not
be at practice and explained why. His wife was going to have a
baby. Chilo Rachal, Jr., came into the world weighing 8 pounds
and 22 inches—sports fans love statistics, so here they are—and
his father was there for his son and of course for his wife.

And Chilo Rachal, Sr., was punished for it!

I love the National Football League, but this story is bothersome.
And I love San Francisco coach Mike Singletary, a former player
for my beloved Chicago Bears, but in this case, I believe he erred.

We vilify professional athletes and guys in general when they
are deadbeat dads. All Chilo Rachal (323 pounds and 77 inches,
in case you are interested) did was the right thing, and he voiced
no complaints about the consequences. I guess that's my job.

Welcome to the world, Junior. Your dad loves you, and that's what really matters.

ANNOTATION

After I wrote this reflection, several *Psychology Today* readers commented that I did not understand football. Rachal was *not* being punished for missing practice. Rather, holding him out of the game was a sound football decision by Coach Singletary because Rachal had missed learning what he needed to know about the upcoming game. Okay. I can see that as an alternative account.

I could observe that the 49ers played much better after Rachal entered the game, so the "sound" football decision was obviously wrong in retrospect. But I won't make that point.

I could observe that the incident received widespread media attention, which is why I knew about it in the first place, and nothing that I read lauded it as a sound football decision. But I won't make that point either.

I could observe that Coach Mike Singletary has since been relieved of his job—fired. But that would be hitting after the whistle, so I won't do that.

And I could even observe that the technical definition of *punishment* was well satisfied: Someone does *X*, after which a negative consequence follows, making it less likely that *X* will be done again. But I won't go there.

I admit that I am not a mind reader, and I have no idea what Coach Singletary intended by benching Rachal. I regret using what may have been a questionable example to make a good point. But the point remains a good one: Families matter, even more than NFL games and their outcomes, and sometimes things get out of kilter in sports (and other venues of life).

62

Streaks in Sports and Life

Not for Men Only

At the time of this writing (December 12, 2010), the University of Connecticut women's basketball team is closing in on one of sport's most revered streaks, the 88 consecutive victories by the UCLA men's basketball team coached by John Wooden.

The pending accomplishment by the UConn team is playing to mixed reviews in the sports pages and on talk radio. "Yes, sure," say many of the skeptics. "That's nice, but you can't compare the UConn women's team to the UCLA men's team."

Well, why not? This is a question to which I will return.

For the time being, let me share with you part of a list that appeared on the website of *Sports Illustrated* of the 34 "greatest" streaks in sports history.

Even a casual sports fan knows about many of the streaks listed, including great individual performances by

- Joe DiMaggio (baseball)
- Rocky Marciano (boxing)
- Orel Hershiser (baseball)
- Edwin Moses (hurdling)
- Brett Favre (football)
- Byron Nelson (golf)

- Lance Armstrong (cycling)
- Cal Ripken (baseball)
- Johnny Unitas (football)
- Sugar Ray Robinson (boxing)
- Jerry Rice (football)

And great team performances by

- Philadelphia Flyers (hockey)
- Los Angeles Lakers (basketball)
- University of Oklahoma Sooners (football)
- Boston Celtics (basketball)
- Miami Dolphins (football)
- Montreal Canadiens (hockey)
- UCLA Bruins (basketball)
- New York Yankees (baseball)
- University of Iowa Hawkeyes (wrestling)

A marvelous list, to be sure, but do you notice what's missing? Women, the 51% minority.

At least as I scrolled through the list and counted on my fingers, *Sports Illustrated* included only one streak by female athletes, the recent Penn State women's volleyball team, which reeled off an unbelievable winning streak of 109 straight games. And there are no beaches for summer practice in Happy Valley.

So what's going on? Maybe women have not participated in sports nearly as frequently or as long as have men, so the well-known streaks are of course dominated by male athletes and male teams. But maybe not. I suspect that the sports-following public does not take women athletes seriously enough even to notice their streaks, much less to celebrate them.

I am as guilty of overlooking the accomplishments of women athletes as are many so-called sports fans, but I spent some time this morning atoning by poking around for information about streaks by female individuals and teams. I call your attention to the following, which deserve checking out, not to mention our acclaim and admiration:

- Sonja Henie (figure skating)
- Martina Navratilova (tennis)
- Félicia Ballanger (sprint cycling)
- Guo Jingjing (diving)
- Iolanda Balas (high jump)
- USA Olympic Women's 4×100m Freestyle Relay
- South Korea Olympic and World Championship Women's Archery Team
- University of North Carolina women's soccer team
- And of course the aforementioned Penn State women's volleyball team

At my own school, the University of Michigan, a very good case can be made that the best varsity team in recent years has been ... not the football team, not the men's basketball team, not the baseball team, and not even the hockey team. The best team has been our (women's) softball team. A T-shirt that I like to wear around campus says "Michigan Softball" on the front. On the back it says "You wish you threw like a girl." The shirt often elicits humorous comments, but only from males. And maybe that's the point.

But it's not my final point. Continuing the sports theme, here is a head fake. This reflection is not about women's sports or about men's sports. It is about "streaks" in any and all venues of life. Some streaks are harder to notice when obvious winners and losers are not tabulated, but they still exist. Like showing up at work every day. Like having a kind word for everyone. Like always remembering your friends' birthdays. Or my personal favorite: My mother writing me a letter every week without fail from the time I went away to college in 1968 until 2007, when her cataract problems made this impossible.

Positive psychology tells us that other people matter. But truly mattering entails more than random acts of kindness.

Truly mattering takes place over time, over years and even over decades. Truly mattering is gritty and difficult. Truly mattering takes no time off. Truly mattering means showing up and doing one's best, over and over and over.

Make a list of the streaks in life that most impress you and who has achieved them. You can include the University of Connecticut women's basketball team if you wish, but if you do not live in Storrs, consider a local list that goes beyond sports. I guarantee that there will be as many women on it as there are men. Indeed, the bookmakers in Las Vegas are saying there will be more women on your list.

ANNOTATION

The winning streak of the Connecticut women's basketball game ended with a loss to Stanford on December 30, 2010, at 90 games.

63

Brett Favre Versus Cal Ripken?

I always turn to the sports section first. The sports section records...accomplish-
ments; the front page has nothing but...failures.
—Earl Warren

I wrote a reflection (62) about streaks in sports that focused on
the University of Connecticut women's basketball team. In
that reflection, I mentioned other well-known sports streaks,
including Brett Favre's streak of consecutive starts by a National
Football League quarterback. That streak just ended, at 297
consecutive games in the regular season and 321 consecutive
games if the playoffs are included.

It wasn't my fault that Favre's streak ended. I did not jinx
him by writing about what was then an in-progress accomplishment. It was an injury that kept him on the sidelines, and if
someone writing about the streak could put the whammy on it,
then it would have ended long ago.

Predictably, the end of Favre's streak resulted in a flurry of
appreciative stories in the sports media. A number of these stories mentioned the streak by Major League Baseball player Cal
Ripken, Jr., who played in 2,632 consecutive baseball games.

All of the stories mentioning Favre and Ripken noted that
it was impossible to compare the streaks, which obviously took
place in two very different games with all sorts of distinctions
between them. And then all of the stories went on to compare
them, usually at great length.

I think I learned something about the appeal of sports to fans, including me. Sports allow us to talk and debate, to compare and contrast, to exercise our heads and hearts over matters that not only are divorced from the real issues of life but also have no definitive answers.

No one debates who the world's fastest man might be. At the time of this writing (December 15, 2010), the world's fastest man is Jamaica's Usain Bolt. We know because he has run faster—by the clock—than anyone else. Is he faster than Jesse Owens? Yes. Bob Hayes? Absolutely. Ben Johnson or Carl Lewis? Sure. There is an answer.

No one debates, at least at the end of the season, which college basketball team might be the best. It is the team that won the NCAA tournament. No one debates about the best college football teams in divisions that have playoffs. There are answers.

Not having an answer is what fuels ongoing debates like Favre versus Ripken, and I think the popularity of sports is thereby served. If anyone cares to read this assertion as implying that there should *not* be a playoff in Division I College Football, well maybe you can—but of course there is no definitive answer.

Sports fans can be criticized for focusing too much on sports to the exclusion of other things in life. I suggest that we be given a small break because what we are doing is using our human nature and maybe—in some cases—perfecting skills that might prove helpful in thinking about fuzzy topics that really do matter, like the great moral and political issues of our time or the more local human issues of our own lives. These also may have no definitive answers, but they nonetheless require us to make judgments and decisions. If these judgments and decisions reflect lots of thought, then that is probably a good thing.

The trick, of course, is to encourage sports fans to put down the last section of a newspaper and then to pick up the first section.

64

Team Sports, Happiness, and Health

I am a member of a team, and I rely on the team. I defer to it and sacrifice for it, because the team, not the individual, is the ultimate champion.
—Mia Hamm

A study by Keith Zullig and Rebecca White (2011) found that U.S. adolescents (seventh and eighth graders) who participated in team sports rated both their life satisfaction and physical health more highly than did their peers who did not participate in team sports. The research was regrettably stark, relying just on self-report and gathering all information at a single point in time. The temptation is of course to conclude that participation in team sports *causes* happiness and health, but things could be the other way around. Or some unmeasured third variable like being coordinated or having access to resources could be responsible for the apparent associations.

Be that as it may, the patterns held for males and females, and an additional finding was that vigorous physical activity (not necessarily participation in team sports) was linked to happiness and health among females but not males. So maybe we can say that there is something about being on a team that is beneficial.

The physical activity inherent in sports is the most obvious benefit, but perhaps playing a role as well are the shared identity that is formed on a team, important lessons about cooperation, and more generally the social communion that team sports allow.

I remember the last time I formally participated in a team sport, decades ago as a faculty member at Virginia Tech. A bunch of us from the Department of Psychology got together to play basketball in a community league. We stunk, although we published lots of papers in professional journals (as if that mattered on the court). Our coach had actually played big-time college basketball back in the day. Coaching us was no doubt a humbling experience for him, although he never said so.

We were winless until the last game of the season, when we actually found ourselves with a comfortable lead and only seconds to go in the game. Our coach called a timeout. He told us, "Guys, when the game is over, please act like you've won before." One of the players objected, "But we've never won before." Our coach reflected, smiled, and said, "Okay. You're right. Go crazy."

And we did.

Being a member of this team is one of the fondest memories I have, and it was not because we won our last game. That makes for a good story, but it was everything else about the team that made us happy. And healthy? Who knows, although we are all still alive and kicking and missing wide-open shots some 30 years later.

I love this game…any game…as long as it is played with others.

REFERENCE

Zullig, K. J., & White, R. J. (2011). Physical activity, life satisfaction, and self-rated health of middle school students. *Applied Research in Quality of Life, 6*, 277–289.

65

Team Celebration and Performance

I encounter many difficult choices in my life. For example, should I work on my current research project or watch a basketball game on television? The basketball game often wins out, to the detriment of my professional career. But I just read a fascinating study by researchers at Berkeley showing that this particular dilemma can be resolved by having it both ways: Watch the game in order to do the research!

Psychologists Michael Kraus, Cassy Huang, and Dacher Keltner (2010) were interested in trust and cooperation among group members and the effects on group performance. That a group high on trust and cooperation would perform better, all things being equal, than a group low seems obvious (cf. the United States Congress), but what made this research notable is that Kraus and colleagues drew on ethology to investigate a possible determinant of trust and cooperation: the extent to which group members deliberately touched one another. Our nonhuman primate cousins may spend up to 20% of their waking hours grooming one another, and grooming leads to many benefits for the group, including trust and cooperation. Is something similar at work among humans?

Most of us do not groom or even touch our colleagues at work, at least not if we want to keep our jobs, but sports are an exception. Players in games like basketball often celebrate with various forms of touching, many well-known enough to have earned their own names: for example, fist bumps, high fives, chest bumps, leaping shoulder bumps, chest punches, head slaps, head grabs, low fives, high tens, half hugs, and team huddles.

Players and teams differ in the extent to which they touch in these ways, and the Berkeley researchers watched National Basketball Association games from early in the 2008–2009 season and coded the extent of touch between and among teammates.* These codes were then related to how well the players cooperated with one another during games later in the season, assessed by coding such cooperation indices as talking to teammates, pointing or gesturing, passing the ball, helping out on defense, and setting screens. Cooperation was then related to individual and team performance, assessed objectively by scoring and victories.

The research was meticulously done, with different groups of coders assessing touching and cooperating. Reading between the lines, I suspect that the coders had a lot of fun doing the research. I know I would have.

Results were clean and clear. Even taking into account possible confounds, such as player status (i.e., salary), preseason expectations for the team, and early season performance by the team, early-season touching robustly predicted later-season cooperation, which in turn robustly predicted later-season performance.

As the researchers concluded, even small acts of celebration, as they accumulate, can have large effects on team performance. The take-home message is simple: Celebrate with those in your

---

* Players particularly high in touch included many of the most acclaimed players in the National Basketball Association: Kevin Garnett, Chris Bosh, Kobe Bryant, Pau Gasol, Shane Battier, Dirk Nowitzki, and Paul Pierce. (Thanks to Michael Kraus for providing this information.)

family or class or neighborhood or workplace, in whatever ways make sense within your group. Good things may result.

There is no "I" in touch.

REFERENCE

Kraus, M. W., Huang, C., & Keltner, D. (2010). Tactile communication, cooperation, and performance: An ethological study of the NBA. *Emotion, 10*, 745–749.

66

The NBA Finals

Does the Best Team Win?

Diligence is the mother of good luck.
—Benjamin Franklin

Like millions of others, I watched the 2011 NBA Finals between the Dallas Mavericks and the Miami Heat. At the time of this writing (June 8, 2011), the best of seven series is tied at 2–2, and the games have been close. I have enjoyed watching the games, but the postgame shows featuring basketball experts have left me a bit confused. Whatever the outcome of the game that just finished, these experts make incredible sense of what happened, calling on the numerous story lines that this series affords.

These experts convince me—almost—that the winner of the last game will of course be the winner of the next game. I keep waiting for someone—anyone—to say, "These teams are evenly matched, and the ball bounced one way for the winner, and another way for the loser. I wonder what will happen in the next game."

Of course, if they said that, why would they have jobs as expert commentators? Anyone can say that kind of thing. Like me, for instance, although I have some evidence to back it up.

Suppose two basketball teams really are evenly matched, so much so that each has a 50-50 coin-flip chance of winning each game in a series. What would we expect to see? A handful of 4-0

Series	Actual	Expected by Chance
4-0	8	8
4-1	15	17
4-2	25	18
4-3	16	21

sweeps, a few more 4-1 series, even more 4-2 series, and most frequently 4-3 series.

I've done a little homework. First, I figured out the numbers of 4-0, 4-1, 4-2, and 4-3 final series in the 64-year history of the NBA, from 1947 through 2010. Then, I calculated how many such series would be expected over the years if each game were a 50-50 toss-up between two evenly matched teams.

Here are the results. I admit my arithmetic is a bit rusty, and if someone can correct my probability estimates, I would welcome the feedback. But assuming I crunched the numbers correctly, consider what I found:

These columns of figures look like they might be different, but an inferential statistics test—the venerable chi-square test, if you recall your Stats 101 course—is available that tells us that the actual results are not at all different from the expected results based on the assumption that the two teams have equal chances of winning each and every game in a series.

This conclusion is of course sports heresy. Said most bluntly, the best team does not win the series because there is no best team, at least not in the NBA finals where two outstanding basketball teams are invariably matched.

I expect readers of this reflection who care about sports to beat me up about this conclusion, observing (correctly) that my simple analyses ignored home court advantage, the format of the series (i.e., 2-2-1-1-1 versus 2-3-2), or the possibility that in some series players might have been injured or suspended in earlier games, thereby influencing the outcome of later games. I did not have the energy to analyze margin of victory, which might yield a different conclusion.

But why not take these data at face value? I bet no one would have predicted my results, even with the simplifying assumptions. I have long believed in the transcendent will-to-win of Michael Jordan, who led the Chicago Bulls to five 4-2 final series wins and one 4-1 series win versus no series losses. But maybe it wasn't the shoes. Maybe it was just the bounce of the ball.

So what's the point for you readers who do not care about the NBA or sports? In some (not all) domains of life, there are winners and losers. That's just how these domains are structured. Someone gets the job. Someone wins the election or the award. Someone earns the hand of the fair maiden or the handsome prince.

And if you are like me, you're usually not the winner. But that does not mean that you are a loser, only that the metaphorical ball may have bounced the wrong way for you. Much as we want to believe in a stable hierarchy of talent and merit, in sports and elsewhere, maybe there is no such thing.

Keep your head in the game, and trust the probabilities. Someday your time will come.

ANNOTATION

The Dallas Mavericks eventually won the playoff series 4-2, an outcome that does not at all change the conclusions drawn here.

Part IX

Enabling Institutions

Geographical Places

Although a person should take responsibility for creating a good life, where the person happens to be makes it easier or harder to have positive experiences, positive traits and talents, and positive relationships. A topic of great interest to positive psychology is identifying the settings that best enable the good life.

Often this interest focuses on geographical settings—states and especially nations. In this section you will find discussions of happy places, from neighborhood hangouts to cities to states to nations.

67

Geography and Happiness

"I broke my nose in two places."
"Really? You should stay out of those places."

There must be a positive psychology analogue of this joke, although I could think of none, and my Internet searches for "happy place" jokes revealed only off-color humor. I must be more naïve than I thought because I had no idea that one's "happy place" had so many interesting sexual meanings.

Be that as it may, the staid meaning of "happy place" seems to be an internal location to which one goes to be happy, serene, and untroubled. Happiness can no doubt be found in an internal place, but that has not stopped people from searching for literal happy places: settings—sometimes neighborhoods and cities but usually nations—where everyone is happy.

Nowadays the popular media and many social scientists are fond of ranking different nations with respect to their overall happiness. Exact ranks differ across surveys and across time, but there is some consensus that Northern European countries have happier citizens than do Eastern European and African countries. Nations in South America have citizens who are happier than one would expect given their relative poverty, whereas nations in East Asia have citizens who are less happy than one would expect given their relative wealth (see reflection 18).

If one wants to understand the happiness of nations and their citizens, a more analytic approach is needed. Happiness is often studied in terms of subjective well-being, an amalgamation of positive affect, negative affect, and life satisfaction—the judgment that one's life has been lived well. Attention to these separate components of happiness results in different rankings of nations. For example, according to one study, people from Mexico reported the highest positive affect, whereas those from Canada reported the least negative affect (Kuppens, Ceulemans, Timmerman, Diener, & Kim-Prieto, 2006). Adults in Switzerland reported extremely high life satisfaction but neither particularly high positive affect nor particularly low negative affect.

Another approach that sheds light on the bases of national differences in happiness attempts to relate the average well-being of citizens across different nations to country-level features such as education, affluence and opportunity, mode of government, concern with human rights, and religiousness (Inglehart, Foa, Peterson, & Weizel, 2008).

Yet another way to understand the literal happy places that may exist on the world is contained in a book by Eric Weiner (2008) titled *The Geography of Bliss: One Grump's Search for the Happiest Places in the World*. Mr. Weiner is not a social scientist, and he did not undertake his search armed with surveys and number 2 pencils. Weiner is a former correspondent for National Public Radio, and for a year, he traveled around the world visiting places reputed to be happy—like Bhutan, Iceland, Denmark, and Qatar—and one place reputed not to be—Moldova—talking to residents, and making observations. These travel accounts became a best-selling book.

Although organized geographically, one chapter per location, the book is less about the 10 nations Weiner visited than it is about the people he met in each. This is a tried and true journalistic method, to tell a story by focusing on one particular person, and it is highly effective as Weiner uses it. Some of his people are natives, others American friends or acquaintances who happen to live abroad and thus have special perspectives. Weiner recounts their interactions and conversations, which center on happiness but usually go much further. He mixes in his own reactions and recollections.

I strongly recommend the book. Weiner is a good observer and really skilled with a phrase. I rarely laugh aloud while reading, but I came close when I encountered such observations as "Dutch sounds exactly like English spoken backward" and "Watching Brits shed their inhibitions is like watching elephants mate. You know it happens, it must, but...is this something I really need to see?"

What about the book from a positive psychology perspective? Weiner knows his psychology. His journey started with an interview of Ruut Veenhoven in the Netherlands, the keeper of the World Database of Happiness. Weiner treats positive psychologists as he treats the other characters in the book—with skepticism but also respect, with humor but also affection. He sees the value of science—information from the World Database of Happiness helped provide his itinerary—but he also has an unconvinced attitude that would serve psychologists well, especially as we are tempted to urge our positive psychology interventions on the entire world.

So, Weiner describes the televised attempt to make 50 residents of Slough happy, by throwing at them over a 12-week period all conceivable positive psychology techniques plus the kitchen sink. It supposedly worked, but Weiner's parting comment was, "Any overlap between TV and reality is purely coincidental....Did these happiness experts really change the psychological climate of Slough, or did they just tickle fifty of its residents for a while?"

Here are some of other things I liked about the book. First, it showed over and over again, with each new interview, that the meaning of happiness is local, richly so. It is useful to ask people around the world to answer the same sorts of survey questions about life satisfaction, but so too is it useful to understand how residents from given cultures think about happiness in their own words and in their own worlds.

Second, Weiner talked to people in bars and restaurants and hotels, in their homes and on the street. If all one were to know of the human condition came from reading what psychology "studies" have to say, we would probably not know that there are bars and restaurants and hotels or for that matter homes and streets (see reflection 75). It is one thing to say, as psychologists do in the abstract, that behavior must be placed in context. It is another thing to see that context in vivid detail, as in Weiner's tales.

Third, Weiner describes himself as a grump, but I think that is literary license. Even he admits that in England he is at best an amateur grump. As I read the book and came to know the part of him that came through in the pages, I saw a man who was thoughtful and funny and not at all full of himself. He could—and did—tell a story at his own expense. I liked him, and I liked his book.

The happiest places on earth are not internal ones. They are not geographical ones. They are the places between us, and the closer they are and the more comfortable, the happier they are apt to be. Weiner apparently agrees. He ends his book by observing, "Our happiness is completely and utterly intertwined with other people: family and friends and neighbors and the woman you hardly notice who cleans your office. Happiness is not a noun or verb. It's a conjunction."

REFERENCES

Inglehart, R., Foa, R., Peterson, C., & Weizel, C. (2008). Development, freedom, and rising happiness: A global perspective, 1981–2007. *Perspectives on Psychological Science, 3*, 264–285.

Kuppens, P., Ceulemans, E., Timmerman, M. E., Diener, E., & Kim-Prieto, C. (2006). Universal intracultural and intercultural dimensions of the recalled frequency of emotional experience. *Journal of Cross-Cultural Psychology, 37*, 491–515.

Weiner, E. (2008). *The geography of bliss: One grump's search for the happiest places in the world*. New York: Twelve.

68

Happy Places

Happy States

A study by Andrew Oswald and Stephen Wu (2010), published in *Science*, attracted deserved attention in the media. These researchers used survey responses from an enormous and representative sample of U.S. adults (1,300,000 of them) to show that on average, U.S. states differ in how happy ("satisfied with life") their residents are. These data are important given previous attempts—often unsuccessful—to show that "state" matters as a predictor of happiness. In several previous blog entries, I have discussed the ongoing search for "happy places," and perhaps some U.S. states now qualify as happy places.

Part of the popular appeal of this research is that it rank-ordered the 50 states. According to this study, the least satisfied state was New York, and the most satisfied states were Hawaii and Louisiana (by the way, the data were pre-Katrina). We the people love lists like this and take pride in being at the top and—perhaps—a wry pleasure in being at the bottom. In any event, the rest of the research entailed aggregating state-level features such as good weather, air quality, commuting time, cost of living, low taxes, low rates of violent crime, and so on—features that "should" make residents happy—and showing that these features were robustly associated with the average self-reported life satisfaction of residents.

These researchers conclude that "subjective well-being data contain genuine information about the quality of human lives."

I agree and further believe that this study is interesting. But I also have some critical observations.

The first is about disciplinary differences in what counts as good evidence. The researchers are economists. Economists tend to distrust what people say. The introduction to the paper by Oswald and Wu indeed dismisses decades of research by psychologists showing that happiness—life satisfaction—as assessed by what people say is associated with all sorts of outcomes that matter, like school success, income, marital stability, and even good health and longevity. In contrast, Oswald and Wu say that "there is little scientific evidence that such data [from self-report] are meaningful."

To them, "meaningful" data are objective and not dependent on self-report, like the state-level features they correlated with self-reports of life satisfaction.* Most psychologists would agree that so-called objective measures have methodological virtues, but we do not privilege such measures, especially when our topic of concern is happiness.

Second, as is the case for any study, unstated theoretical assumptions underlie this particular investigation. Oswald and Wu implicitly endorse one particular theory of happiness known as *objective list theory*. By this view, there are truly valuable things in the world, and happiness entails achieving some number of these: freedom from disease, material comfort, a career, friendships, children, education, and so on.

The methodological implication of objective list theory is that to assess happiness, we need to ascertain whether these truly valuable things have been attained. This is essentially what Oswald and Wu do with their "objective" measure of happiness.

---

* One wonders how such features as crime rates and commuting times can be "objectively" assessed for an entire state without relying on what people report about crimes and times.

The problem is of course deciding what these valuable things are. I believe there is more consensus than a strict relativist might assert, but there are still gray areas and difficult trade-offs among the items on anyone's list of what is objectively good. For many people, lengthy commutes are undesirable, but there are folks who like to drive to and from work, who use their time alone to unwind or—as all of us have seen on frightening occasions—to read books, to work crossword puzzles, to talk on a cell phone, to apply makeup, or to eat. At least until these people crash their cars, they are probably rather content during their commutes.

Third, there is a venerable problem in social science known as the *ecological fallacy*, moving glibly from group-level data to conclusions about individual people. Oswald and Wu seem not to consider this potential problem in interpreting their results. One version of the ecological fallacy is obviously wrongheaded, concluding that each member of a group displays the characteristics of the aggregate. Think of the research finding that a typical family in a given locale has 2.3 children. One would be hard pressed to find many families with 2.3 children.

More to the point, I know people from Long Island (NY) who are quite happy and others from the Big Island (HI) who are quite miserable. The state-level data of Oswald and Wu are impressive, but they do not allow strong conclusions about particular individuals, just groups of individuals.

The more subtle version of the ecological fallacy entails the misattribution of an apparent association. At the level of U.S. states, features like good weather indeed predict the average self-reported happiness of citizens. But most states are large and heterogeneous—think San Francisco versus Los Angeles (CA), Buffalo versus New York City (NY), Chicago versus Carbondale (IL), or—in a favorite example of mine—Heaven versus Hell (MI). Perhaps the self-reported happy people in a state reside mostly in one city, whereas the "objective" features of the state are determined largely by what's going on in another city. Correlation is not causation, and sometimes it's not even correlation.

And along these lines, my thoroughly informal eyeballing of the state ranks suggests that the least happy states are often blue ones, perhaps an unsurprising result given that self-reports of happiness were obtained while George W. Bush was president.

Maybe Oswald and Wu controlled for heterogeneity within states. I could not follow all of their statistical analyses, which differ from those typically used by psychologists—yet another disciplinary difference. If they did this, I apologize for thinking that they may not have done so.

In conclusion, a study showing that self-report matters is going to be taken seriously by a scholarly field that has long ignored self-report. But most psychologists have always taken self-report seriously. As I see it, the importance of the present study is to get economics on the same page as other social sciences and especially psychology.

Welcome aboard. We have important work to do in understanding and building the good life, and many hands make light the load.

REFERENCE

Oswald, A. J., & Wu, S. (2010). Objective confirmation of subjective measures of human well-being: Evidence from the U.S.A. *Science, 327*, 576–579.

69

Are Happy Places Also Deadly Ones?

Suicide Rates Across U.S. States and Cities

In separateness lies the world's great misery; in compassion lies the world's true strength.

—Buddha

Following up an apparent global trend that the happiest countries (judged by the average self-report of their residents) also have the highest suicide rates,* Mary Daly, Andrew Oswald, Daniel Wilson, and Stephen Wu (2011) looked at the suicide rates across the 50 U.S. states as a function of the average self-reported rates of happiness in these states (see reflection 68). This research is more compelling than cross-national research because obvious confounds are reduced when comparisons are made within the same nation.

Nonetheless, the same trend was found: The highest suicide rates in the United States were found in states that were the happiest (like Utah), whereas the lowest suicide rates were found in states that were the least happy (like New York).

The researchers apparently controlled for the respondents' racial makeup, educational attainment, and employment

---

* I am not fully convinced this trend is so simple. In my research for this reflection, I found reports of extremely high suicide rates in such former Soviet bloc nations as Kazakhstan, Belarus, Russia, and the Ukraine, countries notable as well for the low life satisfaction of their citizens. Suffice it to say the predictors of suicide, at the individual or societal level, are numerous and complex.

status in each state. It was not clear whether they controlled for age, religiousness, alcoholism, or access to and familiarity with firearms—factors related to suicide risk.

The story also did not report when the measures of happiness and suicide were done. In other words, what is the sequence? The story was framed in such a way that the happiness (of some) was treated as the cause of suicide (of others), but I will have to wait for the publication of the actual study to understand this important issue.

As a positive psychologist, I am invested in the notion that happiness is a good thing (see reflections in Part II). Research usually supports this notion, but perhaps happiness in the aggregate results in some collateral damage.

If we take the results at face value, they mean that happy places are also deadly ones. This is important to know. If we are surrounded by happy people when we ourselves are not happy, does the implied comparison push us from unhappiness to depression to suicide (see reflection 76)? Mind you, there would be many exceptions, and suicide remains a relatively rare occurrence. But a plausible case can be made that we judge how we are doing in life by comparison to others, including their apparent happiness, and if we seem to be doing more poorly than those around us, then we will suffer.

That said, although I respect these data, they seem too counterintuitive. Positive psychology is often obsessed with counterintuitive results from what I call *gee whiz investigations.* Mind you, imaginative studies can be valuable, and the results of surprising studies attract the attention of the general public or undergraduates who are snoozing or text-messaging during a lecture. But no scientific field can be based on cuteness (cf. Ring, 1967) and positive psychology should not be boiled down to media sound bites.

To make the argument most strongly that happy places are deadly ones, we would need to know that those who commit suicide really are immediately surrounded by those who are happy. It is not obvious that those in one's "state" provide a typical comparison group. Rather, it is one's immediate family members, friends, colleagues, or neighbors to whom most of us compare and contrast ourselves.

Accordingly, Nansook Park and I recently did a follow-up investigating whether the same result occurred when the unit of analysis was the city (Park & Peterson, 2011). Indeed, the association between happiness (of most) and suicide (by some) might be stronger in cities versus states because those in a city provide a more immediate comparison. We examined suicide rates in 44 large U.S. cities as a function of the average happiness reported by residents. According to our results, happier cities had *lower* suicide rates, implying that cities may be a more meaningful unit of analysis for psychological studies than states. Why the previous researchers found what they did is unclear, but our investigation—unsurprising in its results and unlikely to be featured in the *New York Times*—at least sets the record straight.

I want to close with a moral point. If we are happy, we have a psychological gift that does not belong just to us. We have an obligation, perhaps, to turn our happiness into compassion and to reach out to others who are less happy. It is clear that social isolation, in whatever city or state it may occur, is a breeding ground for alienation, depression, and suicide, so what are we doing as happy people to reduce the unhappiness of others?

REFERENCES

Daly, M. C., Oswald, A. J., Wilson, D., & Wu, S. (2011). Dark contrasts: The paradox of high rates of suicide in happy places. *Journal of Economic Behavior and Organization, 80*, 435–442.

Park, N., & Peterson, C. (2011). *Happiness and suicide in large US cities.* Unpublished manuscript, University of Michigan.

Ring, K. (1967). Experimental social psychology: Some sober questions about some frivolous values. *Journal of Experimental Social Psychology, 3*, 113–123.

70

Gauging the Happiness of a Nation

Happiness is never stopping to think if you are.
—Palmer Sondreal

In recent years, calls have been made for an expanded con-
ception of a nation's well-being, going beyond the economic
indicators long used to include psychosocial indicators (Diener,
2000). Consider Bhutan's explicit concern with "gross national
happiness" and the Gallup Organization's ambitious surveys of
psychological well-being in dozens of nations. It seems only a
matter of time before the happiness of all nations is routinely
assessed and tracked, perhaps to influence policy decisions.
Indeed, steps are already under way in the United Kingdom
and the European Union to do precisely this, with the United
States apparently lagging behind.

Two issues need to be considered. First, what do we mean by
psychosocial well-being (i.e., "happiness")? Is it the presence of
positive feelings or the absence of negative feelings? Is it a summary judgment by a citizen that his or life is satisfying? What
about close relationships with others, engagement with one's
work, a sense of community, or meaning and purpose? All of
these figure into the definition of happiness, and the good news
as it were is that they tend to co-occur, although the mix will no
doubt vary across time and place.

Second, how can these components of happiness be assessed?
I am a survey researcher, and my first thought is that assessment

would entail asking people about these components, using our tried-and-true 7-point scales. Doing surveys at the level of nations seems daunting, but only logistically, no different from what social scientist researchers have done for years with more modest samples of respondents.

But upon reflection, I worry that a sole reliance on surveys to gauge the happiness of nations might be misleading. The pitfalls of self-report surveys are familiar, and in the present case, consider that most measures of "happiness" are thoroughly transparent. If some or many respondents believe that policy decisions will hinge on their answers (e.g., more funding for unhappy communities), can we really trust what they say? Maybe yes, maybe no, but how could we know for sure?

The thing about economic indicators of well-being, incomplete though they may be, is that they refer to verifiable things.

I am not suggesting that surveys have no use in gauging the happiness of nations. They are a great place to start. I am suggesting instead that additional methods of gauging happiness be used, those that are unobtrusive.

I am not on Facebook, but I may be among the last people on the planet who can say that. Anyway, a story caught my eye about a new use of Facebook entries. Perhaps you readers are well aware of it, but it was new to me.

Apparently it is possible to count up the number of "happy" and "unhappy" words in updated posts, and use them to gauge the collective mood of some large group of people (Facebook has 300,000,000+ users) over time and as a function of events. Not surprisingly, folks are happier on holidays. The unexpected deaths of famous people (e.g., Michael Jackson) result in unhappy days.

These results are hardly surprising, but that is the point: They imply a modicum of validity.

Should Facebook be used to gauge the happiness of nations? Probably not, considering issues of privacy and the nonrandom groups who use Facebook, within and across nations.

But the general method suggested by this example—to use naturally occurring cultural products, like newspapers, books, popular songs, whatever—seems intriguing. The more products assessed for happiness, the better the results.

REFERENCE

Diener, E. (2000). Subjective well-being: The science of happiness and a proposal for a national index. *American Psychologist, 55*, 34–43.

71

How Can You Tell If Someone from France Is Happy?

This sounds like the setup for a joke, a good one, you can only hope. Sorry. This reflection is about the call by French president Nicolas Sarkozy for his nation's economic progress to be monitored by various "happiness" indicators (Samuel, 2009). Sarkozy trumpeted his idea as revolutionary, but others have made similar proposals, as I have earlier discussed in my reflection "Gauging the Happiness of a Nation" (70).

Be that as it may, Sarkozy's ideas have their own twist worthy of attention and perhaps emulation because part of his proposal entailed suggestions about *how* happiness might be measured among the French. His list of possible indicators—to my disappointment—did not include per capita consumption of good wine, *foie gras*, and *pommes frites* or having a really, really attractive spouse. (Maybe I'm still looking for some humor here.) But consider these indicators of happiness that he suggested:

- Work-life balance—what is the ratio of hours worked and hours of leisure?
- Reduced traffic congestion—how much time is spent sitting in traffic jams?
- Mood—how much time is spent feeling happy or sad?

- Chores—do people have enough time to carry out child care, cleaning, and DIY? (I'm not completely sure, but I believe DIY is an acronym for do-it-yourself activities.)
- Recycling—do people recycle?
- Gratification—is life filled with short-term pleasures and more fulfilling long-term satisfaction?
- Insecurity—do people feel financially secure and safe in their homes?
- Gender—are men and women treated fairly in the workplace and home?
- Taxes—do people get their money's worth from the government?
- Relationships—do people have enough time to see friends and relatives regularly?

Not a bad list at all, and what I want to highlight is that while some of these indicators can be measured only by subjective report (e.g., mood), many of the others allow more objective measurement.

Here Sarkozy joins forces with a philosophical approach to happiness known as *objective list theory* (Nussbaum, 1992; Sen, 1985). By this view, there really are truly valuable things in the world, and happiness entails achieving some number of these: freedom from disease, material comfort, a career, friendships, children, education, knowledge, and so on. The methodological implication of objective list theory is that we need to ascertain whether these truly valuable things have been attained by an individual. Furthermore, we need not even talk to them. The problem is of course deciding what these things are. I believe there is more consensus than a strict relativist might assert, but there are still gray areas and difficult trade-offs among the items on anyone's list of what is objectively good and indicative of consensual happiness.

Nonetheless, Sarkozy's list is a bold start.

What would you include in your objective list of criteria for happiness, for the nation in which you live or just more locally for the life you lead? I suspect a U.S. list might mention choice and freedom, and maybe something about religion— considerations not mentioned in the French list. My idiosyncratic list would include whether on a given day I finished doing something (like my laundry or a letter of recommendation for a student), had a good meal, gave a good lecture, saw an *NCIS* rerun that was new to me, and—of course—had an engaging conversation with a friend. Happiness may not be all that complicated.

REFERENCES

Nussbaum, M. (1992). Human functioning and social justice: In defense of Aristotelian essentialism. *Political Theory, 20*, 202–246.

Samuel, H. (2009, July 7). Nicolas Sarkozy wants to measure economic success in "happiness." *The Telegraph.* Retrieved from http://www.telegraph.co.uk/news/worldnews/europe/france/6189530/Nicolas-Sarkozy-wants-to-measure-economic-success-in-happiness.html.

Sen, A. (1985). *Commodities and capabilities.* Amsterdam: North-Holland.

72

Gross National Happiness

We cannot measure national spirit by the Dow Jones average, nor national achievement by the gross domestic product.
—Robert F. Kennedy

British prime minister David Cameron has joined other world leaders—notably President Nicolas Sarkozy of France (see reflection 71)—in making a public commitment to a national policy that takes seriously the happiness of citizens (Stratton, 2010). Money matters, as captured by familiar ratings of GDP, but so too does well-being, whether it be deemed GNH (gross national happiness) or GWB (general well-being). Research over the years by positive psychologists and others has shown conclusively that money and well-being are related but not redundant, at neither the individual level nor the national level (Diener, 2004; Diener & Seligman, 2004).

The devil is always in the details, and in the present case, the details entail not just how well-being information might inform national policies but also how to ascertain well-being in the first place. Surveys? Content analyses of Facebook pages? Objective indicators like time stuck in traffic jams? I suspect that there is no best way to ascertain well-being, just lots of ways, each with its own pros and cons. Multimethod assessment is as good an idea in tracking a nation's well-being as doing a pointy-headed research project.

I am not privy to what goes on behind the scenes in the U.S. government, but missing to date in this worldwide trend are public calls by national leaders in the United States to start to take the well-being—happiness—of U.S. residents seriously. This would be neither a left nor a right issue. Goodness, perhaps folks across existing political divides in the United States could even agree that the matter is important. That may be asking too much at the present time.

Perhaps there has been a reluctance for a U.S. leader to call for the assessment of national happiness out of fear that he or she would be criticized as a socialist or as a reactionary, as being out of touch with the very real problems faced by folks in today's United States. But appreciate that the suggestions by Sarkozy and Cameron were made precisely because business-as-usual approaches (pun intended) in their respective nations were missing something essential.

Given all the desirable consequences that seem to follow from happiness—like health, longevity, achievement, good relationships, and indeed work productivity—maybe it's about time for the United States to join the movement.

Information about the gross national happiness of the United States may prove useless, or the mere fact of gathering this information may have unintended consequences (think "No Child Left Behind"). But I would still like to see the possibility discussed. As it stands now in the United States, what we seem to have is a great concern with GNA (gross national anger). And there's more to the good life than that.

REFERENCES

Diener, E. (2000). Subjective well-being: The science of happiness and a proposal for a national index. *American Psychologist, 55*, 34–43.

Diener, E., & Seligman, M. E. P. (2004). Beyond money: Toward an economy of well-being. *Psychological Science in the Public Interest, 5*, 1–31.

Stratton, A., (2010, November 14). David Cameron aims to make happiness the new GDP. *Guardian.* Retrieved from http://www.guardian.co.uk/politics/2010/nov/14/david-cameron-wellbeing-inquiry.

73

Positive Psychology and China

China is a big country, inhabited by many Chinese.
—Charles de Gaulle

During August 2010, I spent 2 weeks in mainland China, giving keynote addresses with my colleague Nansook Park at two conferences in Beijing, the first hosted by Tsinghua University and the second by Beijing Normal University. These were the first conferences in China devoted to positive psychology.

I have not yet written any reflections on my experiences in China, perhaps because these were so personally meaningful. I have always said that there are two sorts of experience that matter: those one enjoys in the moment and those one enjoys after the fact because one can think and talk about them (see reflection 17). My China experiences were so much in the former category that I have resisted placing them in the second category. A lifelong dream of mine—starting as a kid growing up in the Midwest of the United States—was to visit China, and it finally happened (see reflection 99). Between the conferences, we tried to visit as many places as possible, including the Forbidden City, Tiananmen Square, the Great Wall, and the city of Xi'an to see the Terra Cotta Warriors. And the food was unbelievable, especially the dumplings in Xi'an.

Although I enjoyed very much my sightseeing and my meals, the highlights of my trip all involved my experiences with people. I loved the Chinese people I met. We did not talk politics with anyone—they were after all our hosts—and I am sure we would have disagreed on things. But our hosts were decent, diligent, and gracious…and funny. That's an important part of what matters, regardless of national policies.

In particular, we met a number of undergraduate and graduate psychology students—mostly female, like in the United States—who were bright beyond belief but also kind and gentle and supportive. They did everything possible to make their guests—us—feel comfortable and to ensure that we enjoyed our visit. Their helpfulness was genuine and went above and beyond anything that I have ever experienced. The point is that positive psychology should not simply be an export endeavor. It should also entail import, and those of us in the Western world have much to learn from those elsewhere, including in particular China and how the Chinese treat visitors.

Contributing to the enjoyment of my China experience was the fact that I am a tall (6′3″) and big (i.e., fat) American who provided a frequent photo op for the citizens there. Apparently the Chinese love taking pictures, and I lost count of how many times I had my picture taken at the conferences as well as on the street by random folks. I guess I looked different—exotic?—to the typical Chinese resident. Cool. I have never in my entire life been exotic.

During my visit to the Great Wall, I took a break and rested while the rest of my party forged ahead. But my time was not idle, because numerous Chinese visitors approached me and asked if they could take a picture of me, invariably with a child (presumably their own). My self-esteem is just fine, thank you, but I never thought I was among the Seven Wonders of the World. Still, I happily complied.

Children often followed me around. We laughed and smiled, even if we could not otherwise communicate. All children are cute, and the Chinese children who followed me around melted my heart.

One of my favorite encounters was with a boy—maybe 8 years old—in Xi'an who boldly walked up to me and craned his neck. He said "hello" tonally, pronouncing it like the Mandarin *nee-how* (hello). I said hello back.

He then told my host something that she did not want to translate, but I insisted. Apparently he said, "I'm glad I'm not an American."

I asked why, which was dutifully translated by my uncomfortable host.

He replied, "If I were an American, then I would have to speak English, and I do not speak English very well."

It was a Piagetian moment beyond precious. My host tried to explain to him that if he were an American, he would indeed speak English. I interrupted her, saying (to her) that counterfactual reasoning was not where he was at. I simply bumped fists with the little boy, and we both smiled. I had made a friend for life.

Anyway, I have decided that it might be of interest to share some of my impressions of China vis-à-vis positive psychology.

First, there was great interest in the perspective of positive psychology. With the increasing affluence of China, there is worry about the negative impact of wealth on the mental health and well-being of its people due to materialism and conflicts with traditional values. There is a special concern about the younger generation. They are not only are part of a global culture but also subject to huge pressures for success. These pressures are exacerbated by the "one-child policy" because family expectations necessarily focus on that one child. We were told by numerous young people that they grew up lonely and stressed.

We originally thought that we should use euphemisms for happiness in speaking to our hosts, lest we be dismissed as shallow hedonists. But no worries. The Chinese want their people, and especially their children, to be happy. Then their problems might be minimized. I agree, but the Chinese openness to happiness theory and research was nonetheless surprising. There are of course cultural differences in what constitutes legitimate happiness, but it is also obvious that happiness is a universal desire.

Second, China is big—really big—not just geographically but population-wise—and highly centralized. Something I learned that I still have trouble wrapping my head around is that since 1949, China has had only one time zone, as opposed to the five time zones it would warrant anywhere else in the world. The point is that if and when China decides to implement ideas and interventions from positive psychology, the scale of so doing would be mind-boggling. The conference at Beijing Normal University, on positive psychology and education, was attended by educators collectively responsible for almost 300 million students in primary and secondary schools.

Third, China is different from Western nations and especially the United States in terms of important cultural values with implications for the reception of positive psychology. China is not only a highly collectivist culture but also one that takes a very long time perspective on things. We often heard mention of the "seven generation" view, which means that the Chinese take into account the consequences of policies for at least seven future generations. Positive psychologists in the United States often focus on the individual and short-term benefits of attention to happiness and well-being. A rationale framed in these terms would miss the boat in China. Instead, emphasis should be on the benefits of positive psychology for the group and for future generations.

It has been said that there are very few differences among people. It has also been said that those differences that do exist are very important. My China visit underscored both of these truisms.

Seeing is believing. If you can, visit and experience a different part of the world, especially the people who live there. They will change you, and you in turn will change them.

We can only hope for the better in both cases.

74

Gauging the Happiness of Nations

A View from North Korea

I have written about recent proposals to gauge the happiness of nations, including France (see reflection 71) and England (see reflection 72). A story about a report on a Chinese website therefore caught my attention (Flanagan, 2011). According to the story, North Korean researchers have compiled their own happiness index that ranks China #1 among 203 nations, followed by North Korea at #2 and Cuba at #3. Number 4 was Iran, and #5 was Venezuela. South Korea fared poorly, ranking only #152, whereas the United States (identified in the report as the "American Empire") finished dead last at #203.

The larger point of this story, I think, is that happiness may well be a universal concern. When positive psychology began, some of us fretted that it would be dismissed as a narrowly Western endeavor. But if happiness matters in North Korea, maybe it matters to most everyone.

That said, the report raises questions. Not mentioned were the criteria used to gauge the happiness of nations or whether these relied on respondent self-report, "objective" indices of well-being, or both. In any event, no study done has ever shown or even implied that the happiest nations on the planet include China, North Korea, Cuba, and Iran. No study ever puts the United States at the very bottom.

To be honest, I doubt that there even is such a report,* or if there is, that it is based on data that would pass minimal scientific muster. But as a resident of the American Empire, perhaps I am prejudiced.

National indicators of well-being deserve scrutiny and debate, and the North Korean index—whether or not it is real—broadens the debate to include the unstated political purpose of such indices and their possible role in maintaining a status quo. Any assessment of the psychological well-being of a nation (i.e., its happiness) must be done in a way that is transparent and valid.

To those of us in the United States, the North Korean index seems blatantly biased. But appreciate that "bias" may be more subtle than placing one's political allies or one's own nation at the top of a list. Bias can and does enter into any assessment in terms of the criteria that one chooses to use and emphasize.

Some years ago, I encountered a list of cities in the United States that afforded the highest quality of life. The list was long and fit my preconceptions (as a Midwestern college professor), being topped by Ann Arbor (MI) and Madison (WI). (I assume climate did not figure prominently in the rankings.)

The punch line: The two "researchers" who compiled the list were graduates of the University of Michigan and the University of Wisconsin, respectively, facts they acknowledged with appropriate and explicit irony.

When I first heard about the idea of gauging the happiness of nations, I was intrigued, and I still am. GNP is important but not the only thing that matters in understanding the well-being of a nation. However, I fretted that such assessments—if they relied too much on respondent self-report—might be tilted by a tendency in some regions to complain (see reflection 70). We are

---

* Some commentators on the story have observed that North Korea does not even recognize South Korea as a legitimate nation, which raises the question why South Korea would be included in North Korea's rankings of nations by their happiness.

unhappy—therefore give us more resources. I did not consider that these assessments might alternatively be used to argue that everything is peachy keen. So I have learned something.

Happiness is important, and its assessment should be serious business, no matter where it is done.

REFERENCE

Flanagan. E, (2011) Are China & North Korea happier than America? *Behind the Wall, NBC News.* Retrieved from http://behindthewall.msnbc.msn.com/_news/2011/05/31/6754108-are-china-north-korea-happier-than-america.

75

Happy Places

Third Places

As I have noted in other reflections here (70, 71, 72, and 74), people have long sought happy places—settings where everyone is content and fulfilled. Most who search for these do not believe them to be physical places but rather social places (see reflection 67).

Candidates for happy places include nations and communities, workplaces and homes. A book by Ray Oldenburg (1999)—*The Great Good Place*—has suggested another happy place candidate, perhaps the most viable of all. The book is scholarly but accessible, an anthropological/sociological analysis of cafés, coffee shops, bars, and other hangouts. The book introduced to me a new term—*third place*—that made instant sense.

Third places are where people congregate other than workplace or home. England has pubs, France has cafés, and Austria has coffeehouses. Once upon a time in the United States, common third places included country stores, post offices, barber shops, hair salons, soda shops, and taverns.

As described by Oldenburg, third places share common features. First, they are neutral, meaning that all people can come and go without penalty. If you don't go to your third place for a few days or weeks, your return is greeted with interest and enthusiasm. Contrast that with work or home, where your eventual return after days of absence would be greeted with a pink slip or divorce papers.

Second, they are level, meaning that the status differences that matter so much elsewhere are not relevant. And no one plays host at a third place.

Third, conversation is the main activity in third places, and one of the few ways to offend others present is to be boring.

Fourth, third places are accessible, meaning that they have long hours and are easy to get to. No reservation needed!

Fifth, third places have regulars. Indeed, regulars define a third place, but new people are accepted, not automatically but often easily.

Sixth, third places are physically plain and unpretentious.

Seventh, and perhaps most critically, the dominant mood of a third place is playful. Laughter abounds.

Third places contribute to the life worth living. They root us; they give us an identity; they restore us; they support us. Bottom line: They allow us to be us. And everyone knows our name.

Starbucks and the like are not third places, at least not when everyone has a cell phone and a laptop computer, and not when ready access to an electrical outlet is more important than whoever else might be there.

Fitness clubs are not third places either, at least not when the exercise machines are parallel to one another and not when no one talks.

And alas, bars are not third places, at least not for those of wary of cigarette smoke outside their entrances and alcohol inside.

For much of my life as a young adult, I had a third place, usually a bar: for example, the Wigwam in Champaign, Illinois, Tom's Tavern in Boulder, Colorado, Don's Rok in Clinton, New York, Daddy's Money in Blacksburg, Virginia, LT in Philadelphia, Pennsylvania, and Ashley's in Ann Arbor, Michigan. (It is amazing to me that I can remember all these places without straining, but I guess that's the point.)

But I cut back on my drinking, and I stopped going to bars. It was only when I read Oldenburg's book that I realized what I was missing, and it was not the alcohol. It was a happy place right under my nose.

I love my home, and I love my work, but I think I need to find a new third place.

REFERENCE

Oldenburg, R. (1999). *The great good place: Cafés, coffee shops, bookstores, bars, hair salons and other hangouts at the heart of a community.* New York: Marlowe.

Part X

Rants

Positive psychology proposes that there are genuinely good things in life that deserve scientific study. But a positive psychologist need not be a Pollyanna and proclaim that everything is wonderful. The reflections in this section, which if nothing else were fun to write, all concern themselves with my own pet peeves. I suspect I am not alone in branding these pet peeves things that do *not* make life worth living.

76

Can You Be Too Cheerful?

On the way home from work the other day, I listened to an interesting NPR story about conspicuous conservation, a play on Thorstein Veblen's (1899) notion of conspicuous consumption. In case you need reminding, *conspicuous consumption* refers to over-the-top and blatant materialism undertaken to show others how well off you might be (even if you are not). In parallel, conspicuous conservation refers to over-the-top ecologically relevant actions undertaken to show others how green you might be (even if you are not). A definition of conspicuous conservation that I like is being frugal in high style.

An example from the NPR story that stuck in my mind was people who put solar panels on the front of their house, not on the roof, because neighbors might not see them otherwise, even though the panels would do much more good on the roof where the sun would actually hit them.

I started to think about the positive psychology equivalent of conspicuous consumption and conspicuous conservation. Keeping with the theme of alliteration, I dub this equivalent conspicuous cheerfulness, strident satisfaction, eternal ebullience, or glaring glee. You get the idea: People who evidence a relentlessly positive stance, not because it is sincere but because it signifies to other people how positive they are. Maybe I'm a somber, skeptical, or cynical kind of guy, but I find relentless good cheer a bit forced, at least when I am on the receiving end of it.

"How are you doing?" I might ask someone.

"Great! Unbelievable! I'm walking on sunshine!" is the constant response of the conspicuously cheerful person.

And I shudder, at least when I suspect this is not an honest answer to the question.

Maybe I should not complain. With the growing popularity of positive psychology, people have learned that happiness and satisfaction are not only attractive but also markers of doing well in life. That is probably an improvement over the not-too-distant past in which cheerfulness was seen as a sign of stupidity or denial.

But it seems to me that *appropriate* cheerfulness should be our goal, and that involves taking into account who is on the receiving end of our expressed emotions, not to mention the fidelity of what we say about our moods. Also, some variation in cheerfulness is probably a good idea as well, lest a lack of credibility be invited. We should be cheerful about good things but not about bad things. I hate to break it to you relentlessly cheerful folks, but good things and bad things happen, to you and certainly to the rest of us. Indeed, appropriate discontent with the status quo has likely led to almost everything that has improved the world.

Is positive psychology to blame for conspicuous cheerfulness? Maybe yes, maybe no. But I do know that a gathering of positive psychologists is rather overwhelming, with all the hugs and the nonstop expressions of satisfaction and success. Ugh.

Sincerity trumps satisfaction, and positive psychology as I understand it does not urge us to be insincere and certainly not to be promiscuously positive. We will have a better world when we figure out what really is good and what really is bad, and when we work to make the good more likely than the bad. Conspicuous and constant cheerfulness works against this action plan.

REFERENCE

Veblen, T. (1899). *Theory of the leisure class: An economic study in the evolution of institutions*. New York: Macmillan.

77

"Strong" Accents Define America

In a land of immigrants, one [is] not an alien but simply the latest arrival.
—Rudolf Arnheim

My reflections here are not overtly political, although I assume my liberal leanings are evident. But in the present case, I cannot help myself. What follows is a political rant triggered by a story I read that some legislators in Arizona want to remove teachers with "strong" accents from classrooms in which the English language is being taught.

Never mind that the way most Americans speak English is an abomination to those from England. Never mind that Australians have little idea what Americans are saying because we sound so funny to them. Never mind that many of us in the middle of the United States have trouble understanding people from the Deep South, from Boston, or from Brooklyn. (The first time I met someone from Brooklyn, I innocently congratulated him on how well he spoke English, given—so I thought—that he had just arrived in the country!)

The United States is a wonderful nation, and I think it is a wonderful nation precisely because it is a nation of strongly accented immigrants. Our ancestors came from around the world, some willingly and others not so willingly, but they all arrived, survived, and thrived. Do we speak in one voice or with one accent? Not exactly, and isn't that the point of America?

A movement to remove those with "strong" accents from public life in the United States would get rid of some of my best teachers, some of my most revered colleagues, and some of my closest friends. It would send some of my best students packing. It would kick Henry Kissinger to the curb, and slap Wolfgang Puck away. Bye, bye, Albert Einstein and Cesar Chavez. Farewell, Bela Karolyi. Irving Berlin: Take a walk, and take your damn songs about America with you!

Has America—or at least Arizona—lost its mind? My immediate ancestors, from Sweden, Germany, England, and Ireland, eventually settled in Iowa, where the notion of *hybrid vigor* is familiar. Usually applied to crops, it applies metaphorically to people.

"Strong" accents among English teachers in the United States? Rather than barring them, how about requiring them?

78

Does Anyone Write Letters Anymore?

What a lot we lost when we stopped writing letters. You can't reread a phone call.

—Liz Carpenter

One of the staples of positive psychology is the *gratitude letter*: a written and specific expression of thanks to someone who has been especially kind or important to you but has never heard you express your gratitude—parents, siblings, other relatives, friends, teachers, coaches, teammates, employers, and so on. Over the years, I have asked students in my positive psychology classes to write such letters. If they cannot deliver it by hand, they should mail it. As a positive psychology intervention, gratitude letters "work" 99+% of the time, by which I mean that the recipients are touched, usually profoundly, and so too are the letter writers, despite misgivings they may have had in the first place about doing something that seemed so corny.

In the last few years, though, I have encountered shocking questions after announcing the assignment: "How much does a postage stamp cost, and where can I get one?"

I realize that postage stamp prices keep increasing, and I realize that neighborhood post offices are closing down. I also realize that many people now pay their bills online or through automatic bank account deductions. And of course I realize that there are nowadays many other ways to get in touch with people. Nonetheless, my reaction to such questions is *Wow!*

This reflection is not about postage stamps but about letters. Does anyone write them anymore? I am quite sure that the answer is fewer and fewer people. When the holiday season is upon us, I see more than a few stories about the decline in post office business, not just the catalogues that used to clog our mailboxes but also the cards and letters that used to brighten the season.

I think this is a shame, and I am guilty as anyone. I cannot remember the last time I wrote a letter to someone. However, I do remember the last few letters I received, vividly and fondly. Two were from colleagues of mine at the University of Michigan who wrote to me about recent events in my life, and one was from a student for whom I provided a recommendation. Mind you, many other people communicate with me, by phone or by e-mail, but these three letters are what I remember. I have read each one many times, savoring them. I keep them on my desk, amidst flash drives and paper clips, and I will continue to reread them any time I want to feel good or until they become too faded to be legible.

What makes a good letter? For me, a good letter is personal and personalized. A good letter takes time to write. The thing about writing a letter is that no one can multitask while doing so, unlike e-mails or telephone calls. A letter represents undivided attention and is precious as a consequence. Oh yes, a good letter is handwritten, not a cut-and-pasted, global searched-and-replaced bit of faux intimacy. It need not be written on fancy stationery or an expensive card—the three letters I have been cherishing were written on plain notebook paper! And a good letter is one that required the writer to find a stamp and an envelope and a postbox!

I gave a media interview last week in which I was asked how people might approach the upcoming holiday season if they were on a tight budget. My answer was simple: Write letters.

By the way, in 2012, a stamp costs 45 cents (see http://www.usps.com/prices/).

ANNOTATION

In recent years, whenever I have bought stamps, I have faced a dilemma, even though I know the price of stamps. Should I buy a booklet of the increasingly lovely first-class stamps that the United States Postal Service (USPS) has been issuing, running the risk that the price will be raised before the booklet is used, or should I buy the more mundane Liberty Bell "forever" stamps, knowing they can be used not only forever but also whenever?

The issue is not about saving a penny or two per letter, but rather that I do not want to go to the bother, when postage costs increase, of obtaining 1-cent stamps in order to make up the difference. The dilemma: Go for the lovely stamps, which I know to brighten my day, however briefly, or avoid the hassles, which I know to take a toll on my well-being, again however briefly. I usually avoid the hassles. Sigh.

In a move resulting from budget deficits, the USPS announced a plan that will resolve my dilemma. Starting January 22, 2011, *all* new first-class stamps—including I assume the lovely ones— are forever stamps and thus hold their value.

Since 1987, some 28 billion forever stamps have been sold and now account for 85% of all first-class stamps that are sold, suggesting that many people, like me, have opted against loveliness.

As much as I admire the Liberty Bell and what it stands for, I welcome this pending change, even if it is driven by financial considerations.

Who says the world is not getting better?

79

You Can't Savor a Nutrient

He who distinguishes the true savor of his food can never be a glutton; he who
does not cannot be otherwise.
—Henry David Thoreau

In Defense of Food by Michael Pollan (2008) is a terrific book. I read
it in one sitting, with no skimming. It was a sorry-it-was-done
kind of book. As the title conveys, the book is a defense of food,
which sounds strange. But appreciate that food is something many
love to hate and hate to love, at least in the United States.

The book had several purposes, and it succeeded at all of
them. First, it provides a fascinating history of how science,
big business, and government led to a radical shift in public consciousness and consumption from a focus on food to a
focus on nutrients—the things in food that presumably matter. Second, the book criticizes this shift, arguing that it could
be justified *if* it made people healthier and happier. However,
the evidence seems to point in the opposite direction. Third,
it offers some sensible advice about what and how to eat. In
criticizing a nutrient-driven diet, Pollan does not advocate
an anything-goes approach. Just the contrary. He advocates a
deliberate approach.

I enjoyed the book not simply because of its content, but
because it was wonderfully written. Consider these sentences,
just a few of many that I underlined in appreciation:

- Culture...at least when it comes to food...is really just a
fancy word for your mother. (p. 3)

- As a general rule it's a whole lot easier to slap a health claim on a box of sugary cereal than on a raw potato or a carrot, with the perverse result that the most healthful foods in the supermarket sit there quietly in the produce section, silent as a stroke victim. (p. 39)
- A diet based on quantity rather than quality has ushered a new creature onto the world stage: the human being who manages to be both overfed and undernourished. (p. 122)
- Don't eat anything your great-grandmother would not recognize as food. (p. 148)
- Among eighteen- to fifty-year-old Americans roughly a fifth of all eating now takes place in the car. (pp. 188–189)

The problems with a focus on nutrients are many. We are tempted to divide them into good nutrients and bad nutrients, and we think that the good ones are all that matter. We become concerned with what we eat but not how we eat it. Most generally, a focus on nutrients embodies inappropriate reductionism. The triumph of *nutritionism* (as Pollan calls it, to emphasize that it is an ideology) is one of taking nutrients out of the context of food, food out of the context of diet, and diet out of the context of lifestyle.

While I was reading the book, I worried that positive psychologists might also be guilty of inappropriate reductionism as we search for simple ingredients that make people happier. It is one thing to cite research showing that positive exchanges greatly outnumber negative exchanges in satisfying relationships. But it is another thing to conclude that only the positive to negative ratio matters, regardless of the relationship and the people involved. Then we are coming close to touting a positive psychology nutrient.

I read another book that described a study done some years ago (Coyle, 2009). Two researchers interested in teaching sat in on basketball practices led by legendary UCLA coach John Wooden. They wrote down every discrete "act of teaching" they observed. Of the many thousands of entries they made, only 6.9% were compliments—positive. And 6.6% were expressions of displeasure—negative. The positive-to-negative ratio was about even, hardly healthy according to current positive psychology. But John Wooden is arguably one of the world's greatest teachers and certainly one of the most beloved of coaches. We should not miss the forest for the trees, the food for the nutrients, or the beloved individual for the positive-to-negative ratio of what he says.

Pollan's advice is contained in the first three sentences of his book. "Eat food. Not too much. Mainly plants."

To this advice I would like to add: "Eat with joy, and do so with others."

Bon appetit!

REFERENCES

Coyle, D. (2009). *The talent code.* New York: Bantam Dell.

Pollan, M. (2008). *In defense of food: An eater's manifesto.* New York: Penguin.

80

I Hate E-mail

It's not the mountain that stops you. It's the pebble in your shoe.
—Mountain climber saying

I hate e-mail. And now that I have your attention, I should say more exactly that I hate how I approach e-mail. The habits I have developed in responding to e-mail messages, which once upon a time made sense when I received a mere handful of messages per day, are now hugely punishing given that I receive several hundred messages per day. I spend more time with e-mail than with anything else in my life, professional or personal, other than sleeping. And my sleep is increasingly disrupted by rumination about the hundreds of unanswered messages in my in-box!

When I first started to use e-mail, I thought it was wonderful. I could send messages simultaneously to a large number of folks about a meeting time and place. I could check in with loved ones when I was in a time zone that made phone calls unwieldy or inappropriate. I could ask simple questions or make simple requests of friends and colleagues without writing letters.

But things changed. What I thought was so wonderful about e-mail was what it allowed *me* to do. But e-mail also allowed other people to do things, and all too often, I am on the receiving end of what they are trying to do. I suppose really important people have someone else to handle their e-mail. I'm not such a person. I'm important enough that people ask me to do things, but not important enough that I can delegate or relegate the hundreds of requests I get every day. Can you send me this? Can you read the attached paper (or book!) and comment on it? Can you advise me about whatever?

"Pardon the multiple postings." Excuse me, but I do not pardon these! I am opposed to the death penalty, but I would probably make an exception in this case. Even e-mail messages that require no response still need to be read. Life is short, and I do not want the epitaph on my tombstone to say "He read all of his e-mail."

Most of the e-mail messages I receive are from people I do not know, and they are contacting me in my professional role. Yes...yes...yes...I could just ignore them. But I am still an old-school kind of guy, and I think it impolite to ignore requests, even if I do not know the people making them and even if the requests are bizarre.

Early in my career, I learned that responding quickly to any and all requests paid dividends. As Woody Allen said, 80% of success is showing up, and in my case, showing up meant responding to requests. The problem is that e-mail has allowed the requests to escalate beyond my capacity to honor them. The result is that e-mail is now killing me.

One of the few self-help books I have read cover to cover promised advice about "managing" e-mail. An ostensibly useful bit of advice was dubbed the *3-minute rule*. If you can answer an e-mail message in 3 minutes, always do so upon reading it the first time, because if you leave it for later, it will still take 3 minutes plus whatever extra time it takes to reread it and re-understand what is needed.

The problem with following the 3-minute rule is that it encourages the e-mail sender to send yet another message, usually immediately. Quickly removing the pebble in your shoe that an e-mail request represents results only in more pebbles.

My colleague Martin Seligman has said that to raise roses, you have to pull weeds. But pulling e-mail weeds leads to more of them. The roses are postponed indefinitely.

This book of reflections is supposed to be about the good life, so why I am whining about e-mail? Simply because e-mail can undercut the good life and its pursuit. It can be a hassle and in my case an incredible one.

I doubt I am alone in my discomfort with e-mail. Is there a solution?

Perhaps a 21st-century rendering of the Golden Rule would be useful: Don't e-mail others messages you wouldn't want to receive yourself.

81

Technology and Happiness

A Book Review

Journalist William Powers (2010) has written an interesting book with a wonderful title—*Hamlet's Blackberry*—and a subtitle filled with promises—*A Practical Philosophy for Building a Good Life in the Digital Age*. The book addresses current technology and how it seems to demand that we be connected to other people and the larger world all of the time. I picked up the book because 24–7 connection is one of my bugaboos.

I am a 60-year-old college professor surrounded by 20-year-old college students who are digitally savvy. They think I am quaint and would call me a Luddite if they knew what that meant. I do use e-mail, although I hate it (see reflection 80). I confess that I consult *Wikipedia* on an almost daily basis to find facts and their analogues. I regularly scan the sports news on Cnn.com. And of course I write blog entries for *Psychology Today* and post them myself.

But otherwise, I have not fully embraced the 21st century and the technological connectedness it affords. My reluctance is one part being challenged by new technology and two parts being overwhelmed by the endless information and requests that new technology unleashes.

I am not on Facebook. I write my appointments in a small book that fits in my pocket, and toward the end of a year—before

I have a new appointment book—I make no future commitments because I have no place to write them down. I do not carry my cell phone with me unless I am traveling out of state. I do not text message, and I have yet to grasp what Twitter entails. Someday I may take one or more of these technological leaps and partake in what to me is new technology. For the time being, I have made my own decision about the degree of connectedness I can handle. And I relish disconnection.

The author of *Hamlet's Blackberry* shares some of my reactions, although he draws his own line differently and describes the issues much better than I do. The first half of the book is a vivid description of his conflict between connection, which of course pays dividends, and disconnection (being alone or face-to-face with family and friends), which also pays dividends.

What I enjoyed most about the book was its second half, which was a historical tour of new (at the time) technologies and how they had an impact on the "connect or not" tension. I love historical details, and *Hamlet's Blackberry* abounds in them.

For example, Socrates distrusted reading and writing, believing that they would sap people's mental abilities and preclude communication, which to him required conversations. The book did not quite say it, but I was left with the impression that one of the Western world's most profound thinkers was himself illiterate. Interesting if true.*

Before books became generally available, reading to one's self—that is, not out loud—was unusual and perhaps even an affectation. When books were scarce, of course they should be read out loud to others.

In Shakespeare's time, a new gadget became available that allowed people not only to write down their ideas on specially coated paper but also to erase them later with a sponge. These so-called tables were an improved version of wax tablets, which

---

* There is apparently debate about whether Socrates was illiterate. I do not know the answer.

had been around for centuries, and they helped people bring some order to the information they encountered, acquiring it and just as important disacquiring it. We do not know if Shakespeare used a table, but he gave one to Hamlet, so perhaps Shakespeare did use one himself. Anyway, this is the source of the book's name.

Technology is whatever is new to us. Old technology is simply the way it is, and we are born into it. Of course, books exist. Of course, they should be read silently to ourselves. Of course, we should be able to erase what we have written. Every generation decries new technology, fearing that it will sap our intellectual potential and diminish our relations with others. After reading this book, I realize that none of this has yet happened, that people are infinitely adaptive, and that we have much to learn from the past.

I remember when I first encountered a personal computer equipped with a word-processing program. It was 1977 or thereabout, and the program required that a document be formatted explicitly, on a line-to-line and sometimes even a word-to-word basis. I also remember my reaction: "This will never catch on!" I smile as I sit here drafting this reflection by pointing and clicking with ease on Word, the 2003 version mind you, because the newest version is of course the devil's invention and therefore X-rated.

For a long time, I never thought to check the spam filter of my e-mail account. When I finally started to look at what had been filtered out, I found the usual suspect messages about Viagra and urgent notices that I had won millions of dollars in lotteries. But I also found "real" messages from friends and colleagues that had been filtered out for reasons I do not understand and thus sat unread for months and sometimes years. Guess what? Life went on just fine for all of us. A lesson to be learned.

Hamlet's Blackberry is not self-help. It does not contain five easy steps for dealing with technology and adjudicating the connection-disconnection tension. But the book is provocative

and informative and true to its subtitle about offering a philosophy rather than a fix. That's what matters most. And I take
solace in knowing that my issues with e-mail and other technologies have a long historical precedent.

The important message of *Hamlet's Blackberry* is that being
connected and not being connected both matter. The trick is to
choose the mode we want at a given time. Powers advised readers to find their own solutions to the tension, those that fit the
lives they lead.

I enjoyed the book, and I am happy to recommend it. You
can buy it in hardback or in paperback or in a Kindle edition.
You can read it out loud or silently to yourself. But do read it.
And maybe you could talk to other people about it.

REFERENCE

Powers, W. (2010). *Hamlet's Blackberry: A practical philosophy for building a
good life in the digital age*. New York: HarperCollins.

82

Don't Pick My Brain

Readers of my reflections like it when I go off on a rant. I try to make my occasional tirades relevant to the theme here— the good life—by some hand-waving comments to the effect that what annoys us undercuts our pleasure and fulfillment. But readers probably just like my righteous indignation because I speak for them. And I enjoy writing harangues to let off steam. Sometimes things even seem to change as a result. After my reflection "I Hate E-mail" (80) was posted online, there was a noticeable reduction in detestable e-mail messages in my in-box. I hope that lasts.

So, consider this new pet peeve of mine: People (invariably folks I don't know) who get in touch by e-mail, phone, or occasionally letter asking for an appointment with me "to pick my brain."

I understand that this clichéd phrase is well intended, even complimentary. It means "You know something about whatever, and I would like to get this information from you."

My problem with this phrase is that it is unidirectional. My students, my colleagues, and my friends don't pick my brain, and I don't pick their brains. We talk, discuss, argue, and some-times even reach consensus. Regardless, a good time is had because we interact over ideas.

But when someone wants to pick my brain, I feel like a carcass, a heap of bones in the desert being eyeballed by a buzzard.

So, please, think before you use this phrase. Consider saying, "I would like to talk with you about a topic of concern to both of us." Or consider saying, "I know you can teach me some important things, and maybe I can teach you some as well." And oh my goodness, consider saying, "I want you to help me with my agenda, and I want to know how I can help you with yours."

You may call me a dreamer, but I am not.

And I certainly am not a chicken bone.

83

First, Think Inside the Box

You have to learn the rules of the game. And then you have to play better than anyone else.

—Albert Einstein

I use as many clichés as anyone, but there are a few that I will not trot out because I have come to dislike them immensely. "Think outside the box" is one of these expressions.* Indeed, it is so inside the box! I just did a Google search for the exact phrase and found 1,200,000 hits.

I have no problem with what the expression tries to convey— the importance of looking at things in a new way. That is, after all, one of the defining features of a creative act and a creative person. But increasingly, I hear the expression used as if it were the only defining feature of creativity, which it is not.

Most who think seriously about creativity agree that it entails not only novelty (that outside-the-box stuff) but also utility, and in order to be useful, it has to go above and beyond what is already known (that inside-the-box stuff).

* The origin of the phrase is not clear, but it became popular because of the nine-dot puzzle, now a management consultancy staple that poses a problem: How does one connect nine dots with four straight lives drawn without ever lifting one's pencil? The temptation is to draw a box, which does not solve the problem. Rather, one must draw lines outside the confines of the box shape suggested by the arrangement of the nine dots.

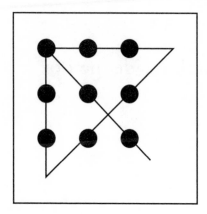

Figure 83.1 The Nine-Dot Puzzle

Whenever I hear people say that they "think outside the box" I cringe, because I have rarely heard folks who are genuinely creative so describe themselves. I also am suspicious because I hear these people saying—and here I may be unfair in some cases—that one need not know what is well accepted.

As a teacher, I want my students to know what is inside the box. This is not because I am a defender of the academic or intellectual status quo. It is because knowing what is inside the box is the only way to get outside the box in a useful way once the basics are mastered.

Psychologists who study prodigious accomplishments, in science, music, or art, speak about the 10,000-hour rule, meaning that in order to do something notable in some field, one must devote 10,000+ hours to mastering the discipline in question (see reflections 23 and 33). Practice, practice, and practice, weedhopper, and appreciate that much of this practice needs to be done inside the box.

If you never venture outside the box, you will probably not be creative. But if you never get inside the box, you will certainly be stupid.

84

It Is What It Is

I have written several reflections about clichés I do not like (82 and 83). So, in the spirit of being fair and balanced (itself a cliché—sorry Fox News), I want to mention a cliché I do like: "It is what it is."

Often used in sports, the expression has much broader applicability. I used it myself recently in my role on a committee charged with evaluating faculty members for tenure and promotion. Our committee always does a conscientious job, carefully looking at what someone has done in the domains of concern to a university: teaching, research, and service. But sometimes we stray into other areas, and we start to criticize folks for what they have not done. That is appropriate up to a point (after all, university teachers need to meet their classes), but when it moves into what someone cannot do—given who he or she happens to be—it requires interruption. Proclaiming that "it is what it is" is one way to halt the cascade of counterfactuals, including those issuing from me.

If someone is hired who is focused and cautious, he or she should not be criticized for later failing to be broad and provocative. It is what it is, and we knew that from the get-go when this person was hired. If someone is hired who works best with individual students or in small classes, he or she should not be taken to task for not teaching mega classes to rave reviews by the masses. Conversely, a teacher who sparkles while giving large lectures but falls short while leading small discussions should not be castigated. It is all what it is, whatever it is, and we should acknowledge and appreciate the strengths of these different types of teachers. If someone is hired who does not work 24/7 (cliché) and has a balanced life (cliché), he or she should not be faulted for taking time with the family. It is what it is, and in this case, it is probably good.

Decades ago, when I was first asked to review a book for a journal, I received some great advice from the journal editor. Do not review the book that the author did not intend to write. Rather, review the book that was written. It is what it is.

The point: Appreciate what people do well, and celebrate who they are, assuming that they do what they do well. After all, it is what it is.

Change is possible, of course, and we want others as well as ourselves to stretch and to grow (compound cliché) at work and at life. But it is what it is, at least until it is not.

I have learned that the point of the reflections I write needs to be presented explicitly to readers. Really explicitly. So, this one is *not* about evaluating faculty members at a university. It is about evaluating anyone doing anything: our country's leaders, our friends, our spouses, our children, and even ourselves. What is being done well? It is what it is, and if it is good, isn't that good enough?

85

Upspeak

Maybe this is just one of my pet peeves as a college instructor who works with 20-something-year-old students. But *upspeak*, as it is called, is not what makes my life worth living. It makes me cringe.

Per *Wikipedia*, upspeak is most common among American and Australian speakers of English and entails a rising intonation at the end of any and all utterances. In other words, upspeak (also known as uptalk, rising inflection, or high rising intonation) turns every sentence into a question.

Linguists have studied upspeak, finding that it occurs most frequently among younger people and among women. Upspeak is reportedly most common among teenage girls from Southern California (aka "Valley girls") and among adults from North Dakota and Minnesota, where it may reflect lingering influences of the Norwegian language. Linguists have further concluded that upspeak serves conversational purposes, discouraging interruption and seeking reassurance.

Be that as it may, upspeak jars me. I spent the past semester listening to my students make presentations, and no matter how brilliant their ideas, their reliance on upspeak distracted me to no end.

Maybe I should let it go. Maybe I should let language evolve. I do know that I have never commented on upspeak to any of my students who do it.

I simply raise the question, as a teacher, about when—if ever—a student should be critiqued on *how* she or he says something, as opposed to *what* she or he says, which seems a legitimate and noncontroversial target for advice.

Along these lines, what about the *likes*, *you knows*, and *whatevers* that intrude into what many of my young students say? Should I call their attention to how annoying these discourse fillers may be, or would that just make them self-conscious and therefore even worse speakers?

Here is a conclusion that makes sense to me, one at which I have arrived during my own career that started 35 years ago as a flip and sometimes profane 26-year-old college professor. What one says is more important than how one says it, and a speaker is well served by *not* using a conversational style that distracts from the message. And I think upspeak distracts.

The issue, of course, is how to decrease it.

ANNOTATION

A reader brought my attention to a wonderful YouTube video by Taylor Mali titled "Like, You Know" that takes on upspeak, and other conversational maladies, much better than I have done in this reflection. See http://www.youtube.com/watch?v=SCNIBV87wV4.

86

Joy in the Misfortune of Others

Sports and Beyond

The comfort derived from the misery of others is slight.
—Cicero

The German word *Schadenfreude* means joy in the misfortune of others. Most of us experience such pleasure some of the time, and some of us most of the time. Schadenfreude is an evil relative of the sorts of topics positive psychologists usually study (see reflection 1). How close or distant a relative, I don't know, but I invite you to consider the issue.

I thought of Schadenfreude during the past week, ever since the news broke that The Ohio State University football coach Jim Tressel resigned amid escalating accusations of wrongdoing by his players. I do not know what really happened—what the players did, what the coach knew, and when he knew it—but regardless, as a sports fan, even one of the University of Michigan football team, I felt sad because these events diminished a game that I enjoy.

I am not saying that those who break the rules should go unpunished, only that punishment, no matter how much it may be deserved, is not an occasion for joy. However, I have been wondering if I am alone in Maize-and-Blue Nation. To and from work (at the University of Michigan), I often listen to a local AM sports station that features talk. Those who call in are usually Michigan fans, and for the past week, callers have been positively giddy with delight over the misfortunes of the Buckeyes and their coach. If their joy were the result of the reasonable expectation that Michigan would benefit down the road from Ohio State's likely loss of football scholarships and exclusion from bowl games, not to mention the resignation of a very good if tarnished coach, I would be more understanding. Those thoughts crossed my partisan mind. But what I have been hearing from most callers is ungrounded joy, simple and hardly pure.

What's going on? Positive psychology holds that the positive is genuine. I guess the unstated corollary is that the negative is also genuine, in this case hatred compounded by over-the-top righteous outrage.* There are truly bad things in the world (pestilence, poverty, prejudice) that deserve to be hated. Their demise may be a morally legitimate cause for joy. But here we are talking about football teams, for goodness sakes. Former coach Tressel's record against Michigan over the past decade was 9–1. Is that a reason to hate him and thus celebrate his fall?

I am a lifelong Cubs fan, but I have never rooted against the White Sox, or the Cardinals, or the Mets, or the Phillies, or the Padres, and so on—a long list could be imagined! I just want my team to do well. Period. Ditto for how I feel about the Michigan football team.

Positive psychology often studies happiness—joy in the extreme case. But happiness about what? Typical survey measures ask only if respondents are satisfied/happy/joyful. I suggest that an authentic positive psychology would take the additional step and ask *why* someone is happy. If the source of happiness is the misfortune of others—like rival political parties and nations, for example, or celebrities, or people at home and work who annoy us—I doubt that this sort of happiness is really what makes life worth living. Why define yourself by what you hate? Does anyone want the epitaph on his tombstone to read "He hated!"?

---

* *Sports Illustrated* writer Steve Rushin made a great comment on the Ohio State and other sports scandals: "Anyone who feels real moral outrage when reading the Sports section has almost certainly skipped the News...section."

87

Bucket Lists and Positive Psychology

Most men lead lives of quiet desperation and go to the grave with the song still in them.

— Henry David Thoreau

I recently spoke with a writer about bucket lists. I had not previously thought much about the phrase, which apparently entered popular use in the wake of the 2007 movie by that name. I'm not wild about the phrase, which has achieved clichéd status, although I understand and can appreciate what it is trying to capture and convey.

A bucket list enumerates things one wants to do before one dies (kicks the bucket). I did a Google search for "my bucket list." The 2.5 million hits, some tiny number of which I read, provide some insight into what many people want to do in order to highlight their lives: travel and see the wonders of the world; have an adventure like white-water rafting; learn a foreign language; meet a celebrity; become rich; or accomplish something really demanding such as running a marathon.

Here are some of my thoughts about bucket lists from the perspective of a positive psychologist.

A bucket list is an attempt to make life memorable and is consistent with Daniel Kahneman's (1999) peak-end theory, which holds that what people remember from hedonic events are their peaks (see reflection 17). No peaks—no memories, or at least not very crisp ones. Whether *life* is an event is an issue to which I will return, but certainly bucket lists, if accomplished, set memories in place that structure life as remembered.

A bucket list can also be an attempt to make life meaningful, depending of course on the specific items. Many of the bucket lists I read contained items that struck me as narcissistic (e.g., get a tattoo), but some did not. These lists contained items that would connect people to something larger than themselves, typically other people and their welfare (e.g., take the entire family on a cruise). Positive psychology research suggests that the latter items are more important for a fulfilled life.

Regardless of their details, bucket lists embody what psychologists have learned about goal-setting. Goals can motivate us to accomplish things, but the most motivating goals are those that are hard and specific. Every bucket list I read on the Internet contained rich details about difficult things. Goals need to be coupled with plans for achieving them, but the right sorts of goals are the critical first step (see reflection 99).

For me, a downside of the phrase bucket list is that it implies a "check off the boxes" approach to life. I hate it when my college students choose courses only to satisfy requirements, and by extrapolation, I hate it when someone approaches life in the same way, even if the requirements are self-set. Here I am probably not being fair to many who create bucket lists. They are likely not saying that only the things on their list matter. I just hear it that way. My apologies.

But I won't apologize for my reaction to people who speak endlessly about single events in their lives, bucket-listed or not (see reflection 36). I get bored, not immediately but eventually. I enjoy hearing about the adventures and accomplishments of people, but I want a dialogue and not a monologue. I want to be convinced that items on someone's bucket list are more than "look-at-how-cool-I-am" badges.

A hypothetical question: How many items on a typical bucket list would be deleted if he or she were not allowed to talk about them to others?

A likely answer: Many of them.

And sometimes we do not know what is worth doing until we actually do it and reflect upon it. A sole focus on a bucket list might lead us to overlook other activities that would be memorable or significant, perhaps more so than what we would have thought years or even decades earlier.

Remember George Bailey in the 1946 film *It's a Wonderful Life*, who never achieved anything on his own bucket list (school, travel), but did—when given the opportunity to reflect—conclude that he had lived a worthwhile life. He never let his own wishes get in the way of other people, and that's why we still cherish this film 60+ years later.

In any event, a bucket list is not about dying but about living, and my chief objection to the phrase is simply that it is misleading. I do not think that most people create such lists with their imminent death in mind. Consider this stringent criterion: If you knew with certainty that you would die tomorrow, what would you do today? Would you really choose to spend your last day getting a tattoo?

So, I like the spirit of a bucket list if not the exact phrase. I like exhilarating memories but not to the exclusion of meaningful experiences. And I like lofty goals if they do not obscure the rest of what matters.

REFERENCE

Kahneman, D. (1999). Objective happiness. In D. Kahneman, E. Diener, & N. Schwarz (Eds.), *Well-being: The foundations of hedonic psychology* (pp. 3–25). New York: Russell Sage.

Part XI

Pursuing the Good Life

If you have read the reflections here in more or less the order they appear, I hope you have come away with the sense that the psychological good life is not only worth having but worth pursuing. Is that possible? The answer is *yes*, and the reflections in this final section provide some practical tips informed by the evidence about how to achieve and sustain a worthy life.

88

Days Are Long—Life Is Short

I have spent my days stringing and unstringing my instrument, while the song
I came to sing remains unsung.
—Rabindranath Tagore

I hope that no one thinks that a writer of reflections about the
good life (i.e., me) has it all together. Competitive soul that I
am, I bet I could trounce most of you who read what I write on
formal measures of neuroticism and rumination. As a writer, I
try to convey a public persona of being somewhat evolved and
somewhat wise. Believe me, it ain't so.

As much as anyone and maybe more than most, I get mired
down in the minutiae and hassles of everyday life. I fret about
the ever-growing number of e-mail messages that inhabit my
in-box (see reflection 80). I worry that people may not like me,
even and especially people I don't like myself. I putter way too
much, sometimes spending as much time formatting a scholarly paper as I do researching and writing it. I fill up many of
my days doing small things that do not matter. I know it, but
sometimes I can't help myself.

A common inside joke among research psychologists is that
we study those topics that we simply do not get. In some cases,
this is obvious. Myopic psychologists seem more likely to study
vision than their 20–20 colleagues. Out-of-shape psychologists
seem more likely to study physical fitness, and unmarried psychologists seem more likely to study marriage.

Following this line of reasoning, are positive psychologists less than positive? Sometimes yes, sometimes no. I could characterize the major players in positive psychology as walking the walk versus talking the talk, but they are my friends and my colleagues, happy or not, and I will respect their privacy. It's probably enough that I have just outed myself as needing further work.

Indeed, gossip is not my point. Rather, my point is to discuss an enemy of the good life, one that is my particular demon but also one that may plague others: getting mired down in the unpleasant details and demands of everyday life.

Sometimes people are urged to live in the moment. I think this advice needs to be qualified by understanding what the moment entails. To paraphrase Albert Ellis, if the moment in which we live is draped in *ought*s and *should*s, it is probably better not to live in it.

Everyday life of course poses demands, and I am not saying that we should ignore those we do not like. I am simply saying—to myself, if no one else—to keep the bigger picture in mind. Things not worth doing are not worth doing obsessively.

There must be an ancient Buddhist aphorism that makes my point profoundly, but I'll just say it bluntly, in plain 21st-century Americanese: Don't sweat the small stuff; and most of it is small stuff.

Days are long. Life is short. Live it well.

89

I Resolve to Take Benjamin Franklin Seriously

Net worth to the world is usually determined by what remains after your bad habits are subtracted from your good ones.
—Benjamin Franklin

I am writing this reflection on the last day of the year. Have you made any New Year's resolutions? I just read an article on the most typical resolutions made by adults in the United States, and I was struck by how many of them embody the strengths of character that have been the subject of my research: spending more time with friends and family (love), saying no to cigarettes and alcohol (self-regulation), getting organized (prudence), learning something new (love of learning), helping others (kindness), getting fit and losing weight (perseverance), and so on. Another common resolution is climbing out of debt, which in today's world probably requires creativity coupled with good judgment.

If you want to make your resolutions happen, I suggest one more: taking Benjamin Franklin seriously.

Benjamin Franklin (1706–1790) is of course widely acclaimed as a statesman and scientist, but he may also deserve credit as America's first positive psychologist. Not only did he enumerate 13 praiseworthy character strengths (virtues), but he also took on the challenge of cultivating each of them, using himself as a research subject (Franklin, 1791/1962).

Franklin characterized each of the virtues of interest to him in terms of what he called their *precepts*. In modern psychological language, these precepts were behavioral markers of the virtue in question. For example, the precepts for *industry* were "lose no time; be always employ'd in something useful; cut off all unnecessary actions" and for *temperance* were "eat not to dullness; drink not to elevation" (p. 67).

From my perspective, too many of Franklin's precepts are phrased in terms of what a person should *not* do, reflecting his concern with what contemporary virtue ethicists call *corrective virtues*, those that protect against human inclinations to act in bad ways. But good character is not simply the absence of bad character. Just because people refrain from mean-spirited actions does not make them kind, any more than being free from anxiety or depression necessarily makes people happy.

Nonetheless, the value of his precepts is that they are behavioral, observable, and countable. The goals they represent are hard and specific, which modern psychologists know are more effective in motivating change than the vague "do your best" (DYB) goals that many of us have.

Franklin's own program of character cultivation was prescient. He recognized that exhortation would not suffice to change anyone, including himself, which is a point still not fully grasped by some proponents of today's character education. Merely hanging a character-relevant poster on a classroom wall (or for that matter, the Ten Commandments) will not lead to change.

I spent my elementary school years staring daily at the periodic table of elements, and that did not make me into a chemist or even into a passable student of chemistry. What is needed is a concrete strategy of changing behavior. Franklin believed, as do I, that most people want to be good and decent. The problem is that we may not know how to do it. One does not tell a depressed patient simply to cheer up or a person prone to procrastination to just do it. If they knew how to be cheerful or how to get things done, then they would do so. What is more helpful is to tell them *how* to do these things. The same point applies to the cultivation of strengths of character.

Franklin also recognized that it would be too daunting to attempt to strengthen all virtues at the same time, so he prioritized them and tackled them in order. He further observed that the strengthening of one virtue might help with the subsequent cultivation of other virtues. For example, Franklin reasoned that the virtue of moderation should facilitate the virtue of silence, given that the latter requires the skills involved in the former.

Anticipating the modern behavior change strategy of "objectively" monitoring progress, Franklin made a book, with one page for each of the virtues he wished to strengthen. He organized each page by the day of the week. At the end of each day, he would think back over his actions and make "a black mark" if he had failed in following the precept. Again, I gently criticize Franklin for emphasizing his transgressions rather than his positive accomplishments, but that followed from the way he defined the precepts for each virtue.

He resolved to address one virtue per week, in the order he had prioritized, so that in 13 weeks he would have addressed all of them in succession. Then he would do it again, and in a year he would have completed four courses. Again, this is very modern, because Franklin anticipated the need for the maintenance of change.

His goal was to have a clean book, and to help him along the way, he included in his log relevant maxims and prayers, much as people today use Post-Its on their refrigerator to keep their goals front and center. For example, my own refrigerator door has a Post-It asking "Are you really that hungry?"

Franklin judged his program a success, in that he accorded himself fewer black marks as time passed. Still, some virtues were harder for him to strengthen than others. In particular, the strength of order gave him great trouble, as he was wont to scatter about his things and could typically rely on his good memory to know where things were amidst chaos. (Does this sound familiar to any of you readers?) In any event, he decided he was incorrigible with respect to this virtue and decided to accept the fault as part of who he was. From a positive psychology perspective, this is okay. No one can have it all, although to Franklin's credit, he tried to change before he accepted the less than desirable conclusion.

Franklin did fret that his "success" with respect to some of the virtues reflected changes in the appearance of the character strength rather than in its reality, but from my vantage point, this is a difficult distinction to maintain if we regard character strengths as habits. "Fake it until you can make it" is one of the slogans of Alcoholics Anonymous, and it means that if we behave in a sober way, no matter how deliberate or stilted our initial attempts, then eventually we will be sober. We are what we do.

Appreciate that Franklin did all of this when he was 79 years of age!

REFERENCE

Franklin, B. (1962). *The autobiography of Benjamin Franklin*. New York: Touchstone. (Originally published 1791)

90

How to Smile

Every time you smile at someone, it is an action of love, a gift to that person, a beautiful thing.

—Mother Teresa

The world is an interesting place, and the Internet provides constant reminders of just how interesting it is. Yesterday a friend alerted me to an Internet story—I assume it is true—about a Japanese train company that is using high-tech scanning to make sure its employees smile properly (Snowdon, 2009).

Smiling is pleasant—to do and to see—and a smiling employee is accordingly likely to provide a more pleasant experience for customers. We all have had the misfortune of dealing with disgruntled employees whose goal is apparently to make us as miserable as they are, never mind that we are trying to pay for whatever they are providing, whether it be lunch, postage stamps, or a new driver's license. So I applaud the attempt to make the folks we deal with more pleasing.

According to the story, each morning the 500 employees of the Keihin Electric Express Railway Company smile into a camera hooked up to a computer. Analyzed are facial features such as lip curvature and facial wrinkles. Spit back at each employee is an overall rating of his or her smile quality, from 0 to 100. If the smile quality is insufficient, the computer provides feedback— for example, "Lift up your mouth corners." The computer also prints out an ideal smile to which employees can refer throughout the day.

The details of how this is all done were not mentioned in the story, but I did some poking around and found that a Japanese company, Omron, has sold several hundred devices called a Smile-Scan to those in the Japanese service industry. Each has a price tag of $7,300 (Toto, 2011). I assume this is the device used by the Keihin Electric Express Company. The Smile-Scan scans a person's face and creates a three-dimensional model. Critical features of the model are then analyzed and quantified to gauge the intensity of the person's smile.

The Omron device even allows two persons to be scanned at the same time, and there is a "battle mode" in which these two people can determine who has a better smile per the algorithm!

One reaction to the Smile-Scan is that it is helping people be phony, and I have previously decried forced cheerfulness (see reflection 76). But maybe branding this strategy phony is too harsh. One of the well-known sayings of Alcoholics Anonymous is "Fake it until you can make it," which means to act how you want to be, even if it is awkward and deliberate in the beginning—eventually, you become how you act (see reflection 89). Maybe if we learn how to smile by heeding computer-provided feedback, we someday will smile as a matter of course.

That said, whether use of the Smile-Scan actually leads to more and better smiles was not mentioned in the story I read, and the long-term effects for service, sales, and customer satisfaction are likely unknown at present.

As a positive psychologist, I believe that most people want to be happy and also to make others happy. The world is less happy than it might be because many of us do not know how to accomplish these goals. Feedback about the quality of our smiles is a start. I doubt that intensity is the only smile parameter that matters, but regardless, if we want to change any habit—good or bad—we need to assess what we are doing with respect to the habit. Indeed, ongoing feedback is critical.

This reflection is not really about smiling, although I hope it made you smile a bit. It is about the importance of concrete advice about how to be more positive to others and the importance of feedback along the way. Whether Smile-Scans will increase the gross amount of happiness in the world is doubtful, but the general premise has promise.

REFERENCES

Snowdon, G. (2009). Get happy!! Japanese workers face smile scanner. *The Guardian*. Retrieved from http://www.guardian.co.uk/money/blog/2009/jul/07/japanese-smile-scanning/.

Toto, S. (2011). Omron updates its Smile-O-Meter. *TechCrunch*. Retrieved from http://techcrunch.com/2011/01/28/smile-scan-omron-updates-its-smile-o-meter/.

91

How to Talk

Make sure you have finished speaking before your audience has finished listening.

—Dorothy Sarnoff

I talk for a living, and I live well. But I don't like how I sound when on occasion I listen to a recording of one of my lectures. Too many pauses and hesitations. Too many corrections and asides. Worse, I usually speak in a monotone, which seems okay when I am trying to deliver a deadpan joke but not otherwise. At least that's how I hear me.

Although I love to talk, I try to avoid hearing my own voice because I sound like an inarticulate Ben Stein. Ugh. I bet many of you have had the same reaction when you hear a recording of your own voice, and maybe you have rerecorded the message on your telephone answering machine countless times because it just didn't sound right to you.

A study described on the University of Michigan website caught my attention because it investigated parameters of how people speak and their persuasive consequences (University of Michigan News Service, 2011). The researchers work at the university's Institute for Social Research (ISR), one of the world's leading centers of survey research. Over the years, ISR social scientists have polled people about their opinions and beliefs via the telephone, and their results are reported frequently in the media.

ISR researchers also study the social psychology of surveys. It is important to know what to do to ensure sincere answers from respondents and more basically what to do to encourage people to consent to a telephone interview in the first place and then to stay with it. Here we have "objective" indicators of how persuasive someone is, and the fact that those doing telephone interviews work from a script—in other words, the content is essentially identical—means that how a person sounds as opposed to what he or she is saying can be studied in its own right.

The researchers, headed by speech scientist Jose Benki, analyzed recordings of 1,380 introductory calls made by 100 male and female telephone interviewers at ISR. They calculated the rate, pitch, and fluency of the calls, and then correlated these scores with whether the potential survey respondent actually agreed to participate.

The results were interesting, and I learned something from them. Some were as I expected, others not.

Really fast talkers were relatively unsuccessful, I guess because they were experienced as fast talkers. Also unsuccessful were really slow talkers, maybe because they were seen as stupid or stilted. So, the middle path—in terms of speech rate—is indicated if one wishes to be persuasive.

Males with a lower pitched voice were more persuasive than those with a higher pitched voice. Perhaps pitch signals age or maturity. Pitch made no difference for females making the initial telephone calls. Interestingly, variation in pitch—which might make a person sound more animated—had little effect on the persuasiveness of speech by males or females. At least for me, a monotone is probably fine, at least if it is not high-pitched.

What about fluency, gauged by pauses in what one says? These findings made me, um, smile. It turns out that pausing—whether empty or filled—is more persuasive than not pausing, apparently because normal (that is, spontaneous) speech entails four or five pauses per minute, and the person who never pauses sounds phony. Fluency is overrated, which I did not know.

This research makes me think of phone calls I am now receiving, with annoying regularity, after I innocently participated some months ago in a brief telephone survey about my "investment" beliefs and attitudes. Apparently, my phone number and whatever information I provided were sold to dozens of investment companies, whose representatives now call me day and night. I doubt I would ever commit thousands of dollars to a stranger over the phone, but I certainly won't do it with any of the folks who have been calling me. They talk too fast. They are too animated and too ready to laugh at my jokes, including the ones I am not making. They are too glib and too rehearsed. And they won't take no for an answer. I actually hung up on someone last week, which I have never before done in my entire life, some years of which have been spent on the telephone.

I have previously written about the importance of feedback if we want to cultivate more pleasing habits, like smiling (see reflection 90). The same point applies about talking in more persuasive ways. And in the case of talking, maybe feedback per se is not enough. We need as well to have a way to make sense of the feedback, and the research results I have described might prove useful: Speak at a moderate pace, sound mature, and pause in natural ways. You can listen to a recording of your own voice with these guidelines in mind, but it might also be useful to have your friends tell you how you sound to them.

Talk is not all about persuasion, of course, but I think these results can be generalized beyond conversations in which you are trying to talk someone into something. When we talk, we want people to listen, whether or not we are trying to persuade, and how we talk influences whether people listen.

REFERENCE

University of Michigan News Service. (2011). *Persuasive speech: The way we, um, talk sways our listeners.* Retrieved from http://ns.umich.edu/new/releases/8404.

92

Finding the Right Bank to Rob

According to an urban legend, 1920s bank robber Willie Sutton was once asked, "Why do you rob banks?" His supposed answer: "Because that's where the money is." In the wake of the world financial crisis, perhaps that's no longer a good answer, but this reflection is not about literal banks. I hope that the title caught your attention and that you'll read my thoughts about metaphorical banks and the good life.

I would like to recommend three very good and interesting books: *Word Hard. Be Nice* (Mathews, 2009), which describes how two young teachers, David Levin and Mike Feinberg, created the KIPP schools; *Mountains Beyond Mountains* (Kidder, 2003), which recounts the story of Paul Farmer's quest to cure the world of infectious diseases; and *Three Cups of Tea* (Mortenson & Relin, 2006), which is the story of mountain climber Greg Mortenson and his peaceful "war" on terror by building schools for girls in Afghanistan and Pakistan.

Beyond being inspiring yet nonsaccharine accounts of remarkable individuals, these books teach a number of lessons consistent with positive psychology, and I will stress one of them here: the importance of finding something to do with one's life that is highly engaging *and* provides meaning and purpose.

Where's the metaphorical money that matters most to you, and how can you get it?

I won't presume to tell you the currency of your realm, but I hope that you have at least considered the matter for yourself. And once you have identified what matters, the stories of David Levin, Mike Feinberg, Paul Farmer, and Greg Mortenson provide excellent advice about how to get it. Hard work and perseverance are essential, as is the advice and counsel of others. And you also need to acquire whatever skills and resources are necessary to make withdrawals. Willie Sutton always carried a weapon into the banks he robbed because "You can't rob a bank on charm and personality." Again, appreciate the metaphorical lesson, not the literal one.

I have found my bank at the University of Michigan, and my work as a college professor is engaging and meaningful, once I sought out the advice of wise colleagues and figured out how to do it. By the way, my work is not always or even frequently fun, but that's okay. For fun, there's always chocolate ice cream.

I close with one more quote attributed to Willie Sutton: "Go where the money is...and go there often."

ANNOTATION

As you may know, a *60 Minutes* story on Greg Mortenson, which aired April 17, 2011, called into question some of the facts in his book as well as how his charitable organization spends funds. This exposé is an all-too-familiar example of a well-known person being brought down to earth for his apparent shortcomings. I do not know the facts of the matter, but the title of this reflection—"Finding the Right Bank to Rob"—has become unintentionally ironic. My metaphorical point remains, if not the literal example. Sigh.

REFERENCES

Kidder, T. (2003). *Mountains beyond mountains.* New York: Random House.

Mathews, J. (2009). *Work hard. Be nice.* Chapel Hill, NC: Algonquin Books.

Mortenson, G., & Relin, D. O. (2006). *Three cups of tea.* New York: Viking Penguin.

93

Ikigai and Mortality

"Only the good die young." While this may have been true in the adolescent fantasies of Billy Joel, it does not square with the results of a 2008 study by Toshimasa Sone and colleagues at Tohoku University Graduate School of Medicine in Sendai, Japan. In a 7-year longitudinal investigation of 43,000+ Japanese adults, these researchers found that individuals who believed that their life was worth living were less likely to die than were their counterparts without this belief.

On focus in this study was the Japanese notion of *ikigai*, translated by the researchers as believing that one's life is worth living. In Japan, *ikigai* is apparently a common term for what English speakers might term subjective well-being, and it includes purpose and meaning, with connotations of joy about being alive. So, one's hobby might provide *ikigai*, or one's family, or one's work. To my thoroughly monolingual ear, *ikigai* sounds like it is created by what positive psychologists call a healthy passion (Vallerand, 2008; see reflection 15).

The notion of *ikigai* is a good reminder to positive psychologists in the United States that our science should not simply be an export business. There are lessons to be learned in all cultures about what makes life worth living, and no language has a monopoly on the vocabulary for describing the good life.

In any event, the study began in late 1994 with a survey of tens of thousands of Japanese adults between the ages of 40 and 79. Among many questions posed to respondents was one about *ikigai*: "Do you have *ikigai* in your life?" Possible answers were *yes*, *uncertain*, and *no*. The vast majority of respondents were followed for the next 7 years. About 7% died during this time, and the cause of death for these individuals was determined by reviewing and coding death certificates.

The researchers took into account such well-known risk factors for mortality as age, gender, education, body mass index, cigarette use, alcohol consumption, exercise, employment, perceived stress, and history of disease. Also controlled was the respondent's self-rated health (bad, fair, good), itself a predictor of subsequent physical well-being (Levy, Slade, Kunkel, & Kasl, 2002).

Almost 60% of the research participants reported a sense of *ikigai* in 1994, and those who did were more likely to be married, educated, and employed. They reported lower levels of stress and better self-rated health.

Even when likely confounds were taken into account, *ikigai* predicted who was still alive after 7 years. Said another way, 95% of respondents who reported a sense of meaning in their lives were alive 7 years after the initial survey versus about 83% of those who reported no sense of meaning in their lives. The lack of *ikigai* was in particular associated with death due to cardiovascular disease (usually stroke), but not death due to cancer. This latter finding is interesting because cancer has long been regarded, at least in the Western world, as a disease of despair (cf. Hippocrates).

The exact mechanisms—biological, psychological, or social—linking *ikigai* to mortality are at present unknown, but these results are worth taking seriously. *Ikigai* does not guarantee longevity, and its absence does not preclude it. Nonetheless, the findings reported by Sone and colleagues (2008) are not just statistically significant; they are also substantively significant.

This study adds to a growing literature showing that the sorts of psychological states and traits of interest to positive psychology are importantly linked to good physical health and long life (e.g., Peterson & Bossio, 1991). A crucial next step for researchers is to understand why and how.

Meaning and purpose in life are unalloyed goods and would seem to require little justification. But just in case a rationale for the life of meaning is needed, the results of this study provide it.

As of this writing, Billy Joel is about 60 years old, and I hope he is well. He once proclaimed that his crowd wasn't too pretty and that it wasn't too proud. But I hope he and his crowd have ample *ikigai*, because only those without it die young ($p < .001$).

REFERENCES

Levy, B. R., Slade, M. D., Kunkel, S. R., & Kasl, S. V. (2002). Longevity increased by positive self-perceptions of aging. *Journal of Personality and Social Psychology, 83*, 261–270.

Peterson, C., & Bossio, L. M. (1991). *Health and optimism*. New York: Free Press.

Sone, T., Nakaya, N., Ohmori, K., Shimazu, T., Higashiguchi, M., Kakizaki, M., Kikuchi, N., Kuriyama, S., & Tsuji, I. (2008). Sense of life worth living (*ikigai*) and mortality in Japan: Ohsaki Study. *Psychosomatic Medicine, 70*, 709–715.

Vallerand, R. J. (2008). On the psychology of passion: In search of what makes people's lives most worth living. *Canadian Psychology, 49*, 1–13.

94

University of Michigan Squirrels

Were I to believe in reincarnation, I would hope to do my next cycle as a squirrel on the main campus of the University of Michigan, Ann Arbor. In terms of quality of life, this would be a step up for me, no doubt, so I better get busy accruing good deeds, just in case dreams really do come true.

Most Michigan squirrels are fat, fluffy, and more than a little feisty. The main campus is bordered by streets but otherwise has no automobile traffic. Trees abound—that is after all why we call it Ann *Arbor*. For reasons that might deserve discussion in another reflection, dogs do not run free on campus. What's not to like from a squirrel's point of view? No bothersome calculus or chemistry exams, no tenure worries, no concerns about the W-L record against other Big Ten teams.

Couple all of this with the tens of thousands of students who walk around campus every day with backpacks loaded with treats that they love to share with the squirrels. A frequent sight on campus is a squirrel eating out of the hand of a student. This may not be the most prudent thing for a student to do, but I have never seen a squirrel chomp down on anyone's fingers. "Don't bite the hand that feeds you" is advice apparently heeded better by Michigan squirrels than by many human beings.

The squirrels expect to be fed, and they have taught Michigan students how to feed them. Not all learning here takes place in classrooms, and Michigan students if nothing else learn their lessons well.

A story in our student newspaper featured the squirrels and inspired me to write this reflection (Menaldi, 2010). I learned that the university has a Squirrel Club with 800+ human members. Whether fans of the chipmunks and groundhogs on campus are allowed to join the Squirrel Club is not clear, although I hope so.

One of my biology colleagues was quoted in the story. He may have been guilty of anthropomorphizing, but he observed that the squirrels act annoyed when they are not fed! He further said that the University of Michigan squirrels are unusual. Not only are they unafraid of people, they also survive the winter well and have two full breeding seasons a year. His punch line: "[Interacting with humans]...doesn't have any detrimental effects on their well-being."

I love it...squirrels described in terms of their well-being! Positive psychology language is taking over the world.

So what's the good life point for those of you who are not squirrels or do not believe in reincarnation? Simply that the Michigan squirrels have figured out what their setting affords, and they have made the most of it by being pleasing. We all should be so savvy.

REFERENCE

Menaldi, V. (2010, November 22). Ann Arbor's pets: Why campus is nuts for squirrels. *The Michigan Daily*. Retrieved from http://www.michigandaily.com/content/ann-arbors-pets.

95

A But-Free Day

According to research by psychologists Shelly Gable, Harry Reis, and colleagues (2004), the way couples respond to each other's good news influences the happiness and stability of their relationships, perhaps more so than how they respond to bad news. This finding is important because so much of couples counseling focuses on resolving conflicts, fighting fairly, and being assertive.

In particular, *active-constructive responding* is beneficial. When someone comes home with what he or she regards as good news, how does the other person respond upon hearing it? Active-constructive responding is enthusiastic and engaged.

"Honey, I got a promotion at work."

"That's great. You deserve it. Tell me all about it. What did your boss say? I want to know all the details."

There are of course other responses, passive and/or destructive.

"That's nice, dear. What do you want for dinner?"

"Does that mean I'll be seeing even less of you?"

"It's about time. You've been there forever."

"I thought promotions were automatic."

"That's terrible. You know how poorly you handle change."

The recommendation follows that people in relationships should use more active-constructive responding. Sounds simple, but proves difficult. I know this because over the years, I have asked students in my classes to try active-constructive responding for a week, not just with their romantic partners but with people in general.

Mind you, some common sense is needed. If your wife tells you she is really happy because she decided to end your marriage and run off with the cabana boy, an active-constructive response on your part is not indicated. But regardless, my students tell me active-constructive responding is difficult.

One of the barriers to active-constructive responding is sincere. We do not want our loved ones to get their hopes up only to be disappointed, to get big heads, or to somehow get in trouble. For example, when I told my friends that I was going to visit Mexico City and give a talk, I was regaled with warnings about kidnapping, disease, weather, traffic, and language problems (*"no hablo español"*). All of these worries were legitimate, I suppose, but they could have been voiced a bit later, after an initial active-constructive response.

Given the difficulty in active-constructive responding, at least for those of us who lack the style in our repertoire, I devised a simpler intervention that can be described as active-constructive light. When someone relates good news, respond without using the word *but*. The generalized version of this intervention is to go through an entire day without using the word *but* or any of its close cousins like *however*, *whereas*, *yet*, *then again*, and *on the other hand*. I call this a *but-free day*, which sounds like an exercise video. Rather than toning up your rear end, this exercise should tone up your relationships.

You skeptics reading this may already be mouthing the word *but*, to which I say, "Get a life...a good life."

REFERENCE

Gable, S. L., Reis, H. T., Impett, E. A., & Asher, E. R. (2004). What do you do when things go right? The intrapersonal and interpersonal benefits of sharing positive events. *Journal of Personality and Social Psychology, 87*, 228–245.

96

Getting Lost in Buildings
...and Life

I love it when research psychologists study real people in real settings doing real things, as opposed to proxy "variables" among proxy research participants (e.g., college students pretending to be someone else) and how these are related to other proxy "variables." Mind you, I have had a solid research career doing the proxy thing, which makes me appreciate the non-proxy thing even more.

A great article was written by Laura Carlson, Christoph Hölscher, Thomas Shipley, and Ruth Dalton (2010) that exemplifies the approach I admire. The title of the article was "Getting Lost in Buildings," and after seeing the title in the journal table of contents, I instantly turned to it and read it straight through in one sitting. Why? Because I get lost in buildings myself.

I have been teaching in East Hall at the University of Michigan for a decade. My office is also in this building, as are 95% of the meetings I attend. But when I am inside East Hall, especially its windowless classrooms, I have no idea where I am in relationship to the outside world. In a lecture, I will refer to Ypsilanti or Detroit, and then wave my hand in the direction where I believe these cities to be located. Many students snicker, and tell me I am pointing toward Marquette, or Lansing, or

Jackson, or—horrors—Columbus, Ohio, home of The Ohio State University.

When in East Hall, I also have no ideas where I am in relationship to other rooms and areas of the building. Sometimes students will stick their head in my office and ask where Room So-and-So happens to be. I invariably take them out in the hallway and help them consult a nearby map—the location of which I do know. I am thanked profusely, as if I were a helpful person. But the fact of the matter is that I have no idea where Room So-and-So might be, so I must consult the map. Helpfulness has little to do with it, just the desire not to appear foolish. But even that secret motive is sometimes frustrated. Just the other day, I helped a student consult the map to find a room that happens to share a common wall with my own office!

Anyway, I read the article by Carlson and colleagues with obvious interest. Summarized were studies showing that getting lost in buildings has several determinants. First, some buildings have a spatial structure that makes them difficult to navigate. Parts of the building may be visually hidden from other parts. Unique features may be minimized. Or the building may be laid out in an overly complex way, apparently common for aesthetically attractive buildings. East Hall has all of these features, although I am dubious about its attractiveness.

A second determinant of getting lost in a building is the cognitive map one forms of it. If the map does not correspond to the actual building, then problems will obviously ensue. I grew up near Chicago, which has numbered streets and a really big lake to the east. The cognitive map I have of Chicago readily fits the actual city. So maybe I got lazy. Or for an even better example, think Lincoln, Nebraska, a checkerboard of streets if ever there were one. It is impossible to get lost in Lincoln, because the cognitive map is so easy to form.

A third contributor to getting lost is the strategy one uses to navigate a place. Two strategies are common: a route-based strategy (remembering the specific path one follows) and a reasoning-based strategy that entails an overall representation in one's mind of the building that allows inferences about one's location. Apparently people differ in terms of how many right turns and left turns they can remember before getting overwhelmed, as well as in terms of their ability to represent the big picture of the building. Oops. I lack both of these abilities, which explains why I get lost not only in East Hall but also in Ann Arbor's only large shopping mall as well as on the streets of the town where I have lived for 25 years.

If you have stayed with me throughout this reflection without getting lost, I hope you see that it is a head fake. I don't care all that much about getting lost in a building (unless I am late to a meeting). This essay can and should be read as a metaphor for life that provides insights about losing our metaphorical way, which most of us do some of the time, and some of us do most of the time. Unhappiness ensues. How can we find ourselves and give ourselves a fighting chance for the good life?

Three strategies follow from the article on getting lost in buildings. First, lead a life that is simple as opposed to complex. Simple lives are easier to navigate. The critic might say that a simple life is boring. I beg to differ, at least when a complex life leaves one lost.

Second, regardless of the simplicity or complexity of your chosen life, have a realistic—in other words, accurate—depiction of it that you can wrap your head around. Understand the rules and the contingencies. This does not mean you have to like them, but you are well served by understanding them. A definition of *insanity* that I frequently quote is "doing the same thing over and over and expecting a different result." So, insanity results from a bad map of life. And fulfillment results from a good map.

Third, find a useful strategy for navigating life. It can be route-based or reasoning-based or most likely a combination. But make sure it is useful. And how can you tell? Pay attention to how satisfied you are with where you think you happen to be.

Too bad AAA does not provide maps for life. But regardless, we can all stop and ask other people for directions when we are lost, even if we are guys.

REFERENCE

Carlson, L. A., Hölscher, C., Shipley, T. F., & Dalton, R. C. (2010). Getting lost in buildings. *Current Directions in Psychological Science, 19*, 284–289.

97

Giving Thanks by Mental Subtraction

We often take for granted the very things that most deserve our gratitude.
—Cynthia Ozick

When Thanksgiving approaches, the thoughts of many of us turn to our blessings. Although counting one's blessings is a proven way to bolster well-being, one study suggests a useful refinement of this strategy that may make it even more effective (Koo, Algoe, Wilson, & Gilbert, 2008). It may matter whether we think about the good things in our lives in terms of their *presence* (e.g., "I have a great job") or in terms of their *absence* (e.g., "Suppose I did not have this great job").

This strategy is called *mental subtraction*, and studies show that instructions to imagine the absence of a good event produce more positive emotions than does the simpler strategy of merely thinking about its presence.

Why does mental subtraction have beneficial effects? The researchers proposed that mental subtraction works against the human tendency to adapt to the good things in our lives and to take them for granted. In support of this explanation were further findings. Research participants who did mental subtraction rated the good event in question as more surprising than those who simply thought about the good event. "This wonderful thing—my job, my spouse, my good health—did not have to happen!"

Mental subtraction keeps the magic alive in ways that counting one's blessings may not. A positive psychology technique is suggested by generalizing this demonstration. Once a day, individuals can be asked to write down three things for which they are grateful. They should be reminded to consider good things that they ordinarily take for granted, like clean water or air conditioning, things that are regarded as comforts as opposed to pleasures—that is, usually notable only when they disappear. Then individuals can be asked to imagine that these good things were absent from their lives. How might this have happened? What would life be like in the absence of these good things?

Like all positive psychology techniques, mental subtraction will have a sustained effect on well-being only if it is practiced regularly and becomes part of one's repertoire. Whether one "adapts" to the benefits of mental subtraction is unknown pending relevant research, but it might be a good idea for individuals to vary the sorts of good events they mentally subtract from their lives.

Why not start this Thanksgiving?

REFERENCE

Koo, M., Algoe, S. B., Wilson, T. D., & Gilbert, D. T. (2008). It's a wonderful life: Mentally subtracting positive events improves people's affective states, contrary to their affective forecasts. *Journal of Personality and Social Psychology, 95*, 1217–1224.

What's in Your Closet?

I wore a vivid pink polo shirt today. I bought it several years ago but never donned it until this morning. The mood finally struck me—and oh yeah, I hadn't done laundry in a few weeks. The shirt aroused attention and commentary from friends and colleagues because I don't do pink.

The attention was nice, although I had to make more than my usual concerted effort to hold in my stomach because people were checking me out. The commentary was supportive—I think—and usually took the form of "That's quite a color for you!"

I usually do black or blue, sometimes dark green, and occasionally brown. But I don't do pink. That was why my shirt attracted notice today.

Why did I even buy a shirt that made me look a giant Pepto-Bismol tablet? I actually remember the sequence of events. I had seen a television show about singer Kanye West, who apparently likes pink polo shirts. Not many rap singers wear polo shirts, much less pink ones, but the show commentary said he was comfortable with his masculinity, so he wore such shirts.

By one of those coincidences that make life so wonderful, the day after I saw the television show, an LL Bean catalog arrived in my mail, and featured was a pink polo shirt. So I ordered it. Maybe I wanted to be comfortable with my masculinity. But as stated, I never wore it until today. However, I don't think reticence about my masculinity had much to do with my delay in wearing the shirt. As the Kinks once sang, "I know what I am, and I'm glad I'm a man"...a man who wears black and blue, green and brown.

Shame on me! I had a lot of fun today, and given that I had already purchased the shirt, it cost me nothing to have so much fun.

So what's in your closet that you don't wear? Put it on, walk among your friends, and have some fun. The feedback I got was positive, but even if you get negative feedback, accept it in the spirit of fun. Hideous is okay if you choose it.

There's a more general point here about the good life. We all wear clothes, assuming we are not members of a nudist colony. As much as anything else about us, our clothes convey to others how we want to be regarded. Soldiers and police are not the only ones who wear uniforms, so I urge you to consider your own uniform. Mine is a black and blue, green and brown one, rather somber and sober, conveying a "don't notice me" message.

What's wrong with conveying another image—one that says "I like to have fun, and I don't take myself all that seriously"?

What's in your closet?

99

The Good Life

Ends and Means

What makes life worth living? For those of us in Ann Arbor, the short list usually includes Zingerman's Delicatessen, a deliberately local business with the following motto: "Food that makes you happy, service that makes you smile." The food at Zingerman's is not cheap, but when Ann Arborites can afford it, and even when we cannot, we happily partake, not only savoring the food and enjoying the service but also remembering that Zingerman's provides health insurance and paid vacations for all employees, that it shares its profits among them, and that it does a lot of wonderful things for Ann Arbor, like sponsoring a farmer's market just off our downtown area.

I described Zingerman's as deliberately local, meaning that despite offers to franchise the brand and go national or global like the now defunct Border's Books (which also began in Ann Arbor), those who run Zingerman's have decided not to do so. They have decided to be great rather than gigantic (Burlingham, 2005).

That said, Zingerman's has grown locally by establishing in Ann Arbor a convoy of other businesses, like a sit-down restaurant featuring "American" food, a coffeehouse, a bakery, a creamery, and recently a candy factory (run by someone, and I kid you not, named Charley). Zingerman's has also established a training program that presents workshops on how to run a successful business.

I attended one of these workshops a few months ago, and I did so wearing my positive psychology hat. Those of us who are positive psychologists acknowledge "positive institutions" to be poorly understood, at least by us, so why not go to the source and learn something? If we want to understand how to do things well, it makes sense to study the excellent examples— individual people or institutions as the case may be.

And indeed I learned a great deal, and one lesson in particular has stuck with me. Obvious when stated explicitly, this lesson was never all that obvious until I heard it spelled out: Distinguish the ends from the means.

In Zingerman's parlance, the end is called one's *vision*, and the vision needs to be in place before the means to the end are considered, created, and enacted. The vision needs to be articulate and specific. And the action plan for realizing the vision needs to be realistic and vetted by those who know about the real world.

The distinction between ends and means is patently important. One need not attend a workshop or read this reflection to appreciate this in the abstract. But the devil is always in the details, and one of the important details is to separate thinking about ends from thinking about means.

For many of us, when we set our goals and figure out how to achieve them, the ends and the means get all jumbled together. This jumbling occurs not only for the biggest goals in our lives, like the college we attend, the person we marry, or the career we pursue, but also for our smaller goals, like looking presentable for the day ahead, having a fun weekend, or—to be very concrete—writing an entry for *Psychology Today* that creates hits but elicits no mean comments from readers (dream on, Chris).

As a research psychologist, my goal is to do studies that are important and interesting, that answer questions about weighty matters, and that suggest ways to enhance the psychological good life. This is a vision with which I am quite happy, although it is of course vague. When I start to flesh out the vision, the process too often gets mired down by my worries about the means. Pragmatic thoughts intrude. Where can I find research participants? How can I encourage them to participate? And most insidiously, where will I find the time to do all of this?

Mind you, questions like these eventually need to be answered, but trying to do so while I am establishing a specific vision about my research is handicapping. The resulting research plan is necessarily compromised, as is the research, as is my long-term satisfaction with my work.

I used to say with pride that one of my signature abilities was knowing how long it took me to do things, from preparing a lecture to washing my clothes to driving to the East Coast. Research suggests that most people most of the time woefully underestimate how long it takes to do even the things that they have done repeatedly. So, I have a useful skill. But after attending the Zingerman's workshop, I realized that this ability is simply a means skill and not an ends skill and that I inappropriately bring it to bear when thinking about my vision.

Do you remember that old—and cynical—definition of a cynic? Someone who knows the price of everything and the value of nothing. In my own life, I know how long it takes to do most anything, but I don't always know what's worth doing, simply because I have not thought enough about my vision.

Most of you readers are not research psychologists, but I hope that the points I am making apply to whatever matters most to you. First, figure out your vision in all of its glory. And only then consider how you might achieve it.

I am writing this reflection at the start of the New Year, 2010. Like many of you, I usually start the New Year with resolutions that I write down January 1. Usually my resolutions jumble together ends and means, and sometimes they are simply about means.

At this very moment, I'm looking up at my bulletin board, on which is tacked my resolutions for 2007. (Maybe I should resolve to clean my bulletin board on a yearly basis.) One of my resolutions was to write a book. I like writing, and I usually write effortlessly. I've written books before. So that seemed like a pretty good resolution.

But guess what? I didn't write a book (until now). How could I have done so? My resolution was about a means to an end, and the end was thoroughly unspecified.

My resolution for the next New Years is *not* to jot down "resolutions" off the top of my head on the first day of the year. It is to establish a vision, for my work and for my life, and maybe that will take the entire year or longer. That's okay.

In the meantime, I'm heading off to Zingerman's for a really good lunch with a friend.

REFERENCE

Burlingham, B. (2005). *Small giants: Companies that choose to be great instead of big*. New York: Penguin.

There Are No Bad Racks

If you're not into games, forget about Scrabble. But if you want a social game—no matter how bad you are, you're always good enough to play.
—Evan Cohen

This reflection is about Scrabble, where one's rack is the seven tiles in front of you that you want to play in a way to produce a high score and/or to prevent your opponent from doing the same and/or to set yourself up for future high-scoring plays and/or to prevent your opponent from doing the same.

This reflection is also about Scrabble as a metaphor for the good life, just in case you are not a dedicated Scrabble player like I am. (But if you do play Scrabble, my advice here is useful.)

Scrabble is deliciously middlebrow, which is why I like the game. When psychologists have studied complex problem-solving, they have often opted to investigate the highbrow game of chess, which in my opinion does not provide nearly as good a metaphor for life. Chess is thoroughly deterministic, whereas Scrabble has an element of chance. Great chess players always beat poor chess players, whereas great Scrabble players sometimes lose to their less talented opponents. If the less talented player draws a lot of power tiles (Q, X, J, K, S, and blanks), good things will happen, *if* they are played well. That's the first lesson about life from Scrabble. Luck can matter...if one takes advantage of it.

Said more positively, anyone can win a Scrabble match against anyone else, not often but at least occasionally. That's a useful metaphor for life, at least for the vast majority of us who are not the best at anything, except of course being ourselves.

More systematically, here are the lessons for a good life that I have learned from playing Scrabble during the past decade.

First, like chess, you don't need to bet on the outcome of a Scrabble match to make it enjoyable. There may be high-stakes Scrabble games, but I've never heard of them. In contrast, other popular games—like poker or the NFL—would likely not be as interesting or engaging without a pot or a wager. Here is a lesson about the good life pertaining to those things that we choose to do. The best activities are those that are intrinsically rewarding.

Second, Scrabble is more of a situational (spatial) game than a verbal game, something I did not appreciate when I first started to play. I have a great vocabulary, so I should be good at Scrabble, right? Wrong, as I learned the hard way in the beginning. It's *where* you play the word, across doubles and triples, more than what the word per se happens to be. Good players see patterns and the possibilities they present. The particulars matter but mainly in the context of the bigger picture. That's another good metaphor for life. Do what you do in situations where doing well has the biggest payoff.

Third, the meaning of a word in Scrabble is not its dictionary definition. It is the worth of the word where it is played on the board. Period. Consider the word SUQ. Every time I throw that one down against a neophyte, he or she looks puzzled and asks, "What does that mean?" I always reply, "It is a three-letter word that ends in Q…and a great play!" "But what does it mean?" they persist. And I repeat what I had just said. Here is the lesson for the good life: The value of anything is contingent and contextualized. A productive play is purposeful and pragmatic. What are we doing with it, where are we doing it, and why are we doing it?

Did you know that some of best Scrabble players in the world don't even speak or read English? They speak Scrabble, as it were, which is what you need to do when playing Scrabble. That's yet one more lesson for the good life: Speak the local dialect!

Fourth, move tiles! If you can't make a high score, then make a low score that frees up your rack. Most of us know that in poker, you cannot draw to an inside straight, and the same principle applies to Scrabble. Don't hold tiles hoping and praying that you'll get the one extra tile that allows a good play. Move them out! Doing so clears out the nonsense and allows new possibilities. If that is not a useful metaphor for the good life, then nothing else in this reflection is.

Indeed, sometimes discarding the 10-point Q can be a great play, and one that is often recommended by Scrabble experts. Another good metaphor, but one that is hard to heed. Even though I know better, sometimes I die ever so slowly by the overly held Q.

Fifth, one of the "best" racks is really mundane— SALTINE—all one-point tiles. Why? Because this ostensibly ordinary rack allows all sorts of plays that can be hooked with the S and produce a bingo (playing all seven tiles and thereby yielding a 50-point bonus), like:

ELASTIN
ENTAILS
NAILSET
SALIENT
SALTINE
SLAINTE
TENAILS

Sixth, bingos rule. The player who makes more bingos than his or her opponent is going to win the vast majority of Scrabble games, even if his or her other plays yield little. The lesson for life? Pretty obvious, I think, and one akin to Kahneman's peak-end theory of what we remember from hedonic experiences (see reflection

17). The peaks are what matter (along with how an experience finishes, which in the case of Scrabble is determined by the peaks—i.e., the bingos).

Seventh, don't rely on what are called *bluehair* moves, those that are cautious, conservative, and constipated (Fatsis, 2002). They block your opponent's future plays, but also your own. Unless they have good reasons for playing defensively, the best Scrabble players open up the board, and their plays create what looks like a spiderweb on the board. The lesson? Go for it!

Eighth, don't *cofffehouse*, a pejorative term used to describe Scrabble playing in which the chatter overwhelms the game (Fatsis, 2002). In my opinion, one can (and should) chatter before and after a match, but when you play Scrabble, you should do so fully, deeply, and sincerely. Flow is thereby produced, even under the time constraints of tournament Scrabble. Yet another good metaphor for life: Do nothing halfheartedly.

Ninth, Scrabble requires that you juggle the here-and-now and the future. If you can play a bingo, you should probably do so, even if it opens up the board for your opponent. But a 30-point play that allows your opponent to make a 40-point play is not preferable to a safer 20-point play.

Tenth, when the game is coming to an end and you are winning, close the board down! Tournament Scrabble matches and even informal games reward margin of victory, but close victories are always better than "should of, could of, would of" losses that resulted from an attempt to pile it on. A lesson for life? I think so.

Finally, and to mention explicitly the title of this reflection, there are no bad racks, only bad players. Good Scrabble players may blame their strategy, but they never blame the tiles they draw. Tiles are to be played, not used as excuses. To be sure, there are less than productive racks (e.g., what I call *irritable vowel syndrome* racks), but these can be fleeting annoyances, if one deals with them by moving tiles or exchanging them. In the latter case, you lose a turn, but you void your rack, as it were, and you make the bad tiles more likely to appear in the rack of your opponent. Another metaphor for the good life, with or without opponents.

Scrabble on, dear reader, whether or not you have a rack in front of you.

REFERENCE

Fatsis, S. (2002). *Wordfreak: Heartbreak, triumph, genius, and obsession in the world of competitive Scrabble players*. New York: Penguin.

Index